The Blessing of Enoch

The Blessing of Enoch
1 Enoch and Contemporary Theology

EDITED BY
Philip F. Esler

CASCADE Books • Eugene, Oregon

THE BLESSING OF ENOCH
1 Enoch and Contemporary Theology

Copyright © 2017 Wipf and Stock Publishers. All rights reserved. Except for brief quotations in critical publications or reviews, no part of this book may be reproduced in any manner without prior written permission from the publisher. Write: Permissions, Wipf and Stock Publishers, 199 W. 8th Ave., Suite 3, Eugene, OR 97401.

Cascade Books
An Imprint of Wipf and Stock Publishers
199 W. 8th Ave., Suite 3
Eugene, OR 97401

www.wipfandstock.com

PAPERBACK ISBN: 978-1-5326-1424-8
HARDCOVER ISBN: 978-1-5326-1426-2
EBOOK ISBN: 978-1-5326-1425-5

Cataloguing-in-Publication data:

Names: Esler, Philip Francis, editor.

Title: The Blessing of Enoch : 1 Enoch and contemporary theology / edited by Philip F. Esler.

Description: Eugene, OR: Cascade Books, 2017 | Includes bibliographical references and index.

Identifiers: ISBN 978-1-5326-1424-8 (paperback) | ISBN 978-1-5326-1426-2 (hardcover) | ISBN 978-1-5326-1425-5 (ebook)

Subjects: LCSH: Ethiopic book of Enoch—Congresses | Ethiopic book of Enoch—Theology.

Classification: BS1830 E6 B36 2017 (print) | BS1830 (ebook).

Manufactured in the U.S.A.   05/30/17

Angus Pryor retains copyright to the image on the cover.

Contents

List of Contributors / vii

Abbreviations / xi

Introduction / Philip F. Esler / 1

1. 1 Enoch and the Biblical Canon / Gordon McConville / 15

2. Plotting "Holy Tradition" in Ethiopian Orthodox Discourse / Alexandra Sellassie Antohin / 27

3. The Contemporary Influence of Ethiopian *Andemta* Traditional Commentary: Examples from the Commentary on 1 Enoch and Other Texts / Ralph Lee / 44

4. The Animal Apocalypse (1 Enoch 85–90) in the Light of Ethiopian Traditional Commentary: The Case of "Open and Closed" Eyes / Daniel Assefa / 61

5. Social and Economic Injustice: Apocalyptic Themes in the Epistle of Enoch and the Apocalypse of John / Archie T. Wright / 70

6. The Political Theology of the Similitudes of Enoch in Its Ancient Context and Its Theological Implications / Crispin Fletcher-Louis / 89

7. Words from the Book of Enoch on the Environment / Loren T. Stuckenbruck / 111

8. The Cry of the Earth in 1 Enoch and Environmental Theology / Daniel Assefa / 124

9. The Identity of the Son of Man: Messianism and Participation in the Book of (1) Enoch / Grant Macaskill / 133

10. Suffering and *Anawim* Identity in 1 Enoch 108: Towards a Theology of Persecution / Sofanit T. Abebe / 147

11. *Deus Victor*: The Nature and Defeat of Evil in the Book of the Watchers (1 Enoch 1–36) / Philip F. Esler / 166

12. 1 Enoch: An Artist's Response / Angus Pryor / 191

Bibliography / 197

Author Index / 213

Scripture Index / 217

Jewish Sources Index / 229

Classical Sources Index / 231

Contributors

Sofanit Tamene Abebe is a PhD student at the University of Edinburgh, School of Divinity and prospective faculty at the Ethiopian Graduate School of Theology, Addis Ababa. Her research interests include Christian origins, early Christian reception and appropriation of Jewish writings, social-scientific and theological biblical interpretation, as well as Ethiopian Orthodox traditions.

Alexandra Sellassie Antohin received her PhD in Social Anthropology from University College London and currently holds a research affiliation with the Institute of Orthodox Christian Studies (Cambridge, UK). For her fieldwork studies, she conducted sixteen months of research in Dessie (an urban center 400 km north of the capital). Topics that were explored included the centrality of the covenant as a prevailing principle in narrative, ritual, material and social dimensions; the culture of commemoration, such as popular observance of feast and fast; and the role of lay associations in mobilizing diocese projects and church expansion. Her publications focus on the patterns of Ethiopian Orthodox religiosity, such as the use of holy water remedies as a conscious open-ended approach to everyday causality and the theoretical and material reconfigurations of the moral body via contemporary Christian tattoo aesthetics.

Daniel Assefa is the Director of the Capuchin Franciscan Research and Retreat Center, Addis Ababa. His research focuses on apocalyptic literature, Second Temple Judaism and Ethiopian biblical hermeneutics. He has published extensively on 1 Enoch, including *L'Apocalypse des animaux (1 Hen 85–90): une propagande militaire?* JSJSup 120 (Leiden: Brill 2007) and "Matthew's Day of Judgment in the light of 1 Enoch," in *Enoch and the Synoptic*

Gospels: Reminiscences, Allusions, Intertextuality, edited by Loren Stuckenbruck and Gabriele Boccaccini, Early Judaism and Its Literature 44 (Atlanta: Society of Biblical Literature, 2016).

Philip F. Esler is the Portland Chair in New Testament Studies in the University of Gloucestershire, Cheltenham. He specializes in the social-scientific interpretation of biblical and extra-biblical texts and Dead Sea legal papyri, biblical theology, and the Bible and the visual arts. He has recently authored *Babatha's Orchard: The Yadin Papyri and An Ancient Jewish Family Tale Retold* (Oxford: Oxford University Press, 2017) and *God's Court and Courtiers in the Book of the Watchers: Re-interpreting Heaven in 1 Enoch 1–36* (Eugene, OR: Cascade Books, forthcoming). He is the editor of *The Early Christian World*, rev. ed. (London: Routledge, 2017). His recent essays and articles include "Pacino de Bonaguida's *Tree of Life*: Interpreting the Bible in Paint in Early 14th Century Italy," in *Biblical Reception* (2014), and "Intergroup Conflict and Matthew 23: Towards Responsible Historical Interpretation of a Challenging Text," *Biblical Theology Bulletin* (2014).

Crispin Fletcher-Louis is an independent scholar, living in Cheltenham, UK. His primary research interests are Jewish apocalyptic, temple theology, Gospels, Philippians, and Christology. Among his many works, he has recently published *Jesus Monotheism. Volume 1, Christological Origins: The Emerging Consensus and Beyond* (Eugene, OR: Wipf & Stock, 2015), which includes a discussion of the relevance of Enochic traditions for New Testament Christology.

Ralph Lee is a Researcher on the 1 Enoch critical Ethiopic text project at Ludwig-Maximilian University, Munich; a Senior Teaching Fellow in Eastern Christianity at SOAS, University of London; and a former Assistant Professor of Eastern Patristics at Holy Trinity Theological College, Addis Ababa, Ethiopia. He is the Chair of the Ethiopic Bible and Literature Program Unit, Society of Biblical Literature Annual Meeting. His primary research interests lie in Ethiopian Christianity, its history, its texts, its commentary tradition, and the contemporary issues that it faces. He is also interested in the hymns of St. Yared. He is the author of *Symbolic Interpretations in Ethiopic and Early Syriac and Ethiopic Literature*, Eastern Christian Studies 24 (Louvain: Peeters, 2016). Among his essays are "The Ethiopic Octateuch" (2016), "Edward Ullendorff" (2015), "The Ethiopic Commentary on Ethiopic Enoch 2 (1 Enoch 6–9) (2014)," and the "The Ten Commandments in the Ethiopic Tradition" (2013).

Grant Macaskill is Kirby Laing Chair of New Testament Interpretation at the University of Aberdeen, having previously taught at the University of St Andrews. He has worked extensively on the Enoch traditions in both Ethiopic and Slavonic and on the theological interpretation of the New Testament, set within early Jewish contexts. His publications include *Union with Christ in the New Testament* (Oxford: Oxford University Press, 2013); *The Slavonic Texts of 2 Enoch*, Studia Judaeoslavica 6 (Leiden: Brill, 2013); and *Revealed Wisdom and Inaugurated Eschatology in Ancient Judaism and Early Christianity*, JSJSup 115 (Leiden: Brill 2007).

Gordon McConville is Professor of Old Testament Theology at the University of Gloucestershire, having worked previously at Trinity College, Bristol and Wycliffe Hall, Oxford. He studied Modern Languages at Cambridge before doing Theology in Edinburgh and doctoral work on Deuteronomy at Queen's University, Belfast. His books include a commentary on Deuteronomy (Leicester, UK: Apollos, 2002), works on the Prophets, *A Guide to the Prophets* (London: SPCK, 2002), and on Old Testament theology and interpretation, *God and Earthly Power* (London: T. & T. Clark, 2006), and *Being Human in God's World: An Old Testament Theology of Humanity* (Grand Rapids: Baker Academic, 2016). He is currently writing a commentary on Isaiah.

Angus Pryor is Reader in Fine Art and Head of the School of Art and Design in the University of Gloucestershire. His research interests are art and biblical interpretation, the impact of 1 Enoch on Ethiopian artistic and architectural heritage, art in anti-institutional contexts and the re-exploration of Modernism within contemporary Fine Art practice. His recent research projects include *New Directions Part 2, 2012–2016*, a series of six large paintings on the theme of biblical interpretation, now installed at Grange Tower Bridge Hotel, London, including the following works: *The Deluge* (oil and caulk on canvas, 2.4m x 2.4m); *Love & Death* (oil, caulk, and plasticine on canvas, 2.4m x 4.8m); *MAD* (oil and caulk on canvas, 2.4m x 2.4m); *The Marriage* (oil and caulk on canvas, 2.4m x 2m); *Canterbury Giant* (oil and caulk on canvas, 2.4m x 2.4m); and *Stack* (oil, caulk, and plasticine, 14m x 3m). Another recent work is *God's Wrath*, 2014, a transcriptional homage to Stanley Spencer's *Angels of the Apocalypse*, 1949, which was hung as part of the *still small voice* exhibition, which he also curated (see below). His recent curatorial practice includes *Plastic Propaganda* (125 Old Broad Street, London, 2015); *still small voice: British biblical art in a secular age (1850–2014)* (curated exhibition of forty biblical art works from the Ahmanson collection at the Wilson Gallery, Cheltenham, 2015); and *Both Ends of Madness*

(A.P.T. Gallery, Creekside, London, 2016), an exhibition on the effects of well-being on contemporary visual arts practice.

Loren T. Stuckenbruck is the Chair of New Testament Studies (with emphasis on Second Temple Judaism) at Ludwig-Maximilian-Univerisity, Munich. His research interests embrace Jewish and early Christian apocalyptic thought; Second Temple literature, including the Dead Sea Scrolls; theological anthropology; evil; Old Testament and ancient Jewish texts preserved in Ethiopic. He has a project funded by the Deutsche Forschungsgemeinschaft to produce the first critical edition of Ethiopic 1 Enoch. He has written a number of monographs including *1 Enoch 91–108*, Commentaries on Early Jewish Literature (Berlin: de Gruyter, 2007) and *The Myth of Rebellious Angels*, WUNT 335 (Tübingen: Mohr/Siebeck, 2014); and he has, with Gabriele Boccaccini, edited *Enoch and the Synoptic Gospels: Reminiscences, Allusions, Intertextuality*, EJL 44 (Atlanta: Society of Biblical Literature, 2016). In addition, he is the author of over sixty articles/essays on or related to the early Enoch tradition.

Archie T. Wright is Associate Professor of Ancient Judaism and Christian Origins, Regent University, Virginia Beach, Virginia. His research areas are Second Temple Jewish Literature and the New Testament. He is the author of *The Origins of Evil Spirits*, rev. ed. (Minneapolis: Fortress, 2015) and several articles and essays relating to the Enochic corpus. They include: "The Book of Watchers: 1 Enoch 1–36 as a Background for the Demonic Pericopes in the Gospels," *Henoch* (2006); "Some Observations on Philo's *De Gigantibus* in Light of the Book of Watchers," *Journal of the Study of Judaism* (2005); "Demonology of *1 Enoch* and the New Testament Gospels," in *1 Enoch and the Synoptic Gospels: Reminiscences, Allusions, Intertextuality*, edited by Loren T. Stuckenbruck and Gabriele Boccaccini, EJL 44 (Atlanta: Society of Biblical Literature, 2016); and "The Astronomical Book in *1 Enoch*," in *The Wiley-Blackwell Companion to the Old Testament Apocrypha and Pseudepigrapha*, edited by Randall Chesnutt (Oxford: Wiley, 2016).

Abbreviations

2TP	Second Temple Period
ÄthFor	Äthiopistische Forschungen
BZNW	Beihefte zur Zeitschrift für die neutestamentliche Wissenschaft
EJL	Early Judaism and Its Literature
ET	English translation
JBL	*Journal of Biblical Literature*
JES	*Journal of Ethiopian Studies*
JJS	*Journal of Jewish Studies*
JSJSup	Journal for the Study of Judaism Supplements
JSNTSup	Journal for the Study of the New Testament Supplements
JSOTSup	Journal for the Study of the Old Testament Supplements
JSP	*Journal for the Study of the Pseudepigrapha*
LCL	Loeb Classical Library
LNTS	Library of New Testament Studies
NT	New Testament
OstSt	*Ostkirchliche Studien*
SHS	Scripture and Hermeneutics Series
SNTSMS	Society of New Testament Studies Monograph Series
WUNT	Wissenschaftliche Untersuchungen zum Neuen Testament

Introduction

Philip F. Esler

We are in the midst of what might be called the third era of modern research into 1 Enoch, which began with the discovery of Aramaic fragments of the text in Cave 4 of Qumran in 1952 and their subsequent publication by J. T. Milik in 1976. The first era had commenced when James Bruce brought copies of the Ethiopic (Geʿez) text of 1 Enoch from Ethiopia to Europe in 1773, an English translation of which was published in 1821 by Richard Laurence, the first in any European language. Critical editions followed shortly after from Laurence in 1838 and Dillmann (in German) in 1851. The second era was inaugurated with the discovery of a Greek version of most of 1 Enoch 1–36 in a monk's grave in Akhmin in Egypt in 1886/87, which was utilised soon after by Charles (1893 and 1906) and Flemming (1902). The rediscovery of 1 Enoch in Ethiopic, then Greek and then Aramaic versions curiously represents the reverse of their actual order of composition. A composite work in five major parts, it was mostly written in Aramaic between the third century BCE and the first century CE, translated into Greek around the turn of the first millennium and then from Greek into Geʿez in the fifth and sixth centuries CE in Ethiopia.

The extent to which scholarship on 1 Enoch is flourishing in this third era of research can be seen in the recent bibliography on the subject by James Charlesworth and Ephraim Isaac that occupies 277 pages.[1] Most research into 1 Enoch today in the West entails historical, textual, and even

---

1. Charlesworth and Isaac 2015.

narrative-based research into Second Temple Judaism and the contexts for ideas taken up in the New Testament (in areas like early Christology). 1 Enoch is particularly significant for our understanding of the origin, nature and function of the apocalyptic genre of Jewish literature. It also valuably contributes to our knowledge of Son of Man theology and the concern for social justice among ancient Israelites.

And yet there is one prominent absence in the current scholarship on 1 Enoch—*its significance as a theological text*, that is, as a text that can speak of human-divine interactions in the present and thus contribute to the topics and concerns of contemporary theology. Virtually all the research undertaken on 1 Enoch so far has been historical in nature; that is, it occupies itself with what the text *meant* in the ancient world and how it casts light on phenomena and other texts in that setting. A limited exception to this is where researchers have raised contemporary theological dimensions of 1 Enoch in what are primarily historical studies.[2]

This lack of interest in the theological potential of 1 Enoch is a surprising and regrettable scholarly lacuna. It also sits oddly with the fact that 1 Enoch is viewed as part of the Old Testament in the Ethiopian and Eritrean Orthodox Churches, while the Epistle of Jude in the New Testament summarizes the fate of the Watchers in v. 6 and quotes 1 Enoch 1:9 (a central verse on God's justice) in vv. 14–15. This book represents the first published output of a project recently initiated to address this egregious neglect of the theological dimensions of 1 Enoch and, accordingly, to inaugurate a new area of theological research. The origins of this project are now described.

During the meeting of the Society of Biblical Literature in Baltimore in November 2013 Loren Stuckenbruck and I had a conversation in which we discovered a mutual interest in and enthusiasm for the role that 1 Enoch could play in contemporary theology. Stuckenbruck had been reflecting on a number of areas where 1 Enoch could play into contemporary theology, while I had been particularly struck by the work's understanding of the nature of evil and the divine response to it. In the years before this conversation Stuckenbruck had made several visits to Ethiopia to seek out further manuscripts of Ethiopic 1 Enoch for the first critical edition of the text (currently being undertaken under his lead with funding from the *Deutsche Forschungsgemeinschaft*).[3] In Ethiopia he had discovered some current interest in the theological use of 1 Enoch, partly in relation to dialogue across ecclesiastical boundaries, which had necessarily to deal with the status of

---

2. For an example of this, see Stuckenbruck's work in relation to disability and mental health (2014:161–86).

3. For a discussion of this project, see Erho and Stuckenbruck 2013.

1 Enoch as a scriptural text for the Ethiopian Orthodox Church, indeed, as a text that brings together many aspects of redemptive history. The indigenous Ethiopian commentary, the *andəmta* (written in Amharic, *floruit* sixteenth to eighteenth centuries CE, with an earlier tradition, the *tərgʷame*, in Geʽez), interprets 1 Enoch as a Christian text and as one that is in harmony with the rest of the Bible. The *andəmta* is both an ancient tradition, but also very much a living and contemporary one. Stuckenbruck explored this interest with Ethiopian theologians at meetings in Addis Ababa on 27 May 2011, 22 March 2013 (with a further meeting held later, on 6 March 2014).

In consequence of our conversation, Stuckenbruck and I agreed to explore undertaking a project in this area. Soon after we discovered that Grant Macaskill shared our optimistic view of how 1 Enoch could enrich contemporary theology. In 2014 the three of us applied to the British Academy/Leverhulme Trust for funding to cover two conferences with Ethiopian researchers, one in Addis Ababa, at the Capuchin Franciscan Retreat and Conference Center, hosted by the Rev. Dr. Daniel Assefa and one in Cheltenham, at the University of Gloucestershire (my home institution) as a way of kick-starting research in this area. The application was successful (with funding supplied by the Leverhulme Trust) and the conferences were held in February and October 2015. The chapters in this book represent a selection of the papers that were delivered on those occasions. The support of the British Academy (which has a long-standing interest in encouraging collaboration between UK researchers and those in Asia and Africa) and the Leverhulme Trust (which provided the funding) is most gratefully acknowledged. In addition, Angus Pryor, Head of the School of Art and Design at the University of Gloucestershire, and himself an artist, having already become interested in 1 Enoch, also took part in both meetings, as a result of which he conceived a plan for twenty-one 2 x 2 metre paintings on themes from 1 Enoch and the creation of a large-scale model of an Ethiopian church decorated inside and out with imagery from the text. He has begun work on the paintings, with the first of them (on God in 1 Enoch 14) the cover illustration for this volume. I will now summarize the contents of the essays that follow.

In Chapter 1 Gordon McConville asks what it means to use 1 Enoch theologically when it is not part of the biblical canon in most of the world's churches, whereas in Ethiopian and Eritrean Orthodoxy it forms part of Old Testament scripture, even though those churches do not have a fixed canon like other Christian traditions. He begins with a consideration of the nature of canon. In the Christian context the canon functions (crucially, in relation to both Old and New Testaments) to provide authoritative testimony to Jesus Christ. That testimony, under the influence of the Holy

Spirit, is, however, open and various, and this renders problematic the idea of a closed canon. McConville then turns to the question of whether the canon is defined "internally," by virtue of its contents (an expression of faith that provides a sort of unity), or "externally," by the decision of an external authority (where the canon may be seen to have less theological unity and more as containing a vibrant diversity, so that scripture is many-voiced). These issues lead inevitably to the question of authority, of who decides how what texts should be read as scripture. Whether texts endorse or subvert power relations is a hotly contested area. The existence of a canon is not able to disguise the huge variety among the texts it contains. Ultimately canon must be subservient to the truth of Christ and various ways have been proposed to explain this, from the early Church onwards. Modern critical approaches provide further resources in this task. This brings McConville to the precise question of the canon and 1 Enoch, which is posed especially by its being Old Testament scripture in Ethiopia (and Eritrea). On one view 1 Enoch was an important text in the biblical period, it was part of the context, and our understanding of the canon of scripture is incomplete without attention to it. On another view the canon is characterized both by its monotheizing thrust and also by an intertextuality that does not respect canonical boundaries. McConville then explores these ideas with respect to the relationship between 1 Enoch and canonical texts, Jude especially (where there are direct quotations of 1 Enoch), but also Hebrews and John. He then considers how 1 Enoch functions in the processes of "inner-canonical comparison" in areas such as angelology, the Son of Man, and the relationship of the wisdom and apocalyptic genres. Lastly, he notes a number of specific areas where 1 Enoch can contribute theologically. We are left with a very lively sense of the importance of standing beside the churches of Ethiopia and Eritrea in solidarity with them in viewing 1 Enoch as a text "by which the various communities of Christian faith learn through the Holy Spirit to be formed in Christ."

In Chapter 2 Alexandra Sellassie Antohin uses the results of her recent ethnographic fieldwork in Ethiopia for a social anthropology doctorate (from University College London) on ritual and devotion in Ethiopian Orthodox praxis to explore the ways that the "Holy Tradition" in the Eastern Orthodox Church finds close parallels in Ethiopian Orthodoxy. She focuses especially on *tabots*, material representations of the Mosaic covenant, which characterize Ethiopian belief and practice. She also indicates the relevance of a text known as the *Dersana Urael* ("The Sermon of Urael"), which is inspired by the activities of the archangel Uriel in 1 Enoch 17–36. She begins by setting out the role of the Holy Tradition in Orthodoxy, a compendium of teachings from the beginning of Christianity onwards, that was regarded as vivifying the "letter" of scripture. The important question arises as to how it is transmitted into contemporary application and relevance. Antohin's essay highlights one aspect: that segment of theological discourse within the Ethiopian Orthodox Church that focuses on the understanding of covenant in its materialized, liturgical and spiritualized forms. In particular, she is concerned with the voices of lay people that are usually peripheral to scholarly discourse. (Her interest finds a parallel in the West in the "ordinary theology" movement that also seeks to address this issue.)[4] As a prelude to this discussion she outlines typically Ethiopian methods of elaborating on the tradition (which is seen as a monotheistic one embracing 1,000 years of Judaism and 2,000 years of Christianity). These include the *andəmta*, an indigenous style of theological interpretation of scripture and the *tabots* that are central to every church, whose nature she explains. From this she proceeds to a discussion of how *Dersana Urael* (see above) was used by some of her informants to help to situate and elucidate phenomena in local churches connected with *tabots* and the foundation or movement of churches. She shows how her informants used this text to prove that *tabot* legends were not self-authored stories but were consistent with the oral and written sources from the Ethiopian Orthodox Church tradition. Central to *Dersana Urael* was the archangel's consecration of ecclesial places in Ethiopia with blood he had collected from the crucified Christ, thus creating a sacred cosmography that could be utilized in the present: a *tabot* might emerge in any place on which a drop of Christ's blood had fallen. Another text from the tradition but used in the present is the *Kebra Negast* ("The Glory of the Kings") that legitimates the claim that the ark of the covenant was brought to Ethiopia in ancient times. At the same time, however, *tabots*, and local legends surrounding them, could be prisms of contestation within and between parishes. She concludes that a notion of "Holy Tradition" is an active discursive category in Ethiopian Orthodox Christianity, reflected both in its historical canonical trends and also in contemporary voices, especially among the laity.

In Chapter 3 Ralph Lee discusses the *andəmta*, a corpus of commentaries on the Geʻez text of the scriptural works (including 1 Enoch) written in Amharic. They were preceded and possibly influenced by an earlier tradition of commentaries written in Geʻez, the *tərgʷame* ("interpretations"). The *andəmta* commentaries originated in Gondar, the Ethiopian capital from 1635–1855 CE, where they were written down from earlier traditions, some of them oral. Lee follows Roger Cowley, who undertook seminal research into the *andəmta*, in regarding this corpus as fundamentally a reflection

---

4. See Astley 2002 and Astley and Francis 2013.

of Antiochene rather than Alexandrian exegesis, which is surprising given the proximity of Egypt and the centuries-old influence of the Alexandrian patriarch on the Ethiopian Orthodox Church. Lee explains the approach taken in the *andəmta* with respect to a range of material. From this Lee proceeds to explain how 1 Enoch fits into this picture. Firstly, he sets out the role of 1 Enoch in the Ethiopian tradition, which is characterized by an open canon (supported by a closed system of doctrines) where there is a fixed number of scriptural books, 81, but variability in the actual books that make up that number. While it is likely that 1 Enoch came to Ethiopia in the fourth century CE, it seems only to have had a firm place in Ethiopian scriptures from the fifteenth century onwards, with its position before that time being controversial. Secondly, he considers the *andəmta* commentary on 1 Enoch, beginning with the observation that the *andəmta* on Psalm 82 demonstrates that 1 Enoch is a point of reference for other texts. Lee's major aim in this section is to reveal how the commentary throws up an array of reflections on 1 Enoch from a context very different from ours that bear directly on the relevance of 1 Enoch for contemporary theology. Thirdly, he considers how the *andəmta* on 1 Enoch comes up in commentary on other biblical texts, as in Psalm 82, mentioned above. One important example is the use of *andəmta* (and the earlier *Tərgʷame Qälämsis*) in the commentary on the Apocalypse, which was the subject of a monograph by Cowley in 1983. The overall message left by this chapter is that 1 Enoch is regarded in Ethiopia as a "Christian" text that allows, for example, a Christian account to be developed of the origin of evil and evil spirits. Enoch emerges, along with St John and others, as a special kind of prophet, who conversed with God, and gives special information about the angelic and diabolic realms.

The first of Daniel Assefa's two chapters in the book, Chapter 4, offers further insights into the operation of the *andəmta* tradition in the way it deals with a prominent aspect of the Animal Apocalypse (1 Enoch 85–90), probably written in the second century BCE. The text is an allegory of the history of Israel set within universal history in which the diverse ethnic groups and individuals mentioned in it are portrayed as various kinds of animals and birds. The aspect focused upon is that of the "open and closed eyes," which is used throughout the text, especially in relation to sheep. Western scholarship on the Animal Apocalypse tends to view the distinction as referring to a good ("open eyes") or bad ("closed eyes") relationship with God, that is, with obedience or disobedience, with turning to God or turning away from him. The central argument mounted by Assefa is that the traditional Ethiopian commentaries keep in view the importance of the distinction as involving knowledge and ignorance. Although there is imagery of open and closed eyes in other parts of 1 Enoch, the greatest concentration of the motif falls in the Animal Apocalypse. Assefa suggests, to cite one of a number of his examples, that the fact that the "sheep" (= Israelites) open their eyes when they have entered the desert after crossing the Red Sea is best interpreted as their gaining knowledge, not that they were becoming obedient. He further notes that the *andəmta* interprets the fact that these eyes are open as referring to when the inner eye of the sheep (their mind) began to examine or to wonder about mysteries. When, soon after, in 1 Enoch 89:32–33, the sheep are blinded, a modern commentator like VanderKam interprets this as disobedience, whereas the *andəmta* speaks again of the inner eye in as much as they were caught up in ignorance and, for this reason, went astray. After further examination, Assefa concludes that the *andəmta* associates the theme of the open and closed eyes with knowledge, but without cancelling out or ignoring the theme of disobedience or apostasy. In doing so it offers a nuanced understanding that combines knowledge and obedience similar to what we find in Genesis 2. In sum, "the larger corpus of Ethiopian biblical commentary proposes an anthropological affirmation whereby receiving the breath of life, opening one's eyes, being faithful to God constitute the vocation of the human person."

In Chapter 5 Archie Wright compares and contrasts how issues of social justice are dealt with in Epistle of Enoch (1 Enoch 92–105) and the Apocalypse. He begins by situating his discussion within the modern context of gross social inequality within and between nations, and by raising questions with respect to the "prosperity Gospel" with its view that faith leads to one's financial improvement. He then explores the biblical foundations of a theology of social justice, especially Deuteronomy 7–15 with its promise of prosperity but only with obedience to God and concern for the poor. He next explains the likely historical social settings for the two texts. The Epistle, for which no evidence exists that it was composed in more than one historical period, is likely to date to the pre-Maccabean period and while it may refer to sectarian division it is not possible to link it in some way with the Qumran group. The Apocalypse is written to Christ-followers in seven cities in Asia Minor, probably in the 90s of the first century CE, although an earlier date is possible. While general social issues can be detected, the diversity among the situations of the seven cities must be acknowledged. The bulk of Wright's essay is taken up with a detailed consideration of social justice themes in the Epistle of Enoch and in the Apocalypse, beginning with an introduction setting out various attitudes to the wealthy in the Epistle and other periods from the second Temple period. Some examples will suffice to illustrate Wright's approach. First Enoch 92:3 offers ultimate hope for the righteous ones who have died, while resurrection is also envisaged in Rev 20:5–6. First Enoch 94:9 offers a stern eschatological warning to the rich that declares the coming day of bloodshed and the "great day of judgment," while Rev 14:20 carries a vivid picture of Endtime blood-letting on a horrific scale. Just as 1 Enoch 95:5 also emphasizes that the wicked will be repaid according to your deeds, so too does Rev 16:11. Wright ends his essay with reflections that return to the broader and contemporary significance of this material with which he began.

Crispin Fletcher-Louis's essay (Chapter 6) identifies a new factor in the generation of the distinctive pre-existent messianic hope of the Similitudes of Enoch (1 Enoch 37–71). Building on an earlier publication in which he has argued that the messianism of the Similitudes is a response to patterns in the Greco-Roman ruler cult (at the end of the first century BCE or the early decades of the first century CE), he argues that it is also indebted to an older and well-established, biblically-based, distinction between the priestly office and the person of the king. Unlike kings, the high priest is an office not a person. The office transcends the identities of those who hold it. The way that works for the high priest is especially clear in Sirach 50. The office pre-exists each incumbent and it will continue to exist after their death. The Similitudes, he contends, projects that distinction onto a mythological, eschatological, horizon. The Son of Man-Messiah (and Elect One) in 1 Enoch 37–71 is almost wholly devoid of personhood. He is simply the one-God-made-manifest, with no separate, individual, identity or personality that would threaten the identity of the one God. He is to the eschatological scenario what the high priestly office is within the real-time liturgical context of the temple-as-microcosm. This interpretation of the Similitudes' distinctive messianism opens up new possibilities for the Enochic text's role as an invaluable *historical* witness to fresh perspectives on the *theological* shape of New Testament Christology and the relationship between Old and New Testaments. In this latter respect, this chapter connects with that by Grant Macaskill (Chapter 9).

The potential for 1 Enoch to enrich environmental theology is amply demonstrated in the next two chapters of the book. The first, Chapter 7 by Loren Stuckenbruck, looks at the big picture. He begins with Lynn White's well-known—and criticized yet still relevant—accusation in 1967 that the Bible and how it has been interpreted has contributed to the ecological crisis. This crisis is not only still with us but becomes ever more acute and theologians have a duty to respond to it using the resources of their religious traditions. The origins of the problem lie in what people do. The sustainability, indeed the survival of life on earth, is at risk. Yet within the larger Christian community there is marked disagreement on what form such a response should take, especially if it means deploying the resources of the Judeo-Christian tradition. Two overarching approaches have emerged. The first, inspired by texts such as 2 Pet 3:10–13 proposes that Christian faith concerns salvation of souls and is heavenly in orientation. Since the world is temporary and we face a Last Judgment, why worry about the environment? In the meantime, texts like Gen 1:26–28 are alleged to justify the view that since human beings essentially own the earth, they can do what they like to it. The second overarching approach views the natural world as having a value in its own right and its proponents look to biblical sources, including Genesis 1 with its stress on the goodness of creation, to justify their position. There are even texts that sideline the place of humans within creation (like Job 38:1—40:2; Psalm 104; and Joel 1:2—2:17). Jesus was also interested in the natural world and incorporated it into his teaching. Yet the use of the Bible in this area is complex and contested and *critical* interpretation must not be abandoned. Into this lively arena Stuckenbruck introduces the new voice of 1 Enoch, here focusing on 1 Enoch 6–11 (which build on Genesis 6). The Giants, progeny of the angels called Watchers and women, ravage humankind, the earth, and themselves, leading the earth itself to complain (1 Enoch 7:6; 9:2). First Enoch recounts an environmental catastrophe that devastates land, animals, and people. In response, God sends the Flood, a reaction not just to the works of human beings as in Genesis but, primarily, to the actions of the angels. Stuckenbruck notes that another take on that catastrophe exists in the Astronomical Book, in Chapter 80, with its image of a universe no longer running how God created it. Unlike the Christian tradition which assigns such events to the Endtime, the Enochic tradition assigns this catastrophe to the past and makes clear that not only is any such use of the earth's resources, including by human beings, a blatant act of rebellion, but it could happen again. Yet 1 Enoch also has a positive side, in looking to a future where "the entire earth will be tilled *in righteousness*, and all of it will be planted with trees, and it will be filled with blessing" (1 Enoch 10:18). At this time, God says, "all humanity will be righteous, and all the nations shall serve and bless me, and all shall worship me" (1 Enoch 10:21–22). Thus, 1 Enoch holds that ultimately the welfare of the created world falls within the sphere of concern addressed by the worship of God.

Daniel's Assefa's second essay in the volume (Chapter 8) further explores these environmental aspects of 1 Enoch by considering one particular contribution that the text can make to a theology of the environment. This is the "cry" which the earth raises to heaven in response not only to bloodshed that the Giants cause but also the damage sustained by the earth's fauna and flora. The expression "the cry of the earth" is used by Richard Bauckham in his *Bible and Ecology* and also, repeatedly, by Pope Francis in his environmental encyclical *Laudato Si'*. Assefa's interest lies in analyzing the cry of the earth in 1 Enoch and in connecting it with contemporary theology on the environment. He begins by exploring the much-used language for "earth" in 1 Enoch, principally *mədra* ("the earth") and *yabs* ("dry ground"). Meanings range from earth, to a piece of land, to a particular land or territory, to the earth as a whole (as in 1 Enoch 9:2). There is in 1 Enoch a focus on the earth in its entirety, and this makes good sense within the current discourse of environmental philosophy and theology, with their stress on the interrelatedness of all things. Assefa next addresses the complaints of the earth. In a text where different characters cry out, the earth itself cries out like a person on several occasions. Here his work resonates with recent research suggesting both that the earth is a character in Genesis and that it finds voice in resisting human violence.[5] A further dimension noted by Assefa is that the earth is capable of receiving righteousness, especially when God comes down from Sinai. The earth will be comforted after all the destruction of the flood. Human beings are even called children of the earth (*wəluda mədr*). In his final section he turns to the contemporary situation. Just as the prophets of ancient Israel received a mixed reception, so too today opinions vary in the face of the environmental crisis. Will we accept responsibility and act, or not? We are the beneficiaries and yet also the victims of our technology. "The situation in the modern world shows great progress paralleled with fragility." Our vulnerability matches that of the human beings in 1 Enoch. In 1 Enoch, however, the trigger for the catastrophe was not human beings but the actions of angels. He concludes by suggesting that if theology is faith seeking understanding, it must be active in helping us understand (and, by implication, respond to) our questionable relationship with the earth.

In Chapter 9 Grant Macaskill explores the Christological dimensions of the Son of Man in that section of 1 Enoch that is called the Parables (or "the Similitudes"), Chapters 37–71, and not as an aspect of past belief but for theologizing in the present. His aim is to show that a human being can be so closely identified with the person of the Son of Man, a title frequently used of Jesus in the New Testament, that the identity of that heavenly person becomes superimposed onto—or realized within—the identity of the earthly individual. This is a difficult concept for modern theology to appreciate, with its post-Enlightenment notions of the person. He begins with a preliminary comment on his own position within the Reformed theological tradition—to the effect that the non-canonical status of a 1 Enoch within that tradition does not prevent its representatives from regarding it as authoritative and inspired. For it is a text that has functioned as part of the Christian tradition. Macaskill then proceeds to the first main section of his argument, to demonstrate the solidarity

---

5. See Jorstad 2016.

or correspondence in the Parables between the Son of Man and the community that he represents: the Chosen. This material connects with Isaiah's picture of the Servant, whose individual identity (and narrative) is constitutive of the corporate identity (and narrative) of a community, just as in the Parables the Son of Man as Righteous One and Chosen corresponds to and is identified with the righteous and the chosen, to whom he mediates divine blessing. Moreover, the Son occupies the Heavenly throne and is depicted as divine. But the Son of Man is not just a representative figure of the community, he is constitutive of that community. Macaskill then considers the different approaches to understanding the divine and human dimensions of Jesus Christ, contrasting the Chalcedonian "two natures" (one human and one divine) joined in hypostatic union of most Christian churches with the *Tewahedo* (= monophysite) understanding of certain Oriental churches, including the Ethiopian and Eritrean Orthodox Churches. The second main part of Macaskill's argument takes up the manner and significance of Enoch, after his transformation into a being fit for the presence of the Lord of Spirits (70:5), being identified with the Son of Man (at 71:4). The Son of Man had previously been identified as a pre-existent figure who would be worshipped by all on earth (Chapter 48). Yet the Son of Man cannot simply be Enoch, who was not pre-existent. Nor is the identification simply typological. Instead, Macaskill proposes that the identification be understood in terms of the Christian theological tradition that deploys the imagery of ascent into heaven and identification with Jesus in relation to the final end of Christian life. "Enoch remains Enoch as he is identified as the Son: he does not become, simply, Jesus." This solution contributes to Christian theology in two ways. First, it takes us back to a pre-Enlightenment yet challenging notion of the person whereby my whole identity, the entirety of myself, might be constituted by the personhood of another. Secondly, it provides a different slant on salvation history. Enoch, the seventh patriarch after Adam, participates in the identity of the Son of Man despite the fact that he died long before "the Christ event," the period of earthly Incarnation. To understand this we must do (what the Ethiopian Church does) and introduce a framework that is at home in older readings of scripture "but alien to much modern discourse, one that starts with the being of God, now understood in terms of the Incarnation, and understands all in this light."

In Chapter 10 Sofanit Abebe examines 1 Enoch 108, a section well styled by Stuckenbruck as the "Eschatological Admonition," within two complementary theological frameworks. The first is a communion of saints theology used to embrace the process that occurs when believers today read the works of biblical authors in dialogue with them in a way that respects their historical alterity. The second is a theology of persecution, specifically adapted to the particular content of 1 Enoch 108. In the first substantive section of her essay, Abebe discusses the character of 1 Enoch 108, both by summarizing its contents and then by setting out how the events in that chapter ("plotted series") can be lined up next to the events to which they refer in the world beyond the text ("referential series"). She next considers the social context for 1 Enoch 108, in particular, its date of composition and addressees. This is followed by an emic explanation of its situation and strategy that links the treatment of the lowly/humble in the text with Israelite depictions of the *anawim*. Abebe next enriches this discussion with a further dimension: etic explorations of the textual phenomena taking the form of social-scientific perspectives on sectarianism (especially from Bryan Wilson) and liminality (especially from Victor Turner). In her last section, "Towards a Theology of Persecution," Abebe discusses the experience of persecution that many Christians face today, especially in Africa, and shows how the thought of 1 Enoch 108 is resonant with and can also contribute to contemporary theologies of persecution.

In my own essay, Chapter 11, I address the question of evil as a dominant theme in 1 Enoch 1–36 (the Book of the Watchers). I begin with a discussion of evil and the way God deals with it as perhaps the central issue in theology. This leads into the phenomenology of evil in the Book of the Watchers. I argue that to appreciate this theme one must distinguish between "narrative time" in the text, meaning the course of events in their chronological order in Israelite tradition, and "dramatic time," meaning the actual order of events in the text itself. The somewhat unusual order of dramatic time (with the Book of the Watchers, for example, beginning with an account of the End) does not mean that the author is insouciant to narrative time. This means that the earliest example of evil recognized in the Book of the Watchers is not the secession of the Watchers from heaven to marry human wives, which occurred in the time of Noah (1 Enoch 6–8), but Cain's slaying of Abel (mentioned in 1 Enoch 22:5–7). The evil activities of the Watchers and their progeny, the Giants, and subsequently the spirits of the latter, are not the cause of evil on earth as is so often suggested, but merely the most egregious example of a phenomenon started by Cain (nothing much being made of the doings of Adam and Eve in the Garden of Eden [1 Enoch 32:6]). I next introduce three unsatisfying explanations for the nature of evil, that is: an illusion; as the absence of good; or as a distinct power in the world. In this context I introduce my preferred means to understand evil, Karl Barth's notion of *Das Nichtige* ("nothingness"), a paradoxical form of reality of which sin is the concrete expression. This proves illuminating in relation to evil in 1 Enoch 1–36, including with respect to the spirits of the

Giants, which continue to roam the earth until the End. One very significant aspect of evil in the text is the centrality of violence. So too is the fact that God is presented as affected by evil. In the penultimate section I note that some Patristic authors ask if God could have dealt with evil in the world apart from by sending his beloved and incarnate Son, but without realizing that this is precisely what we find in 1 Enoch 1–36. In both the Enochian and New Testament understanding salvation-history is a two-stage process, with an intervening event (the Flood on the one hand, or *Deus victor*, and the life, death, and resurrection of Christ, or *Christus victor*, on the other) dealing a mortal blow to evil but without quite killing it off, for which result one must await the End. In the last section I mount a defense of the *Deus victor* motif as an alternative to universal salvation.

The final chapter of the book, Chapter 12, is something distinctively different from the others, yet fully in keeping with their thrust and spirit. Here practicing artist Angus Pryor explains how 1 Enoch and a growing acquaintance with the art and architecture of Ethiopia have inspired him to paint a series of 21 2x2 meter paintings on themes from 1 Enoch and also to create a large-scale model of an Ethiopian church decorated with Enochian imagery, an artistic Church of St Enoch. He reads and re-reads the Enoch text, exploring his own understanding of it and trying to transcribe its words through images. He must first decide what aspect of the text to visualize, working with size, color, and composition. In line with the other authors in this volume, Pryor believes that 1 Enoch can be read as contemporary text, one that outlines many of the challenges of contemporary society: faith; the thirst for knowledge; our relationship with God; and the way the environment impacts on our systems of belief. As an artist, he regards his task as relatively simple. He takes incidents and concepts in the book of Enoch and translates them through the medium of painting so that a new and exciting element is introduced and further interpretation can take place. The imagery he creates honors Ethiopic tradition, for example, in that the facial characteristics and clothes of God, angels, and Enoch are painted in that style, with the palette a muted one of sombre earth colors in line with the color schemes of Ethiopian paintings. As a post-conceptual artist he uses objects that he has collected on trips to Ethiopia, which not only form part of his research but which he has applied directly to the canvas. He concludes with the statement "Painting signifying belief is a powerful medium."

Having now summarized the essays in the volume, one final thing remains to be done—to say something about its title, *The Blessing of Enoch*. The first verse of Ethiopic 1 Enoch, which serves as a superscription for the whole text, runs as follows:

ቃለ፡ በረከት፡ ዘሄኖክ፡ በከመ፡ ባረከ፡ ኅሩያነ፡ ወጻድቃነ፨ እለ፡ ሀለዉ፡
ይኩኑ፡ በዕለተ፡ ምንዳቤ፡ ለአሰስሎ፡ ኩሎ፡ እኩያነ፡ ወረሲዓነ፡

The word of the blessing of Enoch, by which he blessed the chosen and the righteous who will be present on the day of tribulation, to remove all the evil and wicked ones.[6]

Nickelsburg reasonably notes that this verse is closely dependent on the blessing of Moses in Deut 33:27 and suggests that the Book of Enoch is being presented as a testament. He then goes on to state, "Enoch's words are a blessing because they announce the future blessed state of the righteous."[7] This interpretation, however, tying the blessing to events predicted in the text, is far too narrow. The author of v. 1 surely intended that the blessing subsisted not merely in the knowledge of what was to come *but also in the very fact of the existence and transmission of the Enochic corpus of material*. The superscription announces the text itself, "The word of the blessing of Enoch by which he blessed (*Qalä bärakät zähenok zäkämä baräkä*) the chosen and the righteous." And why? Because it was a repository of divinely sourced wisdom on a whole range of issues going to what it meant to be human in a world created by God yet troubled by evil. This was why the various parts of 1 Enoch were preserved by its original scribal tradents. It is also why Ethiopian Christians have treasured 1 Enoch for fifteen hundred years. The fundamental challenge offered by the essays in this volume is that now, in the twenty-first century CE, the time has come to return to these ancient modes of relating to 1 Enoch and to recognize that its riches can and should be brought into creative interaction with the manifold currents of contemporary theology. In sum, just as our Israelite and Christian ancestors in faith were blessed in 1 Enoch, so too are we.

---

6. My translation; the Greek adds at the end of the verse, "and the righteous will be saved" (καὶ σωθήσονται δίκαιοι).

7. Nickelsburg 2001:135.

1

1 Enoch and the Biblical Canon

GORDON MCCONVILLE

The question of 1 Enoch in relation to the biblical canon is raised by the book's special position in the history and spirituality of the churches in Ethiopia and Eritrea. That special position has implications for the nature of canonicity itself. And so, in order to consider the topic in particular, it is necessary to say something about the nature of the biblical canon.

The canon is one of the hard cases of biblical and theological interpretation. There are barely resolved questions about the history of it. When was the Hebrew canon "closed"? How are the relative claims of the smaller (Hebrew) canon and the larger Alexandrian to be evaluated? How did the New Testament canon, in the familiar form that it ultimately reached, relate to actual practice in the churches? For that matter, how does it do so today? Regarding the limits of the canon, the Church has lived with a kind of uneasy (or easy) truce on some of these questions. The Apocrypha have a higher status in the Roman Catholic Church than in the Protestant ones. And in the latter the readiness of theologians to distinguish between levels of authority within the received canon is betokened by Luther's famous disparagement of the letter of James as "a right strawy epistle," because he could not see in it the doctrine of justification by faith in Christ.[1] "Canons within

---

1. Luther expressed his view of James in his Preface to James and Jude. For a text, see for example, Dillenberger 1961:35-36 (http://matt1618.freeyellow.com/preface.html).

His view of James was more nuanced than the well-known sound-bite suggests, and he allowed that it had some useful instruction. However, he evidently doubted its apostolicity, on the grounds of its contents, and so saw it as having lesser authority than

the canon" are a recurring feature of the Church's life, and the contest with Marcion continues to find echoes.

At the heart of the question of canon is the relationship between form and content. What is a canon meant to do? In the Christian context in which the present question is raised, its function is authoritative testimony to Jesus Christ. This function is applicable, crucially, to both Old and New Testaments, the two-Testament canonical structure witnessing to the Church's core claims about the saving work of God in the history of Israel and in Jesus Christ. That twofold witness implies a givenness, expressive of the belief that the meaning of history, which began to be unfolded in God's dealings with Israel, is revealed in a definitive way in Jesus Christ. The acceptance of a canon in the Church is related to the need to speak truly about Christ.

The manner of that testimony, however, is open and various, an ongoing work of the life and thought of the Church, in its relationship with the living Christ, and under the influence of the Holy Spirit. In that sense, the idea of closure in relation to canon is problematical: can ultimate authority in the matter of belief in the Person of Christ be dependent on correctly defining a corpus of books? Perhaps the Church's practical agreement to disagree over the limits of the canon testifies indirectly to this central point.

Canon: Internal or External

One of the questions that has occupied those who have thought about the canon is whether it is defined from within, that is by virtue of its contents, or from without, that is by the decision of an external authority. In the former case, the argument is that the canon virtually defines itself because it expresses faith in the one God Yahweh, and, for the New Testament, the God who is revealed in Jesus Christ. In the latter, the canon is seen less as having intrinsic theological unity, than as the result of various historical factors and ultimately by virtue of the Church's decision to regard it as such.

The argument for intrinsic unity may not ignore the rather obvious diversity of the Bible's contents. There are those who have thought that historical criticism is essentially "anti-canonical," because it deliberately proceeds without reference to a canonical framework, and even functions to disturb canonical interpretations.[2] The warning is well taken, though practitioners of various forms of canonical criticism have attempted to handle it in their own ways.[3]

---

the writings of Paul.

2. For example, Barton 1991:50–51.

3. One thinks of B. S. Childs' careful attention to historical critical factors in his

In regard to the Hebrew Bible, the argument about intrinsic unity draws on the view that the writings have been formed in the conscious opposition of mono-Yahwistic belief to the religious and political syntheses of the Old Testament's environing world. Thus, for Horst Seebass, Deuteronomy is "a historical-political transposition of the specifically Israelite understanding of God into the international world of its day."[4] James Sanders, in his version of canonical interpretation, sees the oneness of God as the key unifying factor, cutting across internal diversity, and coming to expression in the Old Testament's pervasive critique of polytheistic belief systems.[5] This "internal" view of canonical unity has in its favor that it highlights the bond between the core beliefs of the believing community and the written forms that become authoritative in it. However, it is open to the objection that the notion of "believing community" begs the question who that community is, and what power structures exist within it. In recent times, one influential strand of Old Testament criticism has claimed that the formation of the authoritative books, and even their theological content, was determined by the ruling elite in post-exilic Yehud in their own interests. On this view, even "mono-Yahwism" is re-cast as the doctrine of the ruling class, over against a popular Israelite or Judean religion in which diversity, icons, and feminine imagery played an important part. Canon thus becomes a function of social and political power.[6]

On an "external" view of the unity of the canon, according to Michael Wolter, its contents do not depend on inner coherence, but on the contrary reflect the diversity that characterized the early Church's attempt to express what was at the heart of the Gospel.[7] Indeed, the New Testament canon had the character of purposeful compromise. Its plurality even had the positive function of showing that Christian identity is bound to take different forms in different contexts.[8] Examples of this diversity abound in both Testaments. In the Old Testament, there is a frequently observed tension between writings that aim to nurture a religious practice, including the Priestly literature and Chronicles, and those that promote a freer kind of religious expression, as in prophetic and Psalmic texts that evidently disparage sacrificial worship (Pss 40; 50; Hos 6:6). There are tensions between "nationalistic" Israelite perspectives (Deuteronomy, Ezra–Nehemiah) and a more inclusive

---

commentaries on Exodus and Isaiah (1974 and 2001).

4. Seebass 2003:38.
5. Sanders 1987.
6. See Smith 1971; Blenkinsopp 1977; and Davies 1995.
7. Wolter 2003:54–60.
8. Wolter 2003:61–62.

impetus, as in the books of Ruth and Jonah, and in parts of Isaiah. There are royal-messianic strains and others that contend sharply against royal pretensions. In the New Testament, one thinks of texts expecting an imminent parousia, and others that envisage a church that is settling down for a longer haul. In the light of such examples, it is clear that canon does not function as a test of orthodoxy, or an aggregate of that which ought to be believed. It is characterized, on the contrary, by "polyphony." This is not the same as a free-for-all. Rather, it is to suppose that scripture functions in its juxtapositions, highlighting the theological nodes around which the faith of the Church is to be nurtured in different times and places. It follows, however, that no individual text can be heard on its own, but rather in a perpetual dialogue with all other "canonical" texts. Scripture is essentially polyphonous, or many-voiced.[9]

These factors are inevitably at play in the Church's use of scriptural texts. For example, it is a commonplace of the experience of scripture to find certain kinds of text perplexing. How should Christians respond to the Bible's "violent" texts? In practice, interpretation of these often involves a process of comparison and evaluation with texts that offer a more peaceful vision, such that the violent texts are re-read in the light of the latter, or wholly eclipsed by them. The same goes for texts that subordinate women, or even seem to license their abuse, the "texts of terror," in Phyllis Trible's famous phrase.[10] Such texts may either be, in practice, omitted from the effective canon, or re-read from an emancipatory point of view, that is, in such a way as to bring to bear the special interests of the reader. Cases like this shed light on what is involved when the scripture is actually used by the Church. That is, instead of being merely a book of instruction, it finds its meaning(s) within the theologizing and experience of the Church in its many forms. In this regard, a further dimension comes into play, namely what Thiselton, citing Bakhtin, identifies as "alterity," or "the other." There is something in the very alienness of texts, as they come out of their varied ancient biblical worlds into our varied modern ones, that enters into the way in which we are bound to apprehend them.[11]

At this point I have introduced the issue of interpretation in relation to the canonical texts, and implicitly the question of authority. Who is to say how any text is to be read? I have signaled above the possibility that a canon may enshrine certain power interests. So too may prescribed uses of it by

---

9. A. C. Thiselton uses the term "polyphony" in this connection and sense (2006: 24–27).

10. Trible 1984.

11. Thiselton 2006:24–25.

various plausible authorities. Itumeleng Mosala argued concerning the biblical texts, that: "As products, records and sites of social, historical, cultural, gender, racial, and ideological struggles, they radically and indelibly bear the marks of their origins and history. The ideological aura of the Bible as the word of God conceals this reality."[12] Christopher Rowland responded to this claim with reference to the Gospel of Luke. Accepting that some texts tend to be supportive of the *status quo*, he argued that, nevertheless, more subversive texts were also to be found alongside them, and these would not be lost upon readers. Even if Luke emanated from an elite group, the variety of readings preserved in it ensured that the text could not be controlled by its ideology.[13] The artificial boundaries of a canon cannot disguise the huge variety within it, or inhibit the many possibilities of dynamic encounter with the texts. As I have put it elsewhere, "It is the diversity of canon that illustrates the nature of biblical interpretation in practice . . ."[14]

Wolter's contention that the early church defined itself apart from canon makes the important point that canon is secondary to the central criterion of the truth of Christ. Whatever the canon means, in its parts or as a whole, it is subservient to the purpose of testifying to Christ. If there is to be "control" of the meaning of scripture it lies here. Frances Young has shown how the early church expressed its understanding of this by seeking the "mind" of scripture. Irenaeus' "Rule of Truth" functioned as a kind of "hypothesis" about the meaning of scripture, that is, an overarching understanding of it, necessarily Christological, that guided the reading of its parts.[15] How this worked in practice was variously construed. While the Antiochenes looked for the "mind" (*skopos*) of individual books, Origen sought the *skopos* of scripture as a whole.[16] For Athanasius, the notion of the "mind" (*dianoia*) of scripture could justify concepts that were not found directly in scripture itself, such as *homoousios*, but which were essential for understanding its truth.[17]

These theological concepts, applied to interpreting scripture, have a certain kinship with the modern hermeneutical notion of a work's *intentio operis*, as advocated, for example, by Umberto Eco. The *intentio operis*, (the "intention of a work") is distinguished from the *intentio auctoris* ("author's intention") and the *intentio lectoris* ("reader's intention"). The *intentio operis*

12. Mosala 1993:56.
13. Rowland 1995:178–82.
14. McConville 2006b:278.
15. Young 1997:19–20.
16. Young 1997:23–24.
17. Young 1997:29, 34.

is the meaning progressively constructed from the "model reader's" conjectures about it, and is thus unconstrained by meanings that might have been intended by an author, or by interests on the part of the reader.[18] In Wolter's reading of Eco, these distinctions allow us to "understand the *intention* of the canon as a manner of its *use*."[19]

The Canon and 1 Enoch

The special position of the book of 1 Enoch in the Ethiopian Church puts all these issues in a particular light. While the universal Church has never agreed the limits of the canon, the use of 1 Enoch by a portion of the Church pushes the boundaries in a salient way. And if the canon is, in Assmann's phrase, "Kennzeichen einer textual community,"[20] the nature of that community, and how it shares its texts, are brought sharply into focus by the Ethiopian experience. How does the inclusion of 1 Enoch in the broader picture play into questions about the place of individual books in relation to the whole, and how does it affect the "intention" of that whole?

The claims of 1 Enoch to be included in this picture have historical substance. Loren Stuckenbruck has given a comprehensive account of the complex process by which the book (itself developed over a lengthy period) came to be highly valued in the Ethiopian Church. In doing so, he highlights the disputed status of the book in the early Christian centuries, when it, presumably, first entered the Ethiopian tradition, and also notes its renewed prominence in the fifteenth century. He is cautious about the attribution of "canonical" status to it.[21] Christopher Rowland claims, with a slightly different emphasis, that the interpretation of the more widely accepted canonical books requires a hermeneutic that "makes comparison with contemporary extra-canonical (particularly Jewish) literature a necessary part of the interpretative enterprise," and continues: "Our Western canon of Scripture (though we should remember that texts such as *1 Enoch* and *Jubilees* form part of the canon of Scripture of the Ethiopic Coptic church) is incomplete without attention to *1 Enoch* . . ."[22] The phrase "without attention to" leaves

---

18. "Since the intention of the text is basically to produce a model reader able to make conjectures about it, the initiative of the model reader consists in figuring out a model author that is not the empirical one, and that in the end, coincides with the intention of the text"; Eco 1992:64.

19. Wolter 2003:68.

20. Assmann 1999:26.

21. Stuckenbruck 2013:16–20.

22. Rowland 2000:1286.

open the manner in which 1 Enoch might operate theologically in the Church. However, Rowland's point finds echoes in other major theological thinkers. James Barr argued that extra-biblical Jewish work is relevant to the doing of theology because it is the context in which it grows. For him, "if there is a history of salvation, then the historical development of Jewish tradition between the Old Testament and the time of Jesus is part of that tradition."[23] Sanders, pursuing his version of "canonical theology," agrees that the New Testament cannot be understood simply from within its own literature. He has in mind what he calls "the theocentric/monotheizing thrust of the whole," by which he means "all of the literature, Hebraic and Jewish, in whatever language available, from its beginnings through the NT, including the Apocrypha and Pseudepigrapha."[24] For him, canon is characterized not only by this "monotheizing thrust," but also by an intertextuality that has no respect for canonical boundaries, however they might be drawn. Nickelsburg, making a slightly different point, declares that 1 Enoch "can be defined as noncanonical only after the canonical decisions were made."[25]

The position of 1 Enoch as a "minority report" within the larger picture cannot be glossed over. As we proceed, however, it will be helpful to take a cue from Eco's distinction between the *interpretation* and the *use* of a text, a concept that can cope with the untidiness of the outer canonical edges, by pointing up the aspects of community and practice in interpretation. As he argues, the "interpretation" is the critical attention to the nature of a text, while "use" means "to start from [the text] in order to get something else."[26]

In what follows, I want to consider some ways in which 1 Enoch might function in relation to the more widely accepted canonical literature.

1 Enoch and the NT: Jude's Use of 1 Enoch

There are several possible allusions to 1 Enoch in the New Testament,[27] but the most secure is in the Letter of Jude, where Enoch is invoked as having prophesied judgment on sin (Jude 14–15). These verses quote a Greek version of 1 Enoch 1:9, and invoke the image there of the involvement of myriads of angels in the execution of the divine judgment.[28] Echoes

23. Barr 1999:280–81.
24. Sanders 1999:18.
25. Nickelsburg 2001:4.
26. Eco 1990:57.
27. Rowland (2000:1286) cites Matt 25:31–46; 1 Pet 3:19; and Rev 8:8. See also Stuckenbruck 2013:15–16.
28. Stuckenbruck 2013:15.

of 1 Enoch are further embedded in the argument, however. Rowland finds them in v. 1 (1 Enoch 12:5-6), v. 6 (1 Enoch 16:1; 15:3, 7; 17:2), v. 8 (1 Enoch 15:4), v. 12 (1 Enoch 15:11), v. 18 (1 Enoch 15:4), and v. 25 (1 Enoch 12:3; 14:20).[29] While they are concentrated in a short section of the book (chs. 12-17), Rowland also identifies verbal allusions in other places (18:13ff.; 86:1ff.; 89:59ff.). In the argument in Jude, Enoch's preaching to the fallen angels is brought to bear on people of the writer's own day whom he regards as wicked.

Jude thus uses 1 Enoch in order to make his distinctive contribution to the New Testament's argument that the God of Israel is made known in Jesus Christ. Jude is passionately committed to the God of the Old Testament, to the Old Testament's testimony to that God, and to the rigorous distinction between truth and error—Cain, Balaam and Korah having presumptuous "error" in common—and it is in this context that he rather deliberately takes his specific authority from 1 Enoch, in an argument that is evidently reading the Old Testament more widely. For Jude, in his adoption of the theological deposit of Israel, 1 Enoch can be appealed to for its authority in the same way as the Pentateuch. He incorporates it into his reading of biblical history as a story of the judgment of God against evil, a story that is now understood to culminate in the coming of Jesus Christ. This is part of a pattern in New Testament interpretation in which Old Testament passages are held to speak of Christ, conceived (in John and Hebrews) as pre-existent. As Rowland puts it: "The allusions to the *Enoch* corpus are woven into a remarkable tapestry of typological use of Scripture in which the present circumstances are viewed and understood through the lens of these scriptural types."[30]

1 Enoch and Inner-Canonical Comparison

In his use of 1 Enoch for his message of judgment, Jude also takes over some of the distinctive characteristics of the book, notably the Enochian angelology (angels play a big part in this letter). This raises the question of how one reads different parts of the canonical literature in relation to each other. One would not necessarily build a New Testament angelology on Jude's use of 1 Enoch. In a comparative-canonical reading, one would at least have to take account of Paul, in a passage like Col 2:16-19, where angels—and indeed visions—appear in a negative light. Probably, Paul's statements here do not amount to a repudiation of Jude. The New Testament writers, in their application of the Old Testament to Christ, were not

---

29. Rowland 2000:1286.
30. Rowland 2000:1286.

building a systematic theology. The instance exemplifies the presence of counter-voices within the New Testament canon, and 1 Enoch is involved, at this point, in its complex witness.

Inner-canonical comparisons may take many forms. One obvious and important case concerns the Son of Man, a key figure in Daniel and the Gospels as well as in 1 Enoch. First Enoch's Son of Man is apparently composed from a number of Old Testament elements. For example, 1 Enoch 48 evidently conflates "Son of Man" with the Isaianic Servant (as in "a light of the Gentiles," 48:4; cf. Isa 42:6; 49:6). "Son of Man" has become eschatologized here, compared with Ps 80:17[EV], which may imply a reference to the Davidic king, or with the prophet Ezekiel, in which "son of man" is regularly used simply for a human being. First Enoch may have inherited this eschatologized Son of Man along with Daniel 7.[31] As 1 Enoch, therefore, forms part of the broad background to the Gospels on this topic, so the existence of Daniel and the Gospels as co-texts with 1 Enoch allows, in principle, for the Son of Man figure in the latter to be read Christologically.[32]

A further instance concerns the topic of wisdom, and specifically whether a dispute exists between 1 Enoch and Sirach on it. Sirach, as part of the wider LXX canonical form, has a more secure place in the canonical tradition. Yet a dialogue between the two may shed light on intra-canonical relations broadly understood.

Sirach stands firmly within the wisdom tradition. For him, wisdom is taught and learnt, cultivated within a God-given human rationality. For 1 Enoch, wisdom belongs in the heavenly domain. In a telling text in 1 Enoch 42, wisdom looks for a dwelling-place among humans, but cannot find one, so goes home again! In 1 Enoch, wisdom is available to humans only by the disclosure of divine secrets.[33]

For Argall, Sirach argues against esoteric revelatory claims (Sir 4:11–19; 6:18–37; 14:20–15:10; 39:1–11; 3:17–29; 34:1–8).[34] Conversely, he thinks 1 Enoch is aware of the disparagement of Sirach (or a school of thought like Sirach) in 1 Enoch 94:5.[35] Argall admits that the lines cannot be drawn absolutely between the two books: Sirach also knows of the revelation of "hidden things," in his case through the figure of personified Wisdom (Sir

---

31. The relationship of dependence between the two sources regarding the "son of man" is disputed. For different points of view see Goldingay 1989:150.

32. The topic of the Son of Man in 1 Enoch is pursued more fully in the present volume in the essay by Grant Macaskill.

33. Argall 1995:35.

34. Argall 1995:3.

35. Argall 1995:250–51.

24:33).³⁶ Yet he maintains a broad distinction. In Sirach (as in Proverbs) wisdom is *available to all* through the person of Wisdom, while in 1 Enoch it is esoteric and remote.³⁷ On 1 Enoch and the wisdom tradition, he finds that the apocalyptic and the sapiential are bound together, in a way that he thinks has an echo in the Gospel source Q.³⁸

My point here is that in 1 Enoch and Sirach, we may have a case of a theological dispute within "scripture" that is presented to readers of the tradition for theological appraisal. It is a process, furthermore, that is attested elsewhere within the canonical literature. Sirach's conception of divine wisdom as something available to humans, to be taught and learned, is in line with a central contention in Old Testament wisdom literature, exemplified in Proverbs 8. The notion of the body of the faithful as a community of learning is also important in Deuteronomy.³⁹ First Enoch, in contrast, has affinities with the "apocalyptic" strain in the Old Testament, exemplified by the book of Daniel. The point is that, in both the Old Testament case and the New Testament case cited above, the kind of theological process involved in reading across the canonical literature is in principle the same when 1 Enoch is included. It will be an exercise in understanding literary intertextuality within the broad stream of literature that constitutes the received sacred texts that witness to the God of Israel, and in Christian theology, interpreted through the lens of Christ.

Theological Uses of 1 Enoch

I have suggested that in principle, when 1 Enoch is drawn into the cross-canonical theologizing that is an indispensable feature of all theological use of scripture, it participates in a theological process that holds whether the canon is narrowly or broadly defined. A consequent question is in what ways it can fruitfully contribute to contemporary theological discussions. It can be said at this point that the question is not whether the book passes certain theological tests in respect of key Christian doctrines. Nickelsburg, for example, owns an ambivalence in reading 1 Enoch, because he finds it deficient in certain respects. While he applauds its evident sympathy with the oppressed and their laments (9; 103:9–15), he expresses abhorrence at the eschatologized Holy War (95:3). Yet in this regard he finds it no better or worse than the book of Revelation, and he notes the ease with which the

36. Argall 1995:2.
37. Argall 1995:92–94.
38. Argall 1995:255.
39. Finsterbusch 2005.

oppressed turn oppressor under the aegis of such theology.[40] He also thinks it curiously silent on soteriology in terms of "forgiveness, reconciliation, justification, expiation, and the like." Rather, it is "a soteriology of knowledge." In this he finds "roots of gnostic speculation," yet here too 1 Enoch may not stand alone canonically, since (he believes) such roots may also be found in the Gospel source Q, and the Fourth Gospel.[41] Yet it has a strong theology of salvation for the righteous, in which even the Gentiles can participate.[42] Making a slightly different point, though akin, Rowland finds 1 Enoch to be "a text that opens up to readers ... the perversion of human culture by an alien wisdom and the manifold ways in which that culture stands under judgement."[43] Contributors to the present volume have addressed several specific theological topics on which 1 Enoch has a distinctive voice.

The question, for my present purpose, is in what way 1 Enoch contributes to the hearing of scripture in the church. In one sense it simply belongs within that long story of the re-interpretation and re-appropriation of scripture that characterizes much of scripture itself, and that is part of the ongoing mission of the people of God. This is an enterprise that flows over from the canonical literature into the church's historic work of theology and commentary. More particularly, 1 Enoch may be seen as one of those vehicles by which the themes and content of scripture are conveyed to the generations that first heard its many parts, and those who have subsequently embraced it within their worshipping life. An important aspect of this is its interplay between the historical and the metaphorical. Historically, its protests against injustice have their roots in actual experience. Metaphorically, its language presses the limits of historicality, so as to suggest that the hard facts of history have their meaning through and beyond themselves. The point may be illustrated by the so-called Animal Apocalypse (1 Enoch 89). This is a re-writing of the biblical story from the creation up to the beginning of the Hellenistic period, recognizably re-staging the salient events and personalities of Israel's history. But it is cast throughout in the metaphorical or symbolic language found widely in the book, in which, notably, the faithful, or perhaps the elect, are depicted as "sheep," while the enemies of the faithful are "wolves" and other wild beasts. While the historical referents are rather thinly veiled, the detachment from them that is achieved by means of the language is significant, for in principle it makes the events available for the investment of new meaning. There is in this an opening for

---

40. Nickelsburg 2001:5b.
41. Also in the *Didache*; Nickelsburg 2001:6.
42. Nickelsburg 2001:7a.
43. Rowland 2000:1286, with special reference to 1 Enoch 6–15.

Christological reading, and the echoes of the leading metaphors here in the Fourth Gospel (John 10) are readily apparent. This is not to say that John 10 can be only properly understood by means of 1 Enoch. If in one sense the latter is a "feeder" of John by virtue of language and theme, its specific historical and theological concerns and claims are susceptible of being critiqued as well as explicated by the Christological re-framing of "shepherd" and "sheep" (a metaphor which, of course, has other additional antecedents, both in scripture and outside it).

Conclusion

In the story and practice of canon, the use of 1 Enoch in Ethiopia has a special place, and represents perhaps the strongest disturbance of the idea of the canon's fixity and universality. As such, however, it may be said to disturb only an unsustainable view of canon as an aggregate of orthodox truths. When canon is understood, rather, as the scripture by which the various communities of Christian faith learn through the Holy Spirit to be formed in Christ, then the relative place and importance of the canonical books become a matter of ecumenical testimony as to how those books function in the forming of those communities. This is in line with what I have described above as an "external" view of canon. It follows that a theologically appropriate response to the recognition of 1 Enoch by some churches as canonical, or quasi-canonical, is to stand alongside them and to hear their testimony. What are the Ethiopian churches, as part of the one holy catholic apostolic church, telling us of their experience of Christ via 1 Enoch? The question is part of the ongoing task of the worldwide church to understand the Gospel on the broadest canvas, and in relation to the endless challenges posed to it by an ever-changing and infinitely complex world.

2

Plotting "Holy Tradition" in Ethiopian Orthodox Discourse

ALEXANDRA SELLASSIE ANTOHIN

"The law is perfect and imperfect at one and the same time . . . it is imperfect, if the mind of those who are being instructed does not go beyond the letter. The crudity of the letter is only half-knowledge."

—ST. CYRIL OF ALEXANDRIA[1]

For the Church Fathers, the art and science of understanding the foundations of Christian law was a consistent nexus of attention. Theological divisions on the degree of scholastic license permissible for those ecclesiastically learned to illicit truth and meaning from the scriptures have fueled specific approaches to interpretation. Some leaders of early Christianity sought to demonstrate how scriptural law, through careful engagement and interpretation can bring depth of meaning and thereby offer transformative modes for expressing revealed truths as represented in textual forms. St. Cyril (Patriarch from 412–444), drawing on a statement from St. Paul, "The letter kills but the spirit vivifies" (2 Cor 3:6), likened this condition as akin to "peeling off the thickness of the

---

1. Malaty 1995:56.

shadow,"[2] that unlike how law was received before the ancients, Christ's mystery required expansive teaching and reflection: shadows, in concert with the letter, reveal a richness to the law beyond what can be communicated by words alone.

Within Orthodox Christian theological understanding, the means of receiving and interpreting the law is in the "instruction", grounded in what is called "the Holy Tradition", a compendium of teachings from apostolic times that is regarded as an uninterrupted continuum since the establishment of the Christian church. This idea and accepted method of vivifying the letter had benefited from a historical authority that dates back centuries to the Fathers of the Church, anywhere from 325 to 787 depending on the branch of Christianity in question. The encompassability of the term becomes more challenging when trying to relate contemporary engagements of Church life, practice and discourse. Pop (2011) accentuates what is often the most contentious aspect of the concept, the dynamics between "human traditions" and "divine revelation," which he argues is "a confrontational space of argumentation and reasoning." Discerning "the Holy Tradition" from "the human traditions is a typical Orthodox theological task and one that presupposes an ongoing discursive and practical argumentative commitment."[3] If empirical research is able to break through certain institutional biases (here, he is mostly referring to the Eastern Orthodox Church of the Mediterranean and countries east of Europe), then a less investigated domain awaits in the "Orthodox complex space."[4] While social theorists have had much to say about tradition as a social construct of constant reinvention (Hobsbawm and Ranger 1983), this analysis purposefully engages with the specifically Orthodox theological connotation of this word. If the Tradition of the church is regarded as inclusive of human traditions and divine revelation as passed down through the ages, who are the recipients of this tradition and by what processes, pedagogical or otherwise, is it being transmitted into contemporary application and relevance?

The following discussion is both an exploration and a methodological proposal. It seeks to explore one highly active segment of theological discourse within the Ethiopian Orthodox Church and by its adherents: the particularized understanding of covenant in its materialized, liturgical and spiritualized forms. There are ways in which this concept is circumscribed in dogma, and there are ways that covenant is defined in popular narrative discourse. The emphasis of this chapter will be on the latter, to argue how the

2. A. Kerrigan, cited in Malaty 1995:57.
3. Pop 2011:104.
4. Pop 2011:104.

"Orthodox complex space", here characterized by the narrators of providential legends of local church histories, as interacting directly, indirectly and moreover creatively with the institutional church and corpus of recognized sources. By featuring voices that are often considered by scholarly outlooks as peripheral to theological discourse, the evaluation of several narrative formulas aims to consider its authoring processes as inclusive of the generative movements of tradition. The material presented here features how lay people take parts of theological sources and use them to frame their retellings of local legends of saints and their miracles. I focus on the *Dersana Urael* ("The Sermon of Urael"), a composition considered part of the apocalyptic genre, a classification supported by its central protagonist Archangel Urael, who is equivalent to Uriel, a pivotal figure in 1 Enoch, being one of the archangels who guides Enoch through the cosmos in 1 Enoch 17–36. Through the assistance of armies of angels, with specific assistance from Archangel Gabriel, the subject of his own homilies (*Dersana Mikael*, another popular devotional text), he establishes certain pacts with "the Ethiopians," thereby reflecting Urael as a particularly lauded holy personage in Ethiopia.[5] Based on ethnographic investigations conducted with multiple Orthodox Church communities in Dessie (2010–2012), I argue that these legends describe a worshipful elaboration of the dialogic relationship between devotees and the devoted. On a broader level, the analysis is dedicated to two objectives: to take seriously the textual and liturgical engagements of Orthodox worship and devotions as dynamic content for interpretation and elaboration, and to forge humble beginnings to a more ecclesial approach to studies of contemporary theological discourse, by ethnographic engagement with a vaster spectrum of contributors to "Holy Tradition."

The Methodology of Elaboration in Ethiopian Orthodox Christian Discourse

Circumscribing tradition as part and parcel of the sacramental and liturgical life of the Church, which Vladimir Lossky describes as "the mysterial character of Christian knowledge,"[6] has garnered significant attention among Eastern Orthodox theologians as compared to Ethiopian Orthodox Church scholars. Lossky defers to St. Basil, a Church father shared between the Oriental and Eastern schools of thought (prior to the canonical divisions of the Council of Chalcedon [451]), regarding "the unwritten customs . . . necessary for understanding the truth of the Scripture . . . the sign of

5. Caquot 1955:62.
6. Lossky 1974:13.

the Cross, baptismal rites, blessing of oil, eucharistic epiclesis, the custom of turning towards the east during prayer and that of remaining standing on Sunday and during the period of Pentecost."[7] This body of knowledge and the techniques of accessing and engaging with it, have corresponding applications in the Ethiopian Orthodox Church, less defined as "Holy Tradition"—the closest cognate to this term would be *Haymanota Abew* (Faith of the Fathers) or *Serate Bete Kristiyan* (Structure of the Church)—but reflected clearly in the church school training. The Ethiopian Orthodox pedagogical training is part of a gradual learning system, starting as early as age four, taking many decades to advance, and contains levels such as the *Nebab Bet* (School of Reading), *Qedasse Bet* (School of Liturgy) to more specialized arts such as *Zema Bet* (School of Chant) and *Qene Bet* (School of Liturgical Poetry).[8] Traditional Church schooling signifies a developed methodology of scriptural exegesis, one conducted by learned individuals who are theologically guided, that is, not ordinary folks. Therefore, understanding the truth of scripture is a pedagogical process that draws from a developed set of expressive mediums and techniques, making Holy Tradition a highly crafted, learned approach in the Ethiopian Orthodox context.

One school of clerical training deserves special notice in relation to its impact on trends of narrative elaboration, both textual and what I will later argue as oral and performative. *Andəmta*, a term connoting the methodology of theological interpretation (and the subject of the essay in this volume by Ralph Lee), is a school of Ethiopian Orthodox church education, where students are taught a structured method of explicating key Scriptural texts and Church canon. Lee focuses on the legacy of St. Ephrem, an Antiochene theologian, whose style of biblical exegesis has had an enduring impact on Ethiopian Orthodox pedagogy and scholasticism. This Ephremic style of interpretation displays what Lee posits as a blending of Alexandrian and Antiochene schools, by "incorporate[ing] significant influences from the East as well as the West Syriac traditions."[9] In large part, these influences contribute to the pedagogical approach of employing hymns and allegorical imagery to transmit theological ideas, particularly innovative as it draws concrete linkages in order to unify the laws of the Old Testament with its realization (fulfilment of prophecy) in the New Testament. This is consistent with how Orthodox theological discourse in the East Tradition broadly conceives of "Holy Tradition." This comprehensive approach towards scripture as chronicled and instructed by the Church takes on added stress in

---

7. Lossky 1974:147.
8. *The Church of Ethiopia* 1970; Binns 2013.
9. Lee 2011:49; see now Lee 2017.

Ethiopian Orthodoxy, where particular material and historical elaborations of the covenant serve as additional means of connectivity via its liturgical development of the *tabot*.

One distinguishing feature of Ethiopian Christianity is its reputation as an uninterrupted lineage of monotheism, "1,000 years of Judaism, 2,000 years of Christianity" as the late Patriarch Abune Paulos would often proclaim. Related to this characterization, one of the most iconic images of Ethiopian Orthodox devotion is the procession of the *tabot* on significant feast days of the liturgical calendar. A *tabot* is a material representation of the physical Mosaic covenant also known as the Ten Commandments, and holds a particular place in the consecration of Ethiopian Orthodox Churches. This item, dedicated to individual saints and archangels, sits inside the sanctuary (*meqdes*) of every church and is the altar from which the Eucharist is consecrated, thereby establishing its definition as the blood covenant of Christ. Though there are direct correspondences to the placement of the *tabot* or altar slab in other Orthodox churches (see *antimension*), this liturgical feature is greatly underemphasized and ambiguously defined. A historian such as Teshale Tibebu, in his *The Making of Modern Ethiopia* (1995), defines "tabot Christianity" as a type of indigenous cultural psyche: "a church is identified more by the *tabot* inside it than by the Cross sign on the roof top of its building."[10] Alternatively, the *tabot* has been studied as part of the techniques of *andəmta*,[11] as part of Coptic liturgical genesis,[12] as exegesis and homiletic works, such as *Dersana Tsion*[13] and *Dersana Urael*, to be discussed in the following section, and as philosophy and polemics of chosen people.[14] Tadesse Tamrat comes closest to a social history of *tabots* by exploring the emergence of what he termed as "spiritual fiefdoms" of medieval Ethiopia. His analysis provides a rare evaluation of the connectivity between canon composed by the Church and what would be considered by believers as customs of worship. The literary form of *kidan* (solemn promise given by Jesus Christ at the end of a saint's life) is derived from the *gedl* (hagiography) in which their miracles are described. The following excerpt from the *gedl Lalibela* (a twelfth-century Ethiopian royal saint) serves as one example of how *kidans* are composed and read on a their feast day, or *tabot negs*: "Whoever brings in an offering, be it small or be it large, I shall receive it from him: and I shall receive it stretching my right hand . . . If he offers oil

10. Tibebu 1995:7.
11. Lee 2011.
12. Fritsch 2012.
13. Amsalu 2015.
14. Mohammed 2012.

I shall anoint his head with the ointment of my mercy; and even if he brings green sheaths of wheat from the grains of his fields into my temple . . . I shall receive it from him . . ."[15] Tamrat posits that there was a mirroring of patron-vassal dynamics, similar to how intercessory human-divine bonds are cultivated: "it is possible to see the *kidan* as a divine land grant on which the clergy base their claims to the spiritual leadership and the economic support of the local population."[16] Tamrat's analytical framework is clearly Marxist–historical, reflective of Ethiopian historiography in the period after the 1974 revolution. The impact of *tabot* popularity both geographically and through social customs encouraged the development of a particular cultural and political imaginary of synchronic interaction between heavenly and earthly realms, a pattern Tamrat notes as continuing in the contemporary age through practices such as pilgrimages.

Despite the various ways that the topic of covenant has been enumerated in the Tradition of the Ethiopian Orthodox Church, there is a great taboo on the discussion of *tabots*, which are generally regarded as an unseemly topic to address. This is partly due to local restraint by clergy on discussing these highly venerated items with individuals outside ecclesiastical circles, much less with foreigners—the general public never sees the *tabots* and only the high clergy are allowed to handle them. Associated with this reality of the ambiguity of *tabots* is the resistance by individuals, laypeople and clergy alike, to acknowledging the materiality of this ritual item. A *tabot* is the sanctifying component of a church; a bishop consecrates a *tabot* instead of the church proper. It is first planted (*tabot makel*), which refers to a saint's manifestation into the earthly properties, then transfigured as an altar of wood or stone (*tabot hig*), then crowned (*tabot negs*)—a ceremony that consecrates the church, ontologically functioning as its foundation. Popular literature published by churches that describe their church community often include histories of the church's foundations. By way of a brief illustration, the memorial booklet of St. Gabriel's church in Dessie (north–central Ethiopia) describes the historical account of his church *tabot*'s movements, indicating a particular subjectivity of a material covenant: "It came from Ras Mekonnen's *s'il bet* (icon/painting studio) in Harrar then went to an Addis Abba church, then was 'requested in Dessie,' where it was housed in the main diocesan church from 1924–1976." Such idiosyncratic chronicling influenced a certain approach to broaching the topic of *tabots* in contemporary reflections. Open-ended questions such as "how did the *tabot* arrive," "how was it found," "how did the *tabot* come to be," or "what *tabots* does

15. Tamrat 1995:196.
16. Tamrat 1995:196.

your church have," avoiding the words "create" or "made," are based on a socially acknowledged personification of these items.

Furthermore, *tabot* histories opened up a rich social space for how believers vivify their surroundings as spiritually directed or mandated. On a national scale, the *Tsion tabot* in the ancient city of Axum (northern Ethiopia), believed to hold the ark of the covenant that was spirited away from Solomon's temple in the tenth century BCE, is the most foundational legend for Ethiopian Orthodox Christians, and further rationale behind the protective behavior of Orthodox Christians towards their spiritual heritage. The *tabot* of St. George and its role in securing victory against the Italians in 1896 is another instance firmly imprinted on twentieth-century historical accounts. The *tabot* of Sedetinya Medhane Alem (the "exiled" Savior of the World), is another popular legend about the *tabot*'s removal outside Ethiopia and re-deposition to follow Emperor Haile Sellassie's movements during his government's exile during the Second Italian War (1936–1941). These archetypal narratives of "covenant", as a talisman and a potent symbol of national heritage and sovereignty, reveal the degree that local developments of a theological concept find their way into historical framings of modern legends, which I will argue contributes to popular elaborations of Ethiopian Orthodox church discourse.

So far, I have delineated certain trends in Ethiopian Orthodox methodology of interpretation as consistent with definitions of "Holy Tradition" and have proposed how the *tabot*, as a liturgical development and as a domain of narrative elaboration, is constitutive of Tradition. The remainder of this analysis will consider the form and practice of telling *tabot* legends as witnessed during my fieldwork with various church communities in Dessie, in order to demonstrate how its narrators are coming into contact with theological discourse. Here, I approach "discourse" in the Bakhtinian sense, as "the inter-play between systems of social value, linguistic convention, and the world portrayed."[17] My aim is to understand *tabots* within their textual and liturgical contexts, which holds the key for understanding how these stories carry social repercussions for its narrators and audience.

Intertextual Reference of *Dersana Urael*

Contrary to typical aversions to discussing *tabots*, Solomon was refreshingly open about this topic and offered his interpretation about how they might emerge, what I characterize as *tabot* origin legends. An instructor of Information Technology, an engaged member of his community church,

17. Hanks 1987:671.

local Sunday school group, and *Mahibere Kidusan* (a national and politically significant organization of Orthodox Christian professionals), he presented the geneses of local churches as grounded in a certain agency of their *tabot*'s namesakes. The way Solomon phrased it, the consecration of the *tabot* of Kirkos lij (Cyriacus the Child, a third CE century martyr) was a result of the "*tabot* speaking." It spoke due to the predicament of the local community, which suffered from various health problems that he referred to generically as malaria and HIV. Individuals began to appeal to the saint and it was this concentration of local devotion that urged the clergy to request the local parish council have Kirkos lij represented in the form of a *tabot* dedication. Solomon's summation of social dynamics and its impact on individual and communal worship underscored the critical importance of devotion as a dialogic relationship. The prayers of the people living in the neighboring hills "were answered," as he stated, substantiated by what he recounted as the healing effects of the saint's feast day. During the annual celebrations of Kirkos lij, people were cured or experienced great relief from illness on these events, punctuated by the annual or sometimes bi-annual rite of *tabot negs* when the *tabot* is removed from the sanctuary and is ritually processed by the clergy and celebrants together. The respect and honor directed to the saint, and the ritual exposure to the *tabot*, brought about material healing, Solomon explained. Therefore, the emergence of a local *tabot* was reasoned by Solomon as founded on a particular social condition that is solved by spiritual assistance. Kirkos lij would cease to exist without acknowledgement by prayer, this logic extending to all holy personages: to worship is intrinsic to the physical manifestation of the saint in daily life.

A fusion between the divine will that initiates sacred presence on earth and the materialization of that presence in the form of a *tabot*, ergo church—the *tabot* being its edifying component—is an issue at the heart of these *tabot* legends. In the case of Kirkos lij, even though Solomon phrased the events as emanating from the devotion of a particular set of individuals, he never ascribed credit of the *tabot* consecration to human will, that is, all spiritual force reflected the subordination of the believers' love and respect to the saint. Through direct influence and accountability of the devotees is diminished, the significance of witness ("He [the saint] heard their prayers") accounts for a crucial factor of the dialectical movements contained in these *tabot* legends.

However, the content of the narrative, and the specific actions attributed to the *tabot* that allowed it to figuratively "speak," were not a function of personalized imagination but were guided by a certain canonical source. Here, the text of *Dersana Urael* ("The Homily of Archangel Urael") was retold by Solomon, signaling how he presented local *tabot* legends not as self-authored stories but as consistent with oral and written sources from the Ethiopian Orthodox Church tradition. Speaking about the history of Arsema Mariam, a *debal* (secondary) *tabot* of St. Mikael's church, and what Solomon explained as a "*tabot* that can go where it likes," he directly launched into a narration of *Dersana Urael* to substantiate his claim. The homiletic text is dated to the late nineteenth century, though the translator of this work surmises that is it potentially written much earlier, *ca.* fifth century as part of the *Qerrilos*, a collection of patristic writings.[18] Its composition, plainly drawing inspiration from the way Uriel guides Enoch through the cosmos in 1 Enoch 17–36, chronicles the encounters of Archangel Urael as he hovers over holy places, such as monasteries headed by renowned leaders of Ethiopian ecclesiastical history, as well as zones of the unconverted in Ethiopia. This detail is the crucial means by which he dispenses with the sanctification described through the imagery of wings dipped in blood, which Urael collected from Christ's side. The symbolic connection between blood and covenant[19] is a detail important for elaborating this theological concept. In this composition, this action of sprinkling the blood that Christ shed over primarily northern to south-central Ethiopia has the effect of confirming the glory of national Christianity and serves as a history of vanquished heathens. This theme contains a certain symmetry to how Solomon narrated the contemporary legend of Kirkos lij to me. He characterized the neighborhood as originally not very faithful, and only because they were suffering, reflecting what he considered a broader moral malaise, did the turn of events towards greater spiritual engagement occur.

Using the canonical account of how monastic centers in Ethiopia were specifically selected for a sacred pact with God, through the flight of the archangel, Solomon relates and extends this action to how a *tabot* may emerge in any given terrain. According to Solomon, it is Uriel who sows the seed by this blood, and where the blood of Christ dropped, a church will be permitted to be built. This seemingly abrupt eruption of divine presence is based on Solomon's presentation of the design of pre-ordination as described in the homily, and it is from this logic that Solomon can substantiate newly accounted for *tabots*.

It is worth noting how compositions considered part of the Ethiopian Orthodox canon often overlap into the genre of "the epic," popular legends of a land and people's sacred foundations. Smith evaluates how legends, and the popularization of Church histories as national histories, contain

---

18. Caquot 1955:63.
19. Covenant sealed by blood is a recurring theme in Exodus (e.g., Exod 24:4–8).

"regenerative power inherent in the ideal of a myth of ethnic election,"[20] namely the chosen people thesis in multiple national traditions. *Dersana Urael* can be interpreted as a type of manifest destiny of Orthodox evangelism, particularly salient for the socio-political dynamics of a country rapidly consolidating into a national empire at the turn of the nineteenth century. A more well-known text of Ethiopia's Christian history is the *Kebra Negast* ("Glory of the Kings"), which employs the techniques of the *andəmta* interpretative methodology and containing much symbolic elaboration about the *Tsion tabot*/ark.[21] This text written in the fourteenth century is hastily dismissed by scholars as marred by overlying political agendas of the day (i.e. justification of Solomonic dynasty rule), thereby calling into question whether this source can be considered as part of "Holy Tradition" as we have been delineating. While this critique might be summarily accepted by Ethiopian scholars working today, I suggest that the persistence of these legends about the *tabot*, textually and through popular circulation, can and should be considered as traditions of chronicling that are part of a methodology of how contemporary narratives of spiritual histories connect with a church and its people.

Social History of a *Tabot* in Ritual Resistance

Another way of engaging with a theological concept is through its performative rites and the devotional gestures they inspire. The *Dersana Urael* provides some concrete examples about veneration that signify its spiritual and cultural importance, such as hymnal praise, material offerings, and continued prayer by the believing community.[22] More broadly, meta-communicative processes of the transmission can be located in liturgical orientations to church, which Carroll analyzes as the Greek Orthodox *metanoia*, or *mesalem* in the Ethiopian Orthodox context.[23] More than the act of prostration, these are metaphysical postures of acknowledging Godly presence, "an act of humility and obeisance that is done, particularly during periods of penitence, such as Lent, as a way of showing respect to something that is holy."[24] Orthodox Christians regard church not as a locality exclusively, but as a behavioral reaction and a temporal condition. It is what William and Boyd describe as the vital movement of the ritual image, structured

20. Smith 2003:77.
21. Lee 2011.
22. Caquot 1955:82.
23. Carroll 2015.
24. Carroll 2015:61.

simultaneously by "emotive force" and "theological content."[25] Furthermore, to draw connectivity between the liturgical gesture and its accompanying embedded discursive idea permits opening up a space for evaluating how performative rites can inform and interact with Tradition and its associated formats of scriptural interpretation.

The interconnected nature of Timqet (Epiphany), a major feast day in the Orthodox calendar, as the macro-context of *tabot* illumination is part of the matrix of references key to understanding this socio-theological phenomenon, situating the "media of communication," whether, text, ritual or both simultaneously, as creating and "restructuring social interactions rather than merely expressing them."[26] Timqet provides such a space for individual and community commentaries to interpret the idea of covenant. In an outlying neighborhood of Addis Ababa, an incident occurred in 1995 where St. Michael's *tabot* refused to "come out" (*tabot alwetam*) of the sanctuary, and effectively disturbed its participation in the three-day long processional ceremony. As one member of the neighborhood described it, the priests came to release the *tabot* out of its sanctuary on the eve of Epiphany, and they were prevented from coming any closer. The member of clergy that was holding the *tabot* on top of his head became locked in a state of paralysis, not being able to talk or move. The *tabot* developed a reputation of being "repressed," and the church began to be referred to as *Chikun Mikael* ("the repressed Michael"). This characterization became a major thread of how this church's history was narrated, as this neighborhood was robbed of the privilege of assisting their Mikael to his sanctuary in the Entoto hills; only a select number of St. Michael churches have this honor in Addis Ababa, the capital. Retellings of this legend and the agency of the saint via its *tabot* was discussed in the third person; it was he (Mikael) that refused to join Yesus and Mariam (named as persons) to Jan Meda, the location where the baptismal pool and Epiphany festivities in Addis take place. The subjectivity of the *tabot*'s will, another tropic similarity previously discussed, reflects popular understandings of divine agency, here derived by lay commentaries on how *tabots* ceremonially behaved.

But why the nickname, "the repressed Michael"? One basic answer is that this is a form of propaganda, a way of politicizing local affairs. In response to the moniker, another community member seemed to skate over its reputation as being "repressed." She believed this grew out of partisan perspectives on the debacle of the church construction; community members were trying to perpetuate a legend (*afe tarik*) to support their

25. Williams and Boyd 1993:142.
26. Bell 1988:369.

cause (*Sow sime awetalet*—"The people named him/it"). The tensions apparent in parish communities exposed the associated issues of power and authority as parishes strived to fulfil their churches in transition. This point relates to how pseudo-canonical works such as the *Kebra Negast*, the political purposes for which have been criticized, are not a unique historical phenomenon, given how modern day *tabot* chronicling proceeds to follow similar patterns.

Additionally, the qualifier of "repression" was a reflection of the local displeasure of tampering with a promise, a commitment of sponsorship that was voiced publicly and the ramifications of the interference. A local entrepreneur pledged a substantial sum of money to erect a larger church for St. Mikael. This commitment galvanized the church parish council to champion for local support for an expanded church. A local taxi-driver, in his retelling, aligned these positive developments and subsequent thwarting by Yesus church with why Mikael stalled during the Epiphany celebration; the *tabot's* behavior was a clear response to the "injustice," in his opinion, of being denied the honor that was being bestowed by his devotees. This series of developments denoted an active agreement between people and St. Mikael, sidelined by jealousy, rivalry and political squabbling.

A member of a local *mahaber* (devotional society) suggested two reasons behind Yesus church's antagonistic reaction. By leading their own procession, proceeding to the baptismal pool at Jan Meda independently and not co-joining with the other churches in front of Yesus church, St. Michael's was exerting an independence from the local parish network. She was sympathetic to the viewpoint that the shift in dynamics might be interpreted as contrary to the whole spirit of how Timqet was celebrated, as a communal event of churches coming together as one. This poses a contrastive point to the expressed communitarian spirit of churches of Timqet; we witness a vacillating tension between hierarchization and interdependence. The representatives from St. Michael's insisted that there is no lingering animosity, that all churches are united again and any internal conflict was an exaggeration. Despite the harmonious conclusion, many people, either regulars of the church or from the broader neighborhood, continued to refer to the church as the repressed Mikael. Righteousness and vindication by way of retaining the name suggested that there were certain sentimental attachments to struggle in fulfilling devotional promises among Ethiopian Orthodox Christians.

Producing Legends as a Resource of Mobilization

If the first example of *tabot* legends was about reference and citation, and the second a reflection of transmission via ritual movements, then this last case is about how devotional commitments are publically verbalized in the ways conceived as prototypical speech acts. Abba Mekeferia Seb was a well-known monk and often treated as a local celebrity by his admirers who estimated he is responsible for helping initiate over fifty church projects all over Wollo (district of north-central Ethiopia), as well as serving as an avid campaigner for the planting of acres of indigenous trees. Discussing the revitalization of churches in rural areas outside Dessie, the monk phrased many of these foundation stories as scenarios in the exercise of steadfast conviction. I had been prompted by one of his admirers to ask about how the church of St. Michael was envisioned, with Abba Mefekeria Seb as the primary driver. Fifty years ago, Abba Hadis, a local priest, saw a hillside location known as Gerar Amba and suggested that St. Michael should be moved there instead of the lowland swamp where the *tabot* was stationed. Abba Mefekeria Seb saw the place and was emotionally enthralled, convinced that this was the providential location. News about this intention began to circulate locally and about forty people pledged to give a thousand birr each to construct a church. Abba Mefekeria Seb states rather pointedly that the Bishop, Abba Samuel at the time, and the clergy as well saw the advantage of having a church of St. Michael in a more visible location, as it would bring them more revenue and would permit it to be well-endowed into the future. After giving his permission to break ground, the church council faced interference by a pair of influential individuals who were strongly against the decision. In one heated exchange, Abba Mefekeria Seb remembers himself saying to the detractors "when you die, St. Michael will receive it/you," a quintessential "wax and gold" (*semenaworq*) statement, dually predicting the man's encounter with St. Michael from his earthly departure and St. Mikael's rightful glory on earth by assuming a place in his sanctuary. Soon after, the high rains began flooding and graves on the lowland where the original church was located began to be washed away. The people in the area took this as a sign that unless St. Michael was moved similar destructive actions would continue. The residents of this outlying community asked Abba Mefekeria to intercede on their behalf and take this problem to the city administration. The significance of his words is etched into the dramatic memory of the story as Abba Mefekeria states his actions to the administrators. Refusing to be seated for the meeting, he recalls proclaiming: "I cannot sit while St. Michael is standing. His *tabot* is buried in the swamp. We need his miracle and we must free him." While the local government eventually approved construction, the prophetic part of this narrative was that the main instigator of the resistance, died on Tselot Hamus (Holy Thursday) and this was seen as an ordaining moment for the foundational story of the church.

By chronicling a localized instance of a *tabot*'s agency, its circulation by continued narrative-retellings situates this activity as a prospective resource for social mobilization, in this case, as a way to bolster community support for church expansion projects. This story concerned an imagined church, as plans to build a St. Michael's church were yet to be completed at the time of the interview in 2012. For individuals to envision a sacred landscape populated by divine presence that is unrealized (i.e. not made concrete via miracles or *tabot* consecrations) should not be confined to wildly creative reasonings but perhaps to a metaphysical conceptualization of *tabot* that is constituted by events of "witness," which I note carries tropic relation to covenant as a form of constant dialogic engagement. The events that result in *tabots* deposition into permanent sanctuaries are memorialized in local histories and therefore their transformation into repeatable legends are often crucial, what Lévi-Strauss and Moore termed as an activity of prospective historical legitimation of "the past as the beginning of a future that is in the process of taking shape."[27] Therefore, the ongoing nature of faith is located in these materializations of a concept, in this case, a specific saint's covenant with God and his devotees, and is utilized as evocative forces to challenge this–worldly representation and authority.

This story was chronicled as a local legend with its requisite mythical aura, while also revealing a notably removed agency of St. Michael. After all, the labor of the community to found a concrete church was contingent upon carving out a space for divine presence. Many stories of church foundations as a genre of popular theological engagement with Ethiopian Orthodox tradition, centered on how believers prevailed over the fickleness and indeterminacy of human responsibility as a moral challenge. Interpreting these stories through the filter of established tropes of divine intercession also enabled its audience to learn how to read messages through symbolic resonance. Circumstances such as flooding as an impetus for carrying out the construction plan and the promise of St. Michael's impending miracle all set up a tangible position for the holy figure, yet contingent on guided devotional action. As the monk characterized, twenty years of consistent praying was what actualized the *tabot* of Mikael, a devotional commitment to acknowledge always.

A question that I was consistently asked during fieldwork was whether other Orthodox Christians had *tabots*. To answer that such a ritual item

---

27. Lévi-Strauss and Moore 1974:280–81.

had no direct corresponding place in other Orthodox Churches not only confirmed a distinctiveness and honor for my fellow inquiring Orthodox, it also initiated a honest appraisal of alternative Christian perspectives on divine presence elsewhere. To ask if others had a *tabot* too, meant if other Orthodox Christians were also endowed to commune and possess an intimate relationship with God via the accessible realities of heaven on earth. Furthermore, *tabots* in the ways evaluated here, were not purely a reflection of the traditionalism of the Ethiopian Orthodox Church, as many Pentecostal perspectives had voiced to me. What these stories have shown is how individuals create methodologies of interpretation that come into contact with theological ideas. In the case of Solomon, he tangentially analyzed these correspondences by noting the problem of health epidemics locally, by evaluating devotion to a popular saint and the emerging series of events of the saint's *tabot*. His general outlook as a young and aspiring local preacher was shaped by what he believed to be an existing moral malaise to which the devotion to Kirkos lij and his ability to be successfully testified to, via its *tabot* legend, served as a potent means of evangelism. In the case of *Chikun* Mikael, there were similar alignments with analytical interpretation, as the breach in *tabot* refusal was framed as a reflection of fractious state of local diocesan politics. Therefore, through this concern about how the "vitalism" of Orthodoxy was becoming reconciled into "modernity," I came to understand that understanding about the *tabot* implied the future of this much-valued concept, making their question whether other lands outside Ethiopia possess *tabots* all the more consequential.

Conclusion

The focus on narrative retellings about the *tabot*, as a domain where individuals can interact with Church canon, offers a broader theoretical query on the space for innovation within a religious tradition rooted in deep historicity, what Turner (1974) calls the tension between *stasis* and *dynamis*. As a closing thought, the return to the language of symbols, metaphor and allegory, so prolific in the Ethiopian Orthodox Church, is useful for relating how narratives can act as devices that communicate cultural logics and, in some instances, inventively elaborate a theological idea.[28] Turner describes the ritual of building Hindu shrines that starts with planting a pot of seed in the earth, then emerges to correspond to all bodily appendages, representing a cycle of transformation, a model that becomes submerged and forgets its "moving originals" as time and a hierarchized mediation to spiritual

28. Antohin 2014.

realm is installed.²⁹ The recursive image of temple=body=temple, which Turner synthesizes as the structure/anti-structure binary of standing and moving, corresponds with initial forms of corporate bodies of early religion, hierarchized power as definitional to cosmologies in their temporal forms. The vitality of tradition, therefore, is predicated on "spontaneity hav[ing] its own rhetorical structure; no free verse is truly free . . . without a repertoire of structures to rely on, there can be no spontaneity."³⁰

This essay has employed its own interpretative license to argue that a notion of "Holy Tradition" is an active discursive category in Ethiopian Orthodox Christianity, not only reflected in its historical canonical trends but also in contemporary voices and perspectives. Further work on how this category is elaborated in local scholastic literature, as well as how it builds or contrasts to similar conceptions in other Oriental Churches is crucial. In my view, the objective would less be to identify direct corresponding labels than to highlight the differences in approaches that attain the same end: interacting with Tradition as a means of achieving cohesion.

In recent years, the number of empirical studies of Orthodox societies in the modern age has greatly increased, yet they remain distinctly "other" in comparison to anthropological investigations of Christianity, mostly of the Protestant kind. The analysis presented here has been careful to note that individuals are not theologizing—this would work against deeply-entrenched and hierarchized modes of scholasticism—and instead contribute to theological discourse, which connotes the process of adding to an already approved body of knowledge and teachings. The conservative ethos of Orthodox Christians can greatly benefit from research on popular understandings of theology, most substantially due to their adherence to authoritative sources, whether textually derived or passed down by spiritual elders. Boylston (2013) discusses the unique contributions of Orthodox traditions to broader Christian scholarship. Illustrating through an anecdote of personally reading St. John Chrysostom as if conversing with an informant, he proposes that a "key point of development will be to ask how scholarly hermeneutics articulate with the interpretive and epistemological ideas and assumptions of Orthodox Christians in daily life and with different degrees of engagement with their religious traditions."³¹ Studying catechism texts that are part of canonical or even pseudo-canonical literature (i.e. *Dersana Urael, Wudasse Mariam, Tamera Yesus,* etc.) adjacent to individuals' reception of this material can bring insights to how theologically-shaped

---

29. Ramanujan in Turner 1974:282.
30. Turner 1974:289.
31. Boylston 2013: par. 16.

conceptions of sin, salvation, redemption, obedience, and human-divine cooperation, are integrated. Observations regarding the ritualization of chronicles and homilies (i.e. hagiographies and the formula of the *kidan*) further emphasize the liturgical and material dimensions of church canon as part of the instructional process of Orthodox Christians. Equal attention to literalism in ethnographic studies of religious communities, as well as to oral and ritual registers of engagement, holds the potential for demonstrating how contemporary, non-clerical engagements are not as disconnected from theological discourse as commonly perceived.

Acknowledgments

The content presented is based on dissertation research supported by ethnographic field research in Dessie and Addis Ababa (2010–2012). The author would like to thank all the individuals who have served as informants and supplied the core testimonies featured here.

3

The Contemporary Influence of the Ethiopian *Andəmta* Traditional Commentary

Examples from the Commentary on 1 Enoch and Other Texts

RALPH LEE

Introduction

The Ethiopian Orthodox Church has a corpus of commentary on biblical and other sacred texts known within the Church as *andəmta*. The commentaries contain the Geʿez text known as "the scholars' text," a form of the text developed over many centuries in Ethiopia, then an often racy translation of that text into Amharic, followed by different forms of discussion of the text including of grammatical and other explanations, historical background, or plain and symbolic interpretations of the text. The name *andəmta* comes from the repeated use of the phrase *andəm*, "and another," an abbreviation for "and another one says," to introduce different interpretations.

The historical development of this corpus is somewhat unclear. We know that there was an earlier tradition of Geʿez commentary, known as *tärgʷame* or "interpretations," which could be of ancient origin, possibly dating back to the advent of Christianity in Ethiopia, but whose known manuscript tradition dates between the thirteenth and sixteenth centuries CE.[1] The connection of these commentaries with the later Amharic *andəmta* is unclear, as some of the material is repeated, but there are significant differences, with material both added and removed. There is a very important oral component of the transmission of biblical interpretation in Ethiopia that is poorly understood, and the contemporary scholars who are the custodians of this tradition eschew printed versions of the text, because they imply closure to a tradition that is essentially open. The Church would claim very ancient heritage for some of the commentary material, dating it to the time of King Solomon when, according to the Ethiopian national epic *Kebra Negast* or *The Glory of the Kings*, the Ark of the Covenant came to Ethiopia, along with cohorts of Levites and other Israelites with biblical scrolls who were versed in the Jewish understanding of the Old Testament, notwithstanding the fact that the *Vorlage* of the Old Testament text is clearly Greek. This is significant in the study of 1 Enoch, because it would be included in the list of books that came at that time, with the consequence being a clouding of the understanding of the history of 1 Enoch in Ethiopia, making it somewhat difficult to glean information from traditional scholars. Nevertheless, the text of the commentary itself has the potential to betray information, along with some of the oral tradition.

The *andəmta* commentaries originated from around Gondar, the capital of Ethiopia from 1635–1855 CE, and were developed in the Amharic language. The origin of the tradition appears to be primarily oral, but with a significant amount of the material being compiled and written down by imperial decree around 1674 EC (that would be around 1681–82 CE), to resolve confusion over different approaches to interpretation, and in particular to develop commentary in Amharic, since by this stage Geʻez had become relegated to an ecclesiastical language, and was not understood by the laity.

The seminal work of Roger Cowley remains the most analytical and penetrating work on this tradition, and of this corpus his two books stand as the most important works for understanding this complex tradition.[2] Since his work there have been several critical studies, with translations into English,[3] and a small part of the 1 Enoch commentary has been published.[4]

1. See Garcia 2010.

2. See Cowley 1971a; 1971b; 1972; 1974a; 1974b; 1977; 1978; 1980a; 1980b; 1983a; 1983b; 1985a; 1985b; 1987; 1988 and 1989.

3. See Ande Berhan 1994; Garcia 1999; Alehegne 2011; and Pedersen 1995.

4. Lee 2014.

Surprisingly, Cowley's view is that the commentary is fundamentally the fruit of the Antiochene tradition, rather than an Alexandrian connection that might have been expected, but that "it cannot be claimed that Antiochene exegetical theory is generative of Ethiopian Bible commentary—it is rather that Antiochene theory has generated Antiochene exegesis, and that this has been transmitted to Ethiopia."[5] This conclusion is very important, since it points to the fact that the tradition is very much an Ethiopian one, which has drawn on many sources, with a large number of those being connected with the "Antiochene" approach.

The tradition appears to transcend the historical divisions of the Church, with primary sources mentioned by name including John Chrysostom, St Basil and St Ephrem, but Cowley identified *Abu'l-Faraj 'Abdallāh ibn aṭ-Ṭayyib al-'Irāqī*, an eleventh-century CE Church of the East commentator on the whole Bible, sometimes referred to as "John Chrysostom of the East" in the *andəmta*, as a major source. One of the most quoted writers identified by Cowley is known as መሥፍቃን (*maśafqan*), the Ge'ez version of the Syriac name for "the interpreter," otherwise known as Theodore of Mopsuestia. Some of Origen's material is quoted, particularly some of his "spiritual" interpretations, although he himself is referred to as "the wicked Origen." This poses interesting questions in relation to the commentary on 1 Enoch, because the potential sources are more limited than those for other sacred texts, and this commentary is likely to be a more specifically Ethiopian development.

The tradition explains its approach to interpretation in the introduction to the commentary on the Pauline epistles. The interpretation opens with a colloquial Amharic translation, often with alternatives that may reflect textual variants. Other techniques employed include: grammatical analysis including the discussion of alternative punctuation; clarification of ambiguous or unclear Ge'ez words; illustrate homophones or situations where gemmination of a consonant alters the meaning; elucidation of the meaning through poetical rearrangement; the supplying of words implied in the text; the identification of other biblical passages with similar meaning; the explanation of important details that might not be understood well by the listener; the retelling of related biblical stories; the reconciliation of the meaning with other apparently contradictory biblical passages often employing diverse authorities; and the explanation of the mystery or hidden meaning of the text, often utilizing the classical Ethiopic "wax and gold"

---

5. See Cowley 1988:376. Cowley also notes here that "Antiochene" itself is a difficult entity to define, but clarifies that he is talking of the interpretative tradition associated with Antioch, and the names of Lucian, Paulinus, Eustathius, John Chrysostom, and Theodore of Mopsuestia.

method for conveying meaning.[6] Reading the commentary, although not articulated in this explanation, typology is frequently employed, and the commentaries will quote diverse sources to give a broad view of the understanding of a particular issue. Although clarification may be one intention, it is not always the aim to resolve all understanding, illustrated by the thirteen or so different interpretations of the white horse in Rev 6:4.[7]

Ethiopian commentary comes in various forms, and indeed its strongest characteristic is the diversity of the style and the content of the commentary. There are clear examples from the Syriac tradition, probably mediated through Egypt, although it is by no means certain that it was through this route alone.

For example, the commentary on Gen 22:5 states:

> ANDM: The ram is a symbol of the Lord, Isaac is a symbol of the believers. The ram became a substitute for Isaac, and the Lord became a substitute for believers. Some say the ram descended from heaven, the Lord was to descend from the heaven of heavens. Some say it was found from the Wood of the Thicket, showing that he would be born from sealed virginity, from Our Lady. It is a symbol that because he came from the flock of Abraham, he would be born from the tribe of Abraham.[8]

This is a fine example as it shows West Syriac symbolic interpretation alongside East Syriac plain interpretation. It is also characteristic of trend in this tradition to include interpretations that cannot both be true alongside each other.

Many of the interpretations are clearly there to explain ideas that would be difficult for rural Ethiopians to comprehend. The curtain of the Tabernacle, supported by hooks and eyes are compared with the means of joining a skin used for warmth, a *däbälo*, or of a case for a prayer book, a *ṣäḥafi koräǧo*.[9]

Diverse sources include the midrash, and significantly for 1 Enoch, include expositions of stories related to 1 Enoch. Found in the commentary on Psalm 82, which interprets the line "you will die like men, and like one

---

6. Anonymous 1998:2–3. It should be understood that although Levine's classic study of Wax and Gold in Ethiopia talks of meaning being hidden by the sophisticated use of language, within the Ge'ez and biblical commentary tradition, Wax and Gold is understood to be a means of conveying meaning through association of ideas: see Levine 1965.

7. Cowley 1983:229–32.

8. Anonymous 1999:143.

9. Anonymous 1999:129.

of the princes you will fall" as referring to *Semyaza* and recounts a story of *Nuhem* that amplifies the 1 Enoch account of the fallen angels:[10]

> From those on the holy mountain one desired to go and give a message to the children of Cain, and that one went from where they were, and saw how they fornicated like wild animals, and especially their leader, called Nuhem, who took a drum, and performed traditional dancing right in the middle of the crowd, like a swimmer swimming to the centre of a lake. When he saw this he was pierced with the arrow of adultery and said to the brothers, "What kind of life do we live? All we do is praise like angels, without our flesh being stuck and attached to our bones! The children of Cain really live life!" After this, there were drawn down, and when they looked, and when they copulated with each other like animals, they looked and said, "Come! Let's go down, and let us look at and take one for each of us!" Their chief was called Semyaza said to them, "Stop! Do not do this thing!" "Why do you tell lies?"[11]

This interesting account may be traced to the *Midrash ha-Gadol on Genesis*,[12] which is probably sourced in the *Pirke de-Rabbi Eliezer*.[13] This should not be used to claim any direct contact with Jewish interpreters, since this material would have been in wide circulation, although neither should it be ruled out—the picture of how various sources came to Ethiopia is poorly understood.

1 Enoch in the Ethiopian Tradition

Many do not understand well the Ethiopian canon, mostly because they do not grasp the rather different view of an open canon, supported by a closed system of doctrine that the Ethiopians have. This, I hope, will be clarified soon with the publication of Dr Bruk Asale's paper presented at the SBL Annual Meeting in San Diego, 2014.[14] The Ethiopian Church seems bound to a canon of 81 books in number more than it is to any particular collection of those books. Although closed in this way, Ethiopian canon appears to be constrained primarily by doctrine, and is potentially open even today for

---

10. *Nuhem* is most probably *Naamah* mentioned in Gen 4:22, the daughter of Lamech and Zillah.
11. Anonymous 1998:412–13.
12. Schechter 1902:118.
13. Ginzberg 1925:147 n45.
14. Asale 2014.

the inclusion of new books. The 1 Enoch commentary itself states that "if one counts four books of Kings, one should omit Enoch and Jubilees, but if one says that there are two books of Kings one should include Enoch and Jubilees."[15] The commentary itself tells us that "when the Apostles gave the books to Clement they regarded it as canonical in their hearts, but did not say it with their mouths." Furthermore, it suggests that this was because the greater part of the church sought to understand the world through philosophy, rather than through what was revealed by the Spirit to Enoch. This seems rooted in an awareness of the difference in outlook between the Ethiopians and the broader Greek world that probably did not develop in the fourth century! At the same time, it fails to note any possible Greek influence on that content from 1 Enoch.

Ethiopian tradition puts high value on the book of 1 Enoch, and its influence on the theology and on the more general outlook of Ethiopian Christianity is plain, although 1 Enoch seems not to have a clear place in the Ethiopian scriptures before the fifteenth century CE, the Golden Age of Ethiopic literature, and its history before this time is controversial. It seems likely that the Ethiopic version of the book came to Ethiopia before interest in the book had diminished, and so its reception in the fourth century is likely.[16] This is consistent with findings that suggest an influence on the Dəgg^{w}a, a hymn book whose origins lie in the sixth century CE, which demonstrates some affinity with 1 Enoch in its understanding of Paradise.[17] Debate in the fifteenth century about the place of 1 Enoch in the canon is on the basis that 1 Enoch has been precious in Ethiopia for some time, and the conclusion of the debate was to raise it 'to a level that had apparently not yet obtained.'[18] It is possible that a study of the commentary tradition may unearth some evidence here, but so far it is not forthcoming! There are many themes that seem to underlie the interpretation of 1 Enoch in the Ethiopian tradition, so in the astronomical books there is a constant implicit affirmation of the Ethiopian lunar calendar, still employed in the country to this day.

The "scholars' text" recorded in the commentary is very close to the text used by Knibb in his studies on the text, reflecting the fact that this version of the text was dominant around the end of the seventeenth century when the commentary was committed to writing.

15. Anonymous 2003:1 2.
16. Stuckenbruck 2013.
17. See chapter 5 of Lee 2017.
18. Stuckenbruck 2013.

The 1 Enoch Commentary

The commentary on Psalm 82 demonstrates that 1 Enoch is a point of reference for the understanding of other sacred texts, although the extent of this is not yet understood. Nevertheless, the cross-referencing shows that 1 Enoch is typical of the commentary tradition in the way that it is used to illuminate other texts, and its place in the understanding of Revelation will be discussed later. It is probably fair to say that although the commentary is contemporary in Ethiopia, in that it is the primary source of the understanding and the relevance of 1 Enoch for the Ethiopian Church, the broader relevance of the commentary tradition, and in particular to the relevance of 1 Enoch for contemporary theology, is that it contains reflections from a very different context, and therefore produces interpretation that we may not have considered. I offer here a selection of these.

First, the introduction to the commentary informs us that the word *Henok* is said to mean renewal (although it presents no further explanation of this idea), and Enoch is presented as a counter to Adam and Eve: "just as Adam brought old age and physical decay because of food, so Enoch restrained himself from food and brought us renewal." This view underpins the generally ascetic outlook of Ethiopia, and in particular fasting, which is a pursuit of all the devout and which is understood to be the primary way to amend evil in one's life for ascetics and laity alike. Fasting is a regular practice throughout the year, including extended fasts in preparation for Advent, Lent, and other important festivals. Enoch is also seen as the prototype resurrected human, pointing us to the entering of the Kingdom of Heaven with new bodies.[19] This emphasizes the clearly Christian interpretation of 1 Enoch within the Ethiopian tradition.

Secondly, the understanding of the source of evil in the commentary also places the battle in the human world. The battle is between the descendants of Seth, who are "angels" and are pure, and those of Cain, who "expose their nakedness, with pearl belts around their waists." God raises Enoch to rebuke the descendants of Seth who marry the lewd descendants of Cain. The fight is also seen as a contemporary one, reflecting on the life of a monk who may be seduced by worldly affairs into going out from his monastery. Some of this tendency is perhaps not surprising, since the Ethiopians also have Jubilees, where in chapter 5 the events take place on the earth and the offspring of the undesirable are "giants" but also interpreted as "mighty men" and "those who can be seen from afar," but the interpretation of 1 Enoch seems to take things a step further, and relegate the whole struggle

---

19. Stuckenbruck 2013.

to being between holy men and others. It is not clear, but it seems that the implication is that the giant size of the offspring of this union arises from unrestrained consumption of food! In our contemporary world of excess, perhaps here is a message! In fact, the resolution of the problem between the two, or relegating the angels to be holy men, makes the two accounts more consistent—although consistency would not always be the primary concern of the *andəmta*!

Thirdly, the ideas found in the 1 Enoch commentary link up with others. A major concern of Mar Isaac, the ascetic commentary of Isaac of Nineveh (seventh century CE), which is part of the broader list of sacred texts in Ethiopia on which there is commentary, is the interaction between the monastics and the world around them. There are three stages, beginners, intermediates, and the perfect—struggling until the final stage between the temptation of the world and that of the higher spiritual life. The concepts as developed in 1 Enoch seem to resonate well with this outlook, a further confirmation of the unity of the corpus of commentary in Ethiopia.

Fourthly, there are several points of interest relating to the text of 1 Enoch that arise from a study of this commentary, which may be of value for critical study and translation, and the project at the Ludwig Maximilian University of Munich led by Loren Stuckenbruck that is preparing the first critical Ethiopic text of 1 Enoch is evaluating their significance. The commentary contains several points of reflection, and different approaches to the text that should perhaps be considered by any contemporary interpreters of the text especially those who would translate the text. With perhaps centuries of reflection on the text these approached may prove important.

For example, consider Knibb's translation of 1 Enoch 10:2: "and he said to him, 'Say to him in my name and reveal to him the end which is coming, for the whole earth will be destroyed.'" The Ethiopian commentary gives two possible translations depending on whether a particular word is to be treated as an object or not. The phrase አግህድ ሎቱ ፍጻሜ ዘይመጽእ with this word order might be read "reveal to him the completion of the deluge, for the whole earth will be destroyed," or, "reveal to him fully the coming deluge."

There are other points where it is clear that the Amharic translation found in the commentary reflects an understanding that differs from existing translations, and in some cases would reflect very different views of the text, and contrasts somewhat with the translation in Knibb (1978):

- 6:3 "I fear that you may not wish this deed to be done...," with the ensuing discussion emphasising that the Semyaza feels he may alone take the consequences, although he is uncertain. An alternative is offered,

"I fear already," taken to imply that Semyaza knew already that they did not desire to do the deed, and take wives, and so he feared.

- 6:5 The words "Then they all swore together and all bound one another with curses to it" stands in contrast to the Amharic commentary which reads: "they swore an oath on Semazya," implying that the translation should have read "then they all swore together and all bound one another with curses on him." The difference has important implications for our understanding of the nature of the curse, and the significance of the place of this oath.

- 6:8 "these are the leaders of the two hundred angels, and of all the others with them," has the following variation offered, "these are the two hundred leaders, their chiefs."

- 7:5 "and they devoured one another's flesh and drank blood from it," with "it" being understood to be "from the earth," so they drank the blood spilled on the earth. The alternative offered is that they drank "from the organs of their bodies."

- 8:1 "and he showed them the things after these," with the alternative, "and he showed those who came after them," speaking instead of later in time, of a different group of people.

There are some parts of the text where there are clear options in translation, and the Ethiopian reflections would take a different view from Knibb's translation:

- The Ge'ez word ዐራቅ may mean "devastated," and so Knibb translates 9:2 "let the devastated earth cry out with the sound of their cries unto the gate of heaven." The root meaning of the word, however, is not only "empty" but also "orphaned" with the implication of being alone. The word can, therefore, be translated as "only" or "merely" rendering the verse 9:2 "and they said to one another, 'it is only the crying out of the earth that brings the sound of their crying out up to the gates of heaven.'" The variation is also added for this verse, "they said to each other and to the angels" indicating that it is by means of angels that the cries of mankind reached the gate of heaven.

- In 14:1 we have "This book (is) the word of righteousness and of reproof for the Watchers who (are) from eternity." The commentary clearly prefers እም ዓለም to be "from the world" rather than "from eternity."

- In 14:6 Knibb has "and before this you will have seen the destruction of your beloved sons, and you will not be able to enjoy them, but they will fall before you by the sword." Based on the text in the commentary this would be better: "and you will not have their possessions," with the alternative text, "and you will not have their weapons."

A further interesting example of interpretation is found in 1 Enoch 14:8, where the clouds and mist call to Enoch, and he is hastened and driven by the path of the stars and by lightning. Various different readings are resolved because they are all understood to refer to angels, or aspects of an angel's being. Here is the verse: 14:8 "Behold clouds called me in the vision, and mist called me, and the path of the stars and flashes of lightening hastened me and drove me." The following discussion ensues:

> Behold, in the vision clouds were calling me. Since it is a vision, he sees clouds when they call him. Another one says, (showing a textual variation) "angels were calling me," he called them clouds, since clouds are shining, and they [the angels] are shining creatures. Another one says "lofty clouds," since they are lofty ones. Another one says "the ones who rule over the clouds" called me.
>
> "and mist called me," Mist is calling me. It is a vision, so he sees the mist when it calls to him. Another one says, "angels called me"; he called them mist, because mist is immaterial, and they are immaterial. Another one says "the rulers of the mist called me."
>
> "and the path of the stars and flashes of lightning hastened me and drove me," the path of lightening and stars hastened me, since it is a vision. Another one says "the angels hastened me," they distressed me. He called them stars, because stars are shining, and they are shining creatures. Stars are lofty, and they are lofty creatures. Another one calls them the rulers of the stars and lightening, they are astonishing, and they are astonishing creatures. Another one says shining, because they are shining beings. Another one says the rulers of the lightening distressed me.

Others are clearly interpretations reflecting the place the book has in the canon, and the corpus of sacred texts, so the New Testament is used to throw light on the meaning:

- 14:19 "And from underneath the high throne there flowed out rivers of burning fire," from underneath the massive throne a river of fire flows. Another one says [in place of throne]: from his authority, the punishment of sinners. Another one says: the gift of the Holy Spirit is found.

- 90:20 "And I looked until a throne was set up in the pleasant land," that flows with milk, the place called Jerusalem. I watched until the Tabernacle was pitched, until the Temple was built, in Jerusalem. "And the Lord of the sheep sat on it," The Lord, in grace, sat on her. Another one says: I watched when he was prepared in the pure and virgin womb of Mary, Our honoured Lady, and sat and the Lord dwelt. Another one says: I watched when the cross was prepared in the centre of the world, in *qəranyo*. And sat the Lord (who) was crucified on it. Another one says: in the pleasant and beloved centre of heaven, I saw the Kingdom of Heaven prepared. *And sat* the Lord took the saints and sat.

1 Enoch in Other Commentary

The reference to 1 Enoch in the understanding of Psalm 82 has already been mentioned, and whilst a complete study of the use of 1 Enoch in the interpretation of other books is lacking, with the use of Cowley's work it is possible to make a brief study of its use in the commentary on the Apocalypse. As well as the *andəmta*, Cowley also studied an earlier *Tərgʷame Qälämsis*, dating from the sixteenth century, and whose references to 1 Enoch are consistent with the dates at which references appear in other texts.

1 Enoch in the *Tərgʷame Qälämsis*

The writer is familiar with the book of 1 Enoch, and several quotations and allusions can be identified in the text. First Enoch is used primarily as a source to explain references to angels in Revelation in a manner that sees the two books almost as a single unit. In Rev 5:6 the pierced "sheep" is understood to refer to Christ, who stands between the old covenant, whose custodians are the Seraphim led by Michael, and the new covenant, whose custodians are led by Gabriel. Gabriel's role is elucidated by reference to Enoch:

> Explanation 14[20] [Rev V 6]: . . . As for the custodians of the new (covenant)—these are the cherubim, because Gabriel was from

---

20. Which covers Rev 5:6–10.

their tribe, as Enoch says, "And Gabriel is one of the chief angels who is over Gännät,[21] the cherubim, and over snakes."[22]

Furthermore, the four angels who hold back the four winds, in Rev 7:1, are explained with reference to Enoch:

> Explanation 21[23] [VII 1] "The four who stand at the four corners of the earth"—these are angels who are appointed over the winds which are in the four corners of the earth, just as Enoch observed.[24]

This is probably a reference to 1 Enoch 18:1–9, which discusses the four winds, from the four points of the compass, and relates them to the path of the angels.[25]

The "seven angels" carrying cups in Revelation are explained with reference to 1 Enoch:

> Explanation 39[26] [XV 1] The seven angels who carry cups are the seven chief ones whom Enoch, son of Jared, observed when they descended to earth, in order that they should confine the angels who fornicated with the daughters of Cain.[27]

> [XXI 9] "One of the seven angels who carry the seven cups of the wrath of God came"—he is Gabriel, because he has authority over the custodianship of that kingdom, as we recalled previously. Some say that (he is) one of the seven archangels who were sent in the days of Enoch, in order that they might trouble the watchers of Heaven who sinned.[28]

As shown above, the Ethiopic commentary on 1 Enoch explicitly interprets these "angels who fornicated with the daughters of Cain" as men seeking

---

21. The Ethiopic word for Paradise, translated by Knibb as "garden," see note 22. The author has a preference for "paradise" as the connection in the text of 1 Enoch is clear.

22. See Cowley 1983:98, quoting 1 Enoch 20:7. In contrast, the text of 1 Enoch in the commentary on 1 Enoch 20:7 in the Amharic commentary and in Knibb's edition of the text reads, "Gabriel, one of the holy angels, who (is) in charge of the serpents and the Garden and the Cherubim" (Anonymous 1993:45; Knibb 1978:73).

23. Which covers Rev 6:12—7:17.

24. Cowley 1983:105.

25. Knibb 1978:68–69.

26. Which covers Rev 15:1–8.

27. Cowley 1983:130.

28. Cowley 1983:152.

to live a holy life, living in the foothills of Paradise.[29] In 1 Enoch 9:1 four angels, Michael, Gabriel, Suriel, and Uriel, look down from heaven on the iniquity caused by the fallen angels, then in 1 Enoch 10 Gabriel and Michael descend with other angels to deal with them.[30] Altogether there are eight angels mentioned by name in 1 Enoch,[31] although never in one group. It is not clear to which seven the commentary refers. In 1 Enoch 87:2-3 seven white men from heaven are mentioned, who may be regarded as angels, but they are not named, and their descent does not appear associated with the confinement of the fallen angels.

Revelation 14:14 mentions "another angel" who calls to "one who sat on the cloud" to use his sickle to reap. The commentary discusses this at some length, starting with identifying the "one who sat" as Christ with a discussion following:

> Explanation 38[32] [XIV 15] ... Some say that the one sitting on a cloud is Gabriel, because he is custodian of the new era[33] ... He is named 'Son of Man' because of his resemblance to Christ, for he resembled him when he abode in the womb of the pure Virgin Mary ... Further concerning him, Nebuchadnezzar the king, when he saved the three children from the furnace of fire, said of the fourth that his face resembled a son of God ... The angel who asked him to put in his sharp sickle is Raguel, because he perseveres to the passing of this transient world, as Enoch says, "He will take vengeance of the world and the lights."[34]

Regarding the person of Enoch, the books of judgement are understood to have been initiated by him:

> [XX 12] "They opened all the books" it is the book of the errors of the unrepentant sinners, which they did in their life-time, for it was written upon a black tablet by the hand of Enoch, just as it was said, "Behold, judgement must be written."[35]

He is listed amongst the saints of old, as one whose righteousness was praised:

---

29. Lee 2014. Also see Anonymous 2003:10–11.
30. Knibb 1978:23.
31. These are: Michael, Gabriel, Suriel, Uriel, Raphael, Phanuel, Raguel, Saraqael.
32. Which covers Rev 14:14–20.
33. See explanation 14 above.
34. This is 1 Enoch 20:4. See Cowley 1978:128 and Anonymous 2003:44.
35. See Cowley 1978:149, suggesting 1 Enoch 104:1; 108:7 for this quotation.

> [XVII 8] "He [the Devil, the red beast] was not"—(it is) because he did not receive power over them as at first. For as for the former saints, namely Abel and Enosh, Enoch and Noah, Abraham and Job, Moses and Aaron, David and Samuel and Daniel, and the other prophets whose righteousness is praised in the books—these he enslaved and put them in a place of torment, where there is no rest for ever, until Christ the Messiah of true righteousness came.[36]

Enoch is also sometimes identified in place of Moses, as one of the two witnesses along with Elijah:

> [XI 3] "The two righteous ones" these are Moses and Elijah, prophets honoured in Israel.[37]

But here, in the commentary on the verse we read:

> But others refer in this place to Enoch, instead of Moses, saying that Enoch and Elijah are alive until now, nevertheless, the (the two witnesses) are to come and fight in the days of the false Messiah, but Moses completely died, so how shall he die a second time? They spoke falsely! Was he (Moses) not alive at the time when he came on Mount Tabor with Elijah? For his death and his rising are for a sign, just as it was said in the holy gospel concerning the crucifixion of our Saviour, "The graves were opened and many corpses of the righteous arose and entered the holy land."[38]

Cowley found one manuscript that reads "Elijah and Enoch," but here it was evidently an alteration, and was not followed in the subsequent passage.[39] A further discussion on this verse, however, challenges this idea, so it seems that the commentary reflects discussion evident in the manuscript tradition:

> The people who raise queries about Moses will come to understand from the word of this book ... "They have authority over water, that they make it blood, and they afflict the early with plagues, as they desire"—is this not (said) concerning Moses, for he made the waters of Egypt blood, and afflicted them with many plagues? But Enoch did not do this.[40]

---

36. Cowley 1978:133.
37. Cowley 1978:112.
38. Cowley 1978:113.
39. Cowley 1978:112 n4.
40. Cowley 1978:115.

Enoch was clearly a prominent enough figure to be considered as one of the "witnesses," a strong reflection of the importance attached to this figure. This discussion develops further in the *andəmta*.

Enoch in the *Andəmta of the Apocalypse*

The *andəmta* makes fewer direct references to 1 Enoch, but the text is used in a similar manner. The first reference to Enoch that we find is in a brief discussion of the way that God communicates with certain prophets:

> 1.20 "and those seven lampstands are the seven churches" H (explanation). If it is asked, "Does he interpret everything to him?," he clarifies it here and there, when it is too obscure for him, just as he clarified it here and there for Enoch and Daniel. A (another one says). Yes, he interprets it (all) for him. Mal 2:7.[41]

This passing reference to Enoch, along with Daniel seems to point to a special way in which these prophets, and John in the Apocalypse questioned God, and were answered. The commentary seems to see these books of Enoch, Daniel, and the Apocalypse as a unit of special prophecy that arose out of a special relationship that these prophets had with God. And consider the following:

> 6:11 "... until the time when the ones who are like them shall be completed, the servants of God and their brothers who must be killed like them." Until the servants of God who must die in martyrdom like them are completed by martyrdom. H (explanation). When the angel took Enoch around showing him the dwelling place of the souls, (Enoch), having seen the kingdom of Heaven, said to him, "Until when is this great (thing)?" he replied to him, saying, "But you long for (it) for yourself, whereas the Most High longs for (it) for many; and in this way the souls made requests and said, ..."[42]

There is some confusion in the commentary here, since whilst Enoch was shown the dwelling place of the souls in 1 Enoch 22, the quotation is from the Ethiopic ሱቱኤል ዕዝራ, *sutu'el 'əzra* (4 Esdras) 2.32–36,[43] and indeed several of the manuscripts consulted by Cowley say "Ezra."[44] 4 Esdras is

---

41. Cowley 1978:195.
42. Cowley 1978:238.
43. Anonymous 2000:599.
44. Cowley 1983:238 n3.

also commonly used in the Ethiopic tradition with particular importance attached to Ezra's heavenly visions, and this may explain this confusion.

The roles of angels sourced in 1 Enoch are also referred to in the *andəmta*, but no specific reference is made to 1 Enoch:

> 6:4 "... and they gave him a great knife ... and they gave him"—
> St Gabriel appeared, giving a sword to *Səmazya*.[45]

> 8:4 "... The one angel" is St Michael, custodian of the old ...
> "And another came"—he is St Gabriel, custodian of the new ...[46]

The *andəmta* takes up the discussion from the *Tərgʷame Qälämsis* regarding Enoch's role as one of the witnesses in Rev 11:3, but the discussion seems to have been resolved:

> [11.4] "and these are the two trees of oil." These are the two trees of oil, Elijah and Enoch, because "Enoch" means "renewal" and "renewal" comes by oil; also "Elijah" means "oil," as it says, "And she left him beneath a tree of 'Elyas," "And one measure of 'Elyas' will make twelve winepresses full."[47]

But the controversy remains in 11:6, where Moses is asserted instead of Enoch as one able to turn water to blood:

> [11.6] "That they make it blood," that they make it blood. It refers to what happened previously in the time of Enoch. A. It will be done in that time (of the false Messiah). But *Tərgʷame Qälämsis* says "Moses" (instead of Enoch); (this) is better (as the interpretation of this verse).[48]

There are no direct quotations from 1 Enoch in the *andəmta*. This is in contrast to the *Tərgʷame Qälämsis*, which may reflect a greater familiarity of the book by the time the *andəmta* was written, or it may simply reflect the fact that the *andəmta* is a corpus of works, and so detailed quotations are not felt necessary.

---

45. Cowley 1983:232.

46. Cowley 1983:251.

47. Cowley 1983:279–80. Cowley comments in a footnote that one manuscript adds, "if it is asked what corruption there was prior to him, just as Adam brought corruption by eating the fig tree, so (Enoch) was renewed by restraint from food," a view that is also expressed in the introduction to the *Andəmta* on Enoch in Anonymous 2003 EC.

48. Cowley 1983:280–81.

Discussion of 1 Enoch in the Ethiopian Commentary

The extensive commentary on 1 Enoch in the Ethiopian Christian tradition uses it in part to unpack ideas found in the Genesis account, in particular the origin of evil and evil spirits. The interpretation is clearly a Christian one, and despite claims to the contrary, no evidence has been found of any clearly ancient tradition of interpretation, with the nature of the commentary being consistent with the rise of the significance of 1 Enoch in the sixteenth century CE. Nevertheless, the text contains important reflections on the translation, and on the text that may be of significance for critical study and new translations of the text.

The book of 1 Enoch is employed to a limited extent to explain aspects of the Apocalypse, in particular in the *Tərgʷame Qälämsis*, in relation to angels and their roles, consistent with its place as a "Christian" text, illuminating aspects of Christian thought. Enoch is regarded, along with St John and others, as a special kind of prophet, who conversed with God, and gives special information about the roles of angels, with the 1 Enoch angel passages being regarded as complementary to those in Revelation. The important role of Enoch, at least in later Ethiopian thought, is demonstrated by his association with one of the enigmatic witnesses, although this idea is not consistent in Ethiopian interpretation.

4

The Animal Apocalypse (1 Enoch 85–90) in the Light of Ethiopian Traditional Commentary[1]

The Case of "Open and Closed" Eyes

Daniel Assefa

Introduction

Part of 1 Enoch, the Animal Apocalypse, comprising Chapters 85–90 and written probably in the first half of the second century BCE, is an allegory that narrates the history of humanity and, particularly, the history of Israel. It begins from Adam and Eve and goes up to the end of the world, preceded by a universal judgment. As indicated in the appellation of the text, human agents are represented by animals while angels are

---

1. The commentary consulted for this paper is the one printed in 2011 by Tensae Printing Press, in Addis Ababa. The verse from 1 Enoch is presented in Geʿez and the explanation is given in Amharic. The Geʿez-Amharic commentaries are known by the name *andəmta*, a term mentioned before a different interpretation than the one previously given (see Chapter 3 of this work). There are older commentaries for biblical and extra-biblical texts in Geʿez, known by the name *tərgʷame*.

symbolized by human beings. The biblical patriarchs from Adam until Isaac are characterized by bulls, whereas Israelites, from Jacob onwards, are indicated by sheep. Gentiles are denoted by wild animals. God is called the Lord or the master of the sheep. The imagery of "open and closed eyes" is used throughout the text, especially in connection with the sheep. For Dillmann, while to have "open eyes" means to recognize God and his way, to believe in him, and to fear him, while "closed eyes" signifies moral and religious darkness.[2]

There are times when the sheep have their eyes open, and times when they have their eyes closed. Does that mean alteration between a good and a bad relationship with God? Does it denote obedience and disobedience? Does it underline the idea of going astray and of returning to God? While all these explanations and similar ones have been suggested by Western scholars, traditional Ethiopian commentaries emphasize the idea of knowledge and ignorance. How can we understand such an interpretation? This short essay aims at responding to these questions through a closer look of the traditional Ethiopian commentaries on the Animal Apocalypse and a comparison of the latter with the suggestions of Western scholars.

The Imagery of "Open and Closed Eyes" in 1 Enoch

An Important Motif

The imagery of opening one's eyes, although frequently represented in the Animal Apocalypse, is also found in other sections of 1 Enoch. According to 1 Enoch 1:2, Enoch's eyes are open. From the overall context, we may infer that, here, the text is not mentioning conversion. Enoch is not starting to be obedient or restoring a good relation with God. The opening of his eyes has to do with revelation. God opens the eyes of Enoch so that he may discover the mysteries of the otherworld and the future age. The action is a gift from God and not the result of Enoch's effort.

While this reference to the image of "open eyes" from the Book of Watchers (1 Enoch 1–36) is positive, one also finds a negative connotation in 1 Enoch 32:6. Adam and Eve realize that they were naked and they are expelled from the garden because they ate the forbidden fruit and their eyes were open. The traditional Ethiopian commentary speaks here in terms of bad wisdom (*andəmta*, 65–66). The opening of their eyes signified wisdom. Yet it was bad in the sense that it was a result of disobedience.

---

2. Dillmann 1853a:260.

In the Book of Parables (1 Enoch 37–71) one finds an invitation to open one's eyes. The summons is addressed to kings, the mighty, the dignified ones and those who dwell upon the earth (1 Enoch 62:1). In this case there is an implicit criticism. Unlike Enoch, the kings and the mighty are defying God and his Messiah. They are disobedient, in darkness and need to open their eyes in order to recognize the chosen by God.

In the Epistle of Enoch (1 Enoch 106–107), reference is made to the opening of Noah's eyes as soon as he was born. The baby has beautiful eyes; when he opens them the house becomes full of exceptional light (106:2). This marvelous event will disturb both the father Lamech and the grandfather Methuselah. The latter will get an explanation from Enoch who is in Paradise; the marvelous event is a gift and a sign of God (1 Enoch 106:8ff; 107).

In 1 Enoch 99:8, blindness and folly (of heart) stand for "going astray" through idolatry. Both the previous and the following verses mention the worship of stones, idols and evil spirits. According to Nickelsburg, here, the idolaters' lack of knowledge is underlined.[3]

The Imagery of "Open and Closed Eyes" in the Animal Apocalypse

Blindness of Egyptians

In 1 Enoch 89:21 Enoch the narrator affirms that the wolves that were pursuing the sheep, representing the Egyptians pursuing the Israelites, were blinded. That this needs to be read metaphorically; one may deduce that they cannot pursue anything if they were physically blinded. Thus, according to 1 Enoch 89:25, the hyenas were not able to see the sheep. This, for Tiller, is a reference to "literal vision."[4] Would it be possible, nevertheless, to read it as disobedience, on the basis of the Egyptian's refusal to obey God who asks them to let the people go? Nickelsburg suggests a possible connection with the plague of darkness.[5]

---

3. Nickelsburg 2001:492. In traditional Ethiopian commentaries on 1 Enoch, the emphasis on idolaters' lack of knowledge is expanded to all types of sins. To commit sin is to be ignorant, to be blind.

4. Tiller 1993:285.

5. Nickelsburg 2001:379.

Israel and the Imagery of "Open" and "Closed Eyes"

The first time the expression "to open one's eyes" is used, in the Animal Apocalypse, in connection with Israel, is in 1 Enoch 89:28. It is just after the people escaped from the Egyptians, by crossing the red sea (cf. Exodus 14), and entered into a desert; there they run short of food and water. At this stage, it is difficult to understand the opening of the eyes as an image of obedience. If one focuses on Exod 14:31, however, the image may refer to the faith of Israel and to its fear of the Lord. According to Reese, the opening of the eyes should be connected with Exod 14:31, whereby it is said that Israel feared and believed in the Lord. Consequently, for Reese, to have one's eyes open or closed means to be in the right or in the wrong relationship with God.[6] An argument against this reading may be that the sheep open their eyes after they have entered into the desert and not exactly at the very moment of their crossing of the sea (1 Enoch 89:28a).

If, on the other hand, one focuses on Exodus 16–17, the opening of the eyes would be an allusion to God's providence, namely to the gift of manna from heaven and water from a rock. However, the fact that the sheep open their eyes before the manifestation of God's providence, before the Lord starts to pasture them (1 Enoch 89:28b) may weaken the latter interpretation.

For Tiller, the opening of the sheep's eyes in 1 Enoch 89:28 signifies Israel's possession of God's law and obedience.[7] This interpretation connects the imagery of opening one's eyes with the speech of God in Exod 15:25b–26:

> There the LORD made for them a statute and an ordinance and there he put them to the test. He said, "If you will listen carefully to the voice of the LORD your God, and do what is right in his sight, and give heed to his commandments and keep all his statutes, I will not bring upon you any of the diseases that I brought upon the Egyptians; for I am the LORD who heals you." (Exod 15:25–26 NRSV)

Tiller makes an association between opening one's eyes and Israel's possession of God's law and obedience because he looks for an important biblical reference which follows the crossing of the see and precedes Moses' first ascent to Mount Sinai. Nevertheless, 1 Enoch 89:28 has nothing that may symbolize what happens in Exodus 15:25b–26. The text narrates subsequently the crossing of the sea, the entrance in the wilderness, their opening

---

6. Reese 1999:34–36.
7. Tiller 1993:292.

of their eyes, the giving of water and herb by their master. Next to that, verse 29 speaks of Moses' first ascent to Mount Sinai. In other words, the incident that reflects the relationship between God and Israel mentioned in the Animal Apocalypse is the giving of the manna and of water. The giving of Law and obedience is not attested in 15:25b–26. It is hence better to link Israel's opening of the eyes with God's providence.

According to the *andəmta* (230) commentary, the sentence "they began to open their eyes and to see" in 1 Enoch 89:28 means their interior eye (lit. the eye of their mind, of reason, heart: ዓይነ ልቦናቸው) began to examine or to wonder about mysteries. However, at that stage, the commentary does not specify which mysteries are the subjects of scrutiny. The context helps to affirm that the mysteries are divine, albeit the commentary does not mention a particular theme in this regard.

Being Blinded as Going Astray

Not long after the opening of the eyes, one finds the opposite recounted, namely the closing of the eyes. In 1 Enoch 89:32–33, to close one's eyes or to be blinded is clearly associated with the theme of going astray and of transgression God's commandment. In the immediate context, the reference is the incident of the Golden Calf, a transgression committed while Moses is on Mount Sinai. In this connection, Vanderkam affirms that "sight and blindness correspond to obedience and disobedience to God's law."[8]

The *andəmta* commentary speaks again of the interior eye but this time in order to suggest that Israel was caught up by ignorance (ድንቁርና) and, as a consequence, went astray. Not only the association between blindness and ignorance is noteworthy but the term ድንቁርና can also mean deafness, inability to listen.

In 1 Enoch 89:41, the period of judges is summarized by the opening and closing of the eyes of Israel. This may be interpreted as a symbol of the "alternating faithfulness and disobedience of Israel.[9] For Nickelsburg,

---

8. Vanderkam 2004:282. Vanderkam has studied this image and has concluded that the metaphor helps to understand the term Israel as meaning to see God; Israel is the one who sees God. For Vanderkam, the image seems to have come from one etymological meaning of the term Israel, namely the meaning of seeing God. Israel is the one that sees God. If that explanation lies behind the image in the Animal Apocalypse, one may interpret that the sheep become authentic Israelites when they see the Lord. When they become blind they fall short of their vocation as those who see God; see Vanderkam 2004:279–92.

9. Tiller 1993:305; Vanderkam 2004:282.

blindness is mainly associated with Israel's cultic sins.[10] As for the *andəmta* commentary, it keeps its peculiar vocabulary for the interpretation of the imagery. Thus, it refers to Israel's interior eye sometimes open and sometimes veiled by ignorance.

First Enoch 89:44 refers to the opening of Samuel's eyes in the Ethiopic version.[11] In the Greek version the reference is to Israel's eyes.[12] Tiller, who prefers here the Greek reading, associates the opening of the eyes of the Israelites with their observance of Saul's decline. When they grow obedient they become able to see that Saul had lost his glory. According to the *andəmta* commentary, it is Samuel who observes the decline of Saul, who discovers or knows his weakening. Now, whether we opt for the Ethiopic or the Greek version, it is clear that we are not dealing here with obedience or disobedience. The opening of the eyes is just a means for realizing the decline of Saul. It is less about returning to God and more about revelation. The mystery may be reserved to the faithful ones, like Samuel or part of Israel. The imagery however is closer to 1 Enoch 1:2 whose eyes are open to understand what everybody notices.

Another interesting reference to blinded eyes is found from 1 Enoch 89:54 onwards. The negative imagery precedes the Babylonian exile. The text is dealing with Israel refusing to listen to prophets (1 Enoch 89:53) sent by God and preferring to abandon the House of God. This will lead in its turn the abandonment of Jerusalem and the Temple by God. This illustrates Israel's apostasy.[13] While mentioning the apostasy of Israel, the *andəmta* commentary (238), still inserts the motif of ignorance. One may say the same for the blindness of Israel and their shepherds in 1 Enoch 89:74.

Small Lambs, A New Movement

After a long period of blindness, the imagery of sight reappears in 1 Enoch 90:6. Unlike the preceding cases, it is even more difficult to interpret adequately the meaning of the image because one does not know for sure which event is referred to. One has therefore to take into consideration the various meanings of the imagery within the Animal Apocalypse. The next verse, 1 Enoch 90:7, shows a sharp contrast between the small lambs with open eyes and the sheep which are enormously deaf and blind. Perhaps, more than their previous situation, their inability to listen to the call of the lambs

---

10. Nickelsburg 2001:382.
11. Cf. Martin 1906:213; Knibb 1978:2:207.
12. Charles 1912:196; Tiller 1993:309.
13. Tiller 1993:318; Nickelsburg 2001:384.

itself is qualified as deafness and blindness. In other words, part of Israel did not follow the reform or the renewal initiated by a group of Jews.

According to Nickelsburg, revelation, with "salvific function" is attested in various important texts of 1 Enoch. Among these, he mentions 1 Enoch 90:6 whereby the lambs open their eyes as a "first step toward salvation. Close to revelation, one he also adds the motif of wisdom as a gift to the elected and as part of salvation (1 Enoch 5:8; 93:10; 104:12–13).[14]

2.5 Eschatological Blessing

After the account of the last judgment, the imagery of sight is underlined in 1 Enoch 90:35, after the punishment of the blinded sheep (1 Enoch 90:26). Tiller says the following in this connection: "This is the last the definitive statement of the righteousness of surviving Jews and Gentiles ... This verse is very emphatic with three essentially equivalent statements of the sheep's ability to see."[15] Would it be possible that the emphasis on the saved sheep's ability to see implies more than an act of obedience? What would be the need of repeating the motif of sight for Israel which is already participating in the eschatological bliss prepared by God? The *andəmta* commentary suggests here that Israel has started to see beautiful things, to observe heavenly mysteries, to know about the otherworldly.

The Traditional Ethiopian Commentary

An Identical Interpretation for Various Imageries

According to the Ethiopian interpretation, as already mentioned, the imagery of "open and closed eyes" is connected with the motif of knowing. Interestingly, the metamorphosis of Noah and Moses is also explained with the same motif of knowing.[16] This is significant in terms of the meaning of the expression *Balä Ä'əməro*, literally "one who reasons," "one who is capable of reasoning." In the case of the sheep, "reasoning" means to convert

---

14. Nickelsburg 2001:41.

15. Tiller 1993:382.

16. Even the white color of the sheep that are saved is given exactly the same interpretation (1 Enoch 90:32). Noah and Moses, during their transformation, become like white angels; they are associated with light and glory. As for the people, they are associated with light when they open their eyes, and when they sin, with darkness. Nickelsburg (2001:380) affirms that blindness symbolizes lack of religious and moral knowledge.

or to shift from sin into a life of appropriate relationship with the divine. However, Noah, before the construction of the Ark, and Moses, before his transformation into an angelic-like status, were both already in a good relationship with God. Their transformation, far from being a symbol of conversion, was a preparation in order to build the Ark or the tabernacle. One may understand here Noah's or Moses' transformation as acquisition of knowledge. However, does that also imply that angels have more knowledge than human beings, given that in both cases the transformation signifies a becoming like angels? The commentary affirms that the angels are intelligent, wise (*Balä Ä'əməro*).

It is noteworthy here to mention Gen 2:7 whereby the Ethiopian commentary of Genesis uses the same interpretation as one finds in the Animal Apocalypse. "The man became a living being" has been interpreted as the man becomes *Balä Ä'əməro*, meaning capable of understanding, intelligent.

What is more difficult is to understand the conversion or good relation of Israel with God as becoming intelligent. Does to see mean to know? Noah and Moses are presented as people who become intelligent when they provisionally acquire an angelic status. Does it mean they become less intelligent when they return to the status of a human being?

Meaning of the Term *Ä'əməro* (አእምሮ)

As shown above, the *andəmta* commentary has a special or technical vocabulary when it wants to explain the opening of the sheep's eyes or the Israelites' good relationship with God or the reception of revelation. In Amharic, the term *Ä'əməro* signifies reason, ability to reason, intelligence or consciousness.[17] When someone opens one's eye, the commentary says, one becomes a person who has *Ä'əməro*, "*balä Ä'əməro honä*" (ባለ አእምሮ ሆነ). This means one becomes intelligent, wise, knowledgeable or reasonable. The Amharic meaning is not so much different from the Ge'ez one. In Ge'ez too, *Ä'əməro* means knowledge, understanding or intelligence.[18] According to the *andəmta* commentary, the sheep's transgression at Mount Sinai is called "blindness of their spiritual eye."[19]

---

17. Kane 1990:1255.
18. Leslau 1987:25.
19. Dillmann (1853a:728ff) gives several examples whereby the expression is used in Ethiopic literature; accordingly, the term means to know; *cognoscere, nosse, scire*. Under that heading Dillmann mentions to the idea of perceiving, seeing (cf. 1 Sam 26:3: "David saw [learned] that Saul had come"). Dillmann remarks also the idea of "inquiring" and of "observing" (cf. 1Sam 17:56; "Inquire whose son the stripling is"

Conclusion

The relationship of God with the people of Israel in the Animal Apocalypse is depicted through the metaphor of "opening" and "closing" one's eyes. When the text wants to show that Israel has gone astray, it says that the sheep have their eyes closed. When the text wants to affirm that the relationship with Israel is good, it says that the eyes of the sheep are open. The apparent meaning of this metaphor is the theme of conversion and the theme of going astray. To see and experience light means to be in good relationship with God. To have one's eyes closed or to be in darkness means to go astray. Nevertheless, the traditional Ethiopian commentary associates this metaphor with the theme of knowledge. Accordingly, to have one's eyes open is to have knowledge, to understand, but to go even further so as to examine divine or heavenly mysteries.

By this emphasis, the theme of obedience or apostasy is not cancelled or ignored. One may perhaps better speak here of nuance. The link with the theme of knowledge seems to reflect a biblical motif of having or missing a religious knowledge, as well explained by Nickelsburg.[20] For the traditional Ethiopian commentary, to have one's eyes open means to be wise and to have one's eyes closed signifies to fail to reason, to be fool. It signifies the opening of the eyes of the mind, of reason, the spiritual vision, contemplation, Revelation. Besides, according to the *andəmta* commentary, there is a convergence of three imageries. The one of sight and blindness, the one of being transformed into an angelic status (Noah and Moses) and the one of being in white colour converge all into an identical interpretation, the one of becoming wise, of understanding the divine mysteries.

Besides, the fact that this identical interpretation is also the same as the one of Gen 2:7-10 is quite noteworthy. There is thus unity between receiving the breath of life, becoming a living human being in Genesis (Genesis 2), the opening one's eyes in the Animal Apocalypse and all other positive qualities attributed to the righteous in the same Enochian text. In other words, the larger corpus of Ethiopian biblical commentary proposes an anthropological affirmation whereby receiving the breath of life, opening one's eyes, being faithful to God constitute the vocation of the human person. To be a human being is to reason, to listen and to be in good relationship with God, to behave faithfully, to be righteous.

(1 Sam 17:56 NRSV); "Let it be paid back to them, so that they may know it" (Job 21:19 NRSV) to mean "so that they may experience or feel it." Ruth has "observed the place where he lies" (Ruth 3:4 NRSV).

20. Nickelsburg 2001:380.

5

Social and Economic Injustice

Apocalyptic Themes in the Epistle of Enoch and the Apocalypse of John

Archie T. Wright

Introduction

Modern Correlations?

As we approach the discussion of social and economic injustice in the Epistle of Enoch and John's Apocalypse, it would be a missed opportunity if we did not offer some suggested applicable concepts that we can draw from the forthcoming examination.

If one is to read the Gospel accounts, he or she knows that justice, in particular economic justice, is important to God. One might ask the question do the economic policies around the world, in particular in the West, promote economic justice or injustice? Do the wealthy hold the power of the future economic status of the nations? If so, what does this say for the future of the currently impoverished nations and their peoples? Will the greed and manipulative practices of the wealthy be reversed at some point in the future or is there no hope for the poor?

Economic inequality is a very visible aspect of the issue of inequality of opportunity for all; it encompasses gender, ethnicity, disability, and the age of individuals. This problem affects all nations and peoples across the globe. In developed and developing countries it is estimated that the poorest

50% of the population controls less than 10% of the wealth. There are of course many reasons for the state of economic situation around the world including poverty on massive scale, unemployment, environmental issues, political instability, and national and international conflicts.

This is of course not a problem that is predominant in the West, but it encompasses the Sub-Saharan African nations, East Africa (Ethiopia and Somalia, among others), the Far East, and Central and South America among others. Some nations have made progress in addressing the societal causes of such inequality through equity and rights-based policies, and legal initiatives, which have been established and kept in place over a long period of time. Many have suggested that the disparity seen in these poorer nations is a result of the greed and political corruption of the wealthy in those nations, including the West. So what hope is there for the poor? In what follows below we may find some light that may help answer this question.

A second issue more closely related to the theological side of the issue that may be raised concerning our topic is the idea of a "prosperity gospel" and its relationship to "social injustice and economic inequality." The prosperity gospel is defined as a teaching that believers (followers of Christ) have a right to the blessings of wealth and health that can obtained through *positive* confessions of faith and the "sowing of seeds" through the faithful payments of tithes and offerings. Although this "movement" for the most part is viewed negatively, it does have some roots, although questionable, in the biblical texts. One should make known the societal realties in which this particular type of teaching thrives and the "false" measure of hope it holds out to, for the most part, desperate people. Primarily, those who are considered leaders in this movement are allegedly obtaining significant wealth through the donations to their ministries by the desperate. The teachers of this "gospel" promote the idea that financial prosperity is a result of righteous living, similar to what we read in Deuteronomy 7–15; if you are not prospering then something is wrong in your life—i.e., sin, which is often expressed through a lack of faith of the one who is not prospering. This lack of faith of the desperate, of course, brings about God's curse. Thankfully, as we will discover below, this does not appear to be the case, but rather it appears to be the poor who are leading the "righteous" lives rather than the wealthy and powerful of this movement and the world economy.

So one might ask what this issue has to do with Epistle of Enoch and John's Apocalypse. We may be able to identify certain correlations between what we see in the prosperity movement and the current state of income inequality in the world and the description offered of the wealthy and the poor in the two texts. At the risk of identifying all wealthy people as wicked (this is certainly not this author's intention), in particular those who call themselves ministers of the Church and the wealthy and powerful throughout the world, there appears to be some parallels between the behavior of these individuals and the wealthy in the social injustice narrative that is presented in Epistle of Enoch and John's Apocalypse. This is not to say that all those who are drawn into the falsehood of this gospel are the "righteous" described in the two texts under discussion; rather they are the victimized poor who are told they are under the influence of evil spirits, which allegedly maintain their life of poverty ignoring the true causes behind it: exploitation, economic inequality, and political injustice. Instead of the "wealthy" helping the victimized poor, they suggest the poverty they wallow in is their own fault, when in fact it is furthered by the greed of those who make the promises of future wealth. Although this type of action is not paralleled in the Epistle of Enoch and John's Apocalypse, the wealthy do exert their power to increase their riches rather than helping the poor.

Origins of a Biblical Social Justice

Deuteronomy 7:12–14 suggests that if one is obedient to the ordinances of the Torah and remains loyal to the covenant, then the Lord will bless him or her with prosperity in all areas of his or her life. Here the author contends that the righteous are identified with wealth and prosperity. At the same time, in Deut 8:13–14 the Lord warns the Israelites not to forget him in their prosperity: "when all that you have is multiplied, then do not exalt yourself, forgetting the Lord you God." For those who are disobedient to the Torah and reject the Lord, he promises, "I solemnly warn you today that you will surely perish."

The principle of social justice and generosity begins in Deut 14:22 and continues to Deut 15:18; these laws focus on easing the burden of the poor and the slave. Deuteronomy 15:4–5 goes as far as to claim that there shall be no poor[1] among the nation, "if only you will obey the Lord your God by diligently observing this entire commandment that I command you today" (v. 5). The people are warned to give to those in need and not to be "hardhearted or tightfisted toward your *needy neighbor*"[2] (v. 7). They are told "to give liberally and be ungrudging when you do so, for on account of this the

---

1. In Deut 15:4 (also v. 7), the term אביון appears carrying with it a sense of "poor" as in financially needy. In Amos 4:1, the same term is used to describe those who are being oppressed in a religious sense, a similar motif to that found in the Epistle of Enoch and John's Apocalypse.

2. Verse 7 suggests the individual in question is a "blood relative" or a "fellow countryman"—מאחיך האביון. Again here, the term carries the sense of financial need.

Lord your God will bless you [יברכך] in all your work and in all that you undertake" (v. 10). However, the text claims in v. 11 there will always be poor in the land ("Since there will never cease [לא־יחדל] to be some in need on the earth, I therefore command you, 'Open your hand to the poor and needy neighbor in your land.'"). This statement is a bit troublesome when one considers God's promise of "blessing." The answer may be simply that Israel was incapable of keeping this command (15:5), and therefore there would always be poor amongst them; there would always be poor, widows, orphans, and slaves, all of whom need the help of others.

As we will see in what follows, the perspective that the blessings of God in a person's life identified him or her as righteous was not consistently maintained in the literature of the Second Temple Period (2TP). Rather, the righteous are understood as the poor (though not likely all of them), while the wicked, or those who ignored the Torah to some degree or another, were the ones who now appeared to be blessed with wealth and power. In what follows we will examine the Epistle of Enoch and John's Apocalypse as to the language used to speak to this issue of the wicked and the righteous and the blessed and the cursed. The starting point will be a preliminary assessment of the social settings of both texts.

Social Setting

Epistle of Enoch

The issue of dating and social setting are inevitably tied together when speaking of these texts. The date of authorship of the Epistle has been identified by some scholars as the end of the second century BCE or the early first century BCE. This theory of dating is offered with the centerpiece identifying the "economically disadvantaged."[3] Pharisees tend to be identified as the righteous, and the wealthy Sadducees as the sinners. However, as Stuckenbruck argues, "the language of the *Epistle* in general is too imprecise to pin down these particular groups."[4] In addition, due to the accusation of idolatry in the Epistle, we are hard pressed to limit such a description to the Sadducees in this manner. The language of idolatry is used to describe the broader community of Hellenized Jewish people just prior to and during the period of the Maccabean revolt.[5] First Maccabees 1:47 describes the activities of at least a portion of the Jewish people in Palestine who "build

---

3. See discussion of dating Stuckenbruck 2007:212–13.
4. Stuckenbruck 2007:212.
5. See VanderKam 1984:144.

altars and sacred precincts and shrines for idols, to sacrifice swine and other unclean animals" (it should be noted that this practice was commanded by a foreign king; cf. 1 Macc 13:47 and 2 Macc 12:40).[6] George Nickelsburg has suggested the date of the Epistle can be divided between what he calls the frame of the Epistle that is tied to the Apocalypse of Weeks (pre-Maccabean, 167 BCE) and the body of the Epistle dated to the end of the second century or early first century BCE.[7]

Gabriele Boccaccini has identified the Epistle as a "post-sectarian" text that was composed following the breach between the Qumran community and the Enochic community due to their respective understandings of Torah (poss. early first century BCE). Boccaccini understands the Epistle as a polemic against the Qumranites.[8]

There are, however, two difficulties with these two propositions of Nickelsburg. Firstly, there is no clear literary evidence that suggests the work was created in two distinct time periods. Secondly, the author of the Epistle directs the rebuke against the sinners in terms of their wealth, power, idolatry, and their oppression of the righteous. It would be difficult to identify the wicked with the members of the Qumran Community; they considered themselves the righteous/pious ones, and they had very little contact with outsiders that would be required with the oppression of the "righteous." In addition, they were not a group that flaunted their wealth throughout the land. It is likely then, as Stuckenbruck contends, the Epistle was composed in the period prior to the Maccabean revolt as there is no mention of the revolt in the Epistle.

The author of the Epistle has been granted a glimpse into the sacred writings in which he sees the reward of the suffering righteous poor being granted to them in the age to come. In the Epistle he is speaking to and for the righteous community who are suffering the oppression of the wicked (wealthy and powerful). In doing so, he tells of the coming punishment the wicked will face at the judgment. The author may be describing a sectarian dispute in the Epistle, as Boccaccini suggests, although there is little to

---

6. See 1 Macc 13:47: "So Simon was appeased toward them, and fought no more against them, but put them out of the city, and cleansed the houses wherein the idols were, and so entered into it with songs and thanksgiving," and 2 Macc 12:40: "Then under the tunic of every one of the dead they found sacred tokens of the idols of Jamnia, which the law forbids the Jews to wear. And it became clear to all that this was why these men had fallen."

7. Nickelsburg 2001:427–28.

8. Boccaccini 1998:104–13. One might argue that 1 Enoch 98:15, "those who write down lying words" may be speaking of the authors of the *pesharim*.

suggest a Qumran/Essene conflict.⁹ The condemnation of the wicked and the message of hope for the righteous poor establishes a setting of social injustice toward the righteous and a period of wealth and power for the wicked, a reversal of the conditions that were expected in the keeping of the Deuteronomic ordinances.

The Apocalypse of John[10]

The author of the Apocalypse clearly indicates the location of the communities to which he is writing, Asia Minor. The proximity of the seven churches would likely place them under the same jurisdiction of the governor of the Roman imperial province. These congregations are facing a range of issues that involve conflicts with outsiders, disputes concerning pagan practices within the churches, and the abuse of wealth and power.[11] These appear to be social issues similar to what we see in the Epistle that have been in existence for a period of time.

David Aune notes that the prevailing opinion for the dating of the Apocalypse is around the end of the reign of Roman emperor Domitian, ca. 95 CE. Other scholars from the nineteenth century suggested a date between 64 CE and 70 CE as a result of the persecution by Nero and the destruction of the Jerusalem temple. Aune argues that both views are possible as a result of a likely "final" edition of the Apocalypse emerging in the early reign of Trajan. The possible "first" edition of the book was likely written in the 60s CE (in the year of the four rulers: 68–69 CE[12]) due to the apocalyptic traditions found in the book.[13] The rising tide of issues included external conflicts with pagans and Jews and internal differences over the Christian practices in relation to those of the non-Christian society.

One of the difficulties in trying to establish a clear social setting for the Apocalypse is that the boundaries of the various communities were not all the same. This is seen in particular in the internal disputes; as with the issues outlined in the Epistle, the Apocalypse may reflect a Christian sectarian dispute or a "Jewish" disagreement with the Jewish Christians. The church at Ephesus would not accept the pseudo-apostles who are identified as the

---

9. See Matthews 2010:165.

10. Nickelsburg has argued that the Apocalypse of John, in its literary form and in aspects of its content, is "significantly analogous" to the Parables found in *1 Enoch*; see Nickelsburg and VanderKam 2012a:83.

11. See discussion in Hemer 2000.

12. DeSilva 1992:273–302.

13 Aune 1997:lvii–lviii.

Nicolaitans, while the people of Pergamum tolerated the Nicolaitan teaching. The church at Thyatira included followers of Jezebel with whom John had significant differences with her teachings. It may be possible to categorize the issues John had with the churches as sectarian disputes, similar to what we may be seeing in the Epistle.[14]

Another difficulty the churches faced was their involvement with the Roman/pagan society. They faced the problem of trying to uphold their own beliefs and distinctiveness while functioning within the Greco-Roman culture. One area of particular challenge was the economic system under Roman rule. This interaction with the Roman economic society created some uncertain situations for Christians and their contact with things related to the Imperial cult. The region was scattered with temples dedicated to the Roman rulers and the pagan gods, though it appears there was no particular pressure for the people of the churches to participate in its activity during Domitian's reign.

The local trade guilds proved to be a particularly complicated issue for the audiences of the Apocalypse. These guilds included people who operated in the various trades that included certain religious activities such as honoring the pagan deities. During the activities, meals were often offered in honor of the one of the gods. John expresses clear opposition to Christian participation in these activities that he understood as a contradiction to their beliefs; community members at Laodicea appeared to think otherwise. John was opposed to the propensity of the guilds to be obsessed by becoming wealthy and seeking pleasure. As a result many in the province were left poor and destitute if they did not participate in the guild. It may be the case the individuals from the church at Laodicea were part of the group who were oppressing or persecuting those who would not participate in the guilds.

In what follows we will examine several passages in the Epistle and determine if there are any allusions to or parallels of the themes, language, or traditions found in John's Apocalypse.

The Social Injustice Themes

Introduction

Throughout history there has been social stratification in which the wealthy and the powerful have fundamental advantages over the poor and powerless. Things were no different in the 2TP and the late first century CE

---

14. See, e.g., discussion in Koester 2014.

in which financial and social inequality was a key concern for Jews and early Christians in Palestine and the Diaspora. The fluidity of views of the wealthy is evidenced in both Josephus (*Jewish War* 7.260–61) and the Dead Sea Scrolls (e.g., 4QInstruction), and other 2TP texts.[15] In addition, some authors offer polemics against these issues in wisdom texts such as Ben Sira. The author of Ben Sira reveals the struggles of the less privileged individuals who are attempting to maintain financial stability (13:3–5, 18; 31:4).[16] They are given a constant reminder that they are the poor and there will be little opportunity for improving their social status in the future. The promise of reward for virtuous behavior found in Proverbs (e.g. 3:33; 5:18; 10:6; 10:22; 11:22; 24:25) or Ben Sira (7:32; 11:22; 31:8) has changed in the worldview of 2TP Jewish groups.

The primary target of the polemic in the Epistle is the wealthy wicked. The contrast between the ways of the righteous and the ways of the wicked generally begins at 94:1. The author warns his sons "O righteous ones,[17] do not walk in the ways of wickedness (*bä-fənotə 'əkuyə*) or in the ways of death (*wä-'i-bä-fənawatä motə*), and do not come near to them, unless you be destroyed (*kämä 'ə-təḥäg^wälu*)" (v. 3).[18] George Nickelsburg has argued that there are two means of evil activity which these people are involved in: 1) violence and deceit; and 2) social and religious sins.[19] According to v. 5b "sinners will tempt men in order to make what is wicked out of wisdom, so that no place will be found for it, and temptation will not vanish at all." The sinners are guilty of such social injustices as slavery, oppressed labor, non-payment of wages, and abuse (see 103:9; cf. Jer 22:13: "Woe to him who builds his house by unrighteousness, and his upper rooms by injustice; who makes his neighbors work for nothing, and does not give them their wages"). All of these methods were employed to build "their houses in sin" (*äbəyatomu bä-ḥäṭiätə*; 94:7). Nickelsburg goes on to identify three possible methods they used to gain their unjust wealth: 1) stealing land that

---

15. See Adams 2011; see also Tcherikover 1959.

16. See 13:3–5: "³The rich do wrong and boast of it, while the poor are wronged and beg forgiveness. ⁴As long as the rich can use you they will enslave you, but when you are down and out they will abandon you. ⁵As long as you have anything they will live with you, but they will drain you dry without remorse"; and 13:18: "Can there be peace between the hyena and the dog? Or peace between the rich and the poor?"

17. Righteous ones are encouraged in v. 4 "to seek after and *choose for yourselves righteousness* (*wä-ḥəräyu läkəmu ṣedəḳä*) and an acceptable life, and walk in the ways of peace so that you may live and flourish." Unfortunately no Greek text survives, although cf. 1 Macc 2:29: πολλοὶ ζητοῦντες δικαιοσύνην.

18. Variations of spelling and wording occur in other mss for the Ge'ez quoted in this sentence, and no Greek text survives.

19. Nickelsburg 2003:549–50.

did not belong to them; 2) using the judicial system for unjust gain (95:6); and 3) bribing judges (94:7).[20] As a result of their sinful actions the wicked have acquired silver and gold and trusted in their wealth[21] rather than trusting in the Most High (94:7b–8b). In the end the wicked will have no peace (wäälǝbomu sälamǝ, 94:6d).[22]

We see the diverse perspectives concerning the wicked and righteous during the late 2TP. The worldview moved beyond the previous "typologies for reward and punishment" and the "traditional association between virtue and success."[23] Authors of 2TP texts begin to ask the question if one's wealth can be an impediment to the eschatological concept of reward. The author of 4QInstruction affirms the idea that wealth is a sign of favor from God, though the author also notes that God will take care of the lowly poor (4Q417 f2i:17–19). However, the Epistle does not affirm this outlook, rather it asserts that those who are wealthy are primarily wicked and the poor are righteous, adopting an eschatological view of reward and punishment. According to 94:7, at the eschatological judgment the wicked will be quickly destroyed because of their persecution of the poor (cf. Zeph 1:15).[24]

The Epistle offers several persuasive statements about financial inequality and the fact that the wealthy do not accept the responsibility that comes with their riches, i.e. take care of the poor, widows, and orphans (e.g. 99:2a;[25] 103:11)[26], instead they place a heavy yoke upon them that is un-

---

20. Nickelsburg 2003:549–50.

21. We find similar themes in the biblical tradition dealing with the wicked: e.g., Ps 49:5–11; 52:7; Prov 11:28; Jer 9:23; 1 Tim 6:17–18; and in extra-biblical traditions of Wis 5:8 and Sir 5:8.

22. See 98:11, 16; 99:13; 101:3; 102:3; 103:8; cf. biblical tradition: Isa 48:22 (οὐκ ἔστιν χαίρειν τοῖς ἀσεβέσιν λέγει κύριος—אין שלום אמר יהוה לרשעים); 57:21 (οὐκ ἔστιν χαίρειν τοῖς ἀσεβέσιν εἶπεν κύριος ὁ θεός—אין שלום אמר אלהי לרשעים); BW 5:4—4QEn^a 1 ii 14 (לת שלם לכן); Cod Pan BW 5:5; 12:5; 13:1; 16:4—οὐκ ἔσται ὑμῖν ἔλεος καὶ εἰρήνη; also BG 1Q24 8.2—לכון לא שלם; 4Q203 13.3—לא[איתי לכה ש]לם.

23. Adams, "Poverty and Otherness," 191.

24. "That day will be a day of wrath, a day of distress and anguish, a day of ruin and devastation, a day of darkness and gloom, a day of clouds and thick darkness." Cf. also Job 3:4–5; Amos 5:18; Job 15:23; 1QS ii 8; Heb 12:18; 2 Pet 2:17; and Jude 13.

25. "Those 'who pervert the eternal covenant'"—διαστρέφοντες τὴν αἰώνιαν διαθήκην—Eth.—šǝr 'atä lentä lä-'aläm täallǝwu—"violate the eternal law." The eternal covenant referring to the Law given in Deut 14:22 and continues into chapter 15:18; these laws focus on easing the burden of the poor and the slave.

26. Gk.—"[the la]wless ones have made the yo[ke] heavy upon us"—cf. Deut 28:48; ἐγεν[ήθη]νμεν κατάβρωμα ἁμαρτωλῶν [οἱ ἄνο]μοι ἐβάρυναν ἐφ' ἡμᾶς τὸν ζυ[γόν]. Eth.—"and we became food for the sinners and the wicked ones, and they [the iniquitous ones] have made their yoke heavy upon us"—wä-konä mäbälǝ 'tä lä-ḥaṭe'an

bearable. However, from this perspective, the poor are elevated to the role of pious ones who will inherit the eschatological reward (see 104:6;[27] cf. Luke 6:20). These pious poor who were being consumed by evil oppression and tribulations, will, in the eschaton, "shine like the luminaries of heaven" (104:2; also 102:4[28]). The author of the Epistle contends for the deliverance of the faithful ones who have been suffering economic and social oppression during their earthly existence.[29] In what follows, we will look at a few examples of the eschatological/apocalyptic language and ideas that are present in the Epistle and John's Apocalypse.

The Epistle of Enoch and John's Apocalypse[30]

The starting point for this examination begins at 1 Enoch 92:2–3a in which the term "time" or "days" carries apocalyptic and eschatological ramifications. The author states, "let not your spirit be saddened because of the times ((Eth. bä-'äzman; although no Greek is extant, the term is likely καιρός). For the Holy and Great One has appointed days (mäwa'elä; likely Gk. καιρόν) for everything. And the righteous one will rise from sleep; and he will arise and walk in the ways of righteousness (wä-yətnäśśa' ṣadəq 'əm-nəwam wä-yətnäśśa' wä-yäḫälləf bä-fənwatä ṣədq; cf. 91:10; 100:5; 51:1; 61:5; and Dan 12:2)."[31] The author is offering an exhortation to the righteous community (cf. John 14:1: "Do not let your hearts be troubled. Believe in God, believe also in me"), which is an attempt to alleviate the suffering of the audience. The phrase "appointed days" likely refers to the eschatological hope of redemption for the community of the righteous and punishment for the wicked who are the cause of the community's current distress. We find the Greek term καιρόν in Rev 12:14 in the context the last days (καιρὸν

wä-lä-'amaḍəyan 'kb ädu la 'lenä ' är'ätä.

27. Eth. "And now do not fear O righteous ones when you see sinners become strong and prosperous in their ways"—(wä-yə'əzeni 'i-təfərrəhu sobä tərey'əwomu lä-ḥaṭe'ään yəṣennə 'uwä-yədelləwu fənotomu); Gk.—"Do not fear O righteous ones when you see sinners become strong and prosperous in their ways"—(μὴ φοβεῖσθε Ο δίκαιοι ὅταν ἴδητε τοὺς ἁμαρτωλοὺς κατισχύοντας καὶ εὐμένους).

28. "Do not be afraid, you souls of the righteous and be hopeful, O those who have die in righteousness"—Eth.'i-təfärhu ' äntəmu näfsä ṣadəqan wa-täsäffäwu 'əlla motu bä-ṣədq; Grk.—"Take courage, O souls of the righteous who have died, the righteous and the pious" (θαρσεῖτε ψυχαὶ τῶν δικαίων τῶν ἀποθανόντων).

29. Cf. Luke 6:17–49, Sermon on the Plain; Luke 12:13–21, the rich and foolish farmer.

30. For discussion of the various manuscript evidence for the extant Ethiopic and Greek, see Stuckenbruck 2007:5–28, 185–87.

31. All translations are from Stuckenbruck 2007.

καὶ καιροὺς καὶ ἥμισυ καιροῦ) in which the woman giving birth to a child is being pursued by the dragon. Similar language is found in Rev 11:18: "The nations raged, but your wrath has come, and the time (καιρόν) for judging the dead, for rewarding your servants, the prophets and saints and all who fear your name, both small and great, and for destroying those who destroy the earth." It emerges from the author's use of καιρόν that it is employed in the context of the eschatological time period similar to what we see with the use of Ethiopic bä-'äzman and mäwa'əlä. The context for the revelation given to John here is following the second "woe" which introduces the coming Kingdom of God and his Messiah and the beginning of his reign on the earth, analogous to the context of 1 Enoch 92:2-5.

1 Enoch 92:3 offers hope for the righteous ones who have died: "the righteous one will rise from sleep, and he will arise and walk in the ways of righteousness." This passage suggests the possibility the resurrection will take place in the eschaton (cf. Rev 20:5, 6). This can be affirmed perhaps in 100:5 (also 103:4a—"And their spirits which died in righteousness will come back to life" and 104:1-2), which claims the "sleep" of the righteous is a time after death in which the righteous will "rise" (cf. Dan 12:2 when all the dead, wicked and righteous, will awaken to the judgment in which the righteous have nothing to fear—"Many of those who sleep in the dust of the earth shall awake, some to everlasting life, and some to shame and everlasting contempt.").[32] It is likely that 92:3 has in mind the eschatological event when one considers the reference to 'in the light" that follows in 92:4[33] and also the righteous shinning in 104:2. Revelation 20:4-6 offers a similar scenario for the righteous in the eschaton, although this is clearly a portrayal of a heavenly experience:

> 4. Then I saw thrones, and those seated on them were given authority to judge. I also saw the souls of those who had been beheaded for their testimony to Jesus and for the word of God. They had not worshiped the beast or its image and had not received its mark on their foreheads or their hands. They came to life and reigned with Christ a thousand years. 5. (The rest of the dead did not come to life until the thousand years were ended.)

32. Another possibility of the use of "arise" may be understood from 91:10 in which the righteous will "arise" and at the same time wisdom will "arise". This may suggest that the righteous are awakening from a spiritual slumber and will be granted wisdom in order to walk in the path of righteousness.

33. 1 Enoch 92.4: "He will be merciful to the righteous one and to him will be given uprightness, which is eternal. And to him will be given authority, and he will be in goodness and righteousness, and they will walk in eternal light." The phrase "eternal light" certainly hints at a time following the resurrection of the righteous who will then judge in the heavens ("authority") (cf. "as the light in heaven" in 104:2).

This is the first resurrection. 6. Blessed and holy are those who share in the first resurrection. Over these the second death has no power, but they will be priests of God and of Christ, and they will reign with him a thousand years.

A further possible use of apocalyptic language in the Epistle and the Apocalypse can be seen in the series of "Woes" (*älle*) that appear in both texts. The Epistle contains eight "woes" that are found in 94:6—95:2; 95:4-7; 96:4-8; 97:10; 98:9—99:2; 99:11-16; 100:7-9; 103:5-8. The Greek term οὐαί occurs in four passages in the Apocalypse: 8:13 (3x); 9:12; 11:14 (2x); and 12:12. It must be noted that the context of the use of the term in each text is slightly different.

The first instance in the Epistle, 94:6—95:2, presents the initial series of woes that declare the coming judgment upon the wicked.[34] The first set of woes addresses the long held opposition to the unjust gain of wealth, a primary theme of the Epistle, also in Proverbs, the *Sibylline Oracles*, and multiple DSS.[35] 1 Enoch 94:6 makes it clear the author is categorically opposed to unjust gain. The passage reads, "Woe to those who build iniquity and wrongdoing and found deceit.[36] For they will be quickly overthrown and *have no peace* [found also in 1 Enoch 5.4, referring to the unrighteous; 12.5; 16.4, referring to the Watchers; 98.6; 99.13; 101.3; 102.3; 103.8; 105.2, referring to sinners; 98.16, those who write down lying words]."[37] Revelation 6:4 offers a broader sense of the lack of peace in its description of the opening of the second seal in which the rider of the red horse will *remove peace* from the earth, perhaps implying the wicked will *have no peace* as in 1 Enoch 94:6.[38]

The opening "woe" in the Apocalypse appears in 8:13 in which the author repeats the term three times emphasizing the warning of the coming judgment for those who are on the earth.[39] The context of Revelation 8 is a vision granted to the author in which he is seeing the throne room of God

---

34. The woes found in the Epistle can also be found connected to a blessing for the righteous. Parallels are found in Luke 6:20-26 in which we read of the righteous poor and wealthy wicked. See discussion in Stuckenbruck 2007:260.

35. E.g., Prov 1:19; 10:2; 11:28; 13:28; 15:27; 18:11, 16; 20:17, 21; 23:4-5, 23-27; 28:1, 16, 22; 29:3; *Sib. Or.* 2.25, 70-72, 100-102; 1QpHab ix 5; xii 10; 1QS v 14-15, 19, 20; ix 8-9; 1QHa vi 20; CD A vi 14-17; viii 4-6; xi 15; CD B xix 19.

36. Nickelsburg (2001:460) reads, "Woe to those who build iniquity and violence, and lay deceit as a foundation."

37. Brackets and italics are mine.

38. See note 22 above.

39. "Woe, woe, woe to the inhabitants of the earth, at the blasts of the other trumpets that the three angels are about to blow."

where the angels are offering up the prayers of the saints to God. It is unclear in the passage if the righteous are left on the earth; but there are promises of shelter during the testing of those on the earth in 3:10; 7:2-4; and 11:1-2 (which describes those who still worship in the temple of God). The author suggests in 9:4[40] that there are people on the earth who have the seal of God and those who do not, perhaps suggesting that the living righteous will go through the coming calamity alongside the sinners.

A second woe is found in 94.7a that reads, "Woe to those who build *their houses with sin* [this should be understood as an act of social injustice by the wicked—i.e. slavery or forced labor; Eth. *äbyatihomu bä-ḫaṭi'ät*] for they will be overthrown (Eth. *yətnäśśätu*) from their entire foundation and they will fall by the sword." It is a matter of debate as to whether or not the "overthrowing" or "thrown down" is speaking of those who build the houses or the actual houses.[41] Based on other similar passages (e.g., 95:3, among others), the houses appear to be the object in the author's exhortation. The author contends a future judgment awaits those guilty of this sin of building houses through illegal gain will "fall by the sword"; this judgment may suggest an overturning of the favored status of the wicked will end in the last days (cf. 99:16a—Gk. God will "rub out" [ἐκτρίψε] their glory).

Verse 7b reads "And (woe to) those who acquire gold and silver: in the judgment they will be quickly destroyed"; again a harsh warning to those who are gaining wealth unjustly. Here it appears the author is speaking of a specific way in which the wicked gain their wealth and build their houses; i.e. through the sin their own hands. Nonetheless, the sin of how the illegal gain is accumulated is not spelled out; thus, not rejecting the accruing of riches altogether. It is clear from a theological standpoint the author is concerned with the failure of the wicked wealthy to use their wealth in line with Torah, to benefit the poor, again, an issue of social injustice. This is a clear violation of God's direction spelled out in Jer 22:6—"He [the king] judged the cause of the poor and needy; then it was well. Is not this to know me? says the LORD."

In the Apocalypse, the wealth and use of gold by the wicked is mentioned in a negative sense on several occasions. The first is in 9:20 where the author is offering an invective against those sinners who are "worshiping demons and idols of gold and silver and bronze and stone and wood, which cannot see or hear or walk." The emphasis on the wealth of the wicked (gold

---

40. "They were told not to damage the grass of the earth or any green growth or any tree, *but only those people who do not have the seal of God on their foreheads.* They were allowed to torture them for five months, but not to kill them, and their torture was like the torture of a scorpion when it stings someone."

41. See Nickelsburg 2001:462. Cf. 99:16; 91:12; and 98:12.

and other precious items) is found also in 17:4 in which the woman sitting on a beast is adorned in riches. Here she represents the great Babylon (Rome) with whom the wicked in and around the author's community had much economic interaction. A similar understanding of the wickedness of gold and wealth is offered in 18:11–13 that depicts the eschatological ruin of Rome along with the wicked rich who depended on her for their prosperity. Again, the author of Revelation does not rule out the acquisition of wealth as we read in 3:18a, "Therefore I counsel you to buy from me gold refined by fire so that you may be rich." As can be seen, there is a strong polemic against unjust wealth in both the Epistle and the Apocalypse, but they do not rule out the accumulation of wealth provided it is used to fulfil the commandments, i.e. take care of the poor, the widows, and the orphans.

The third woe of the Epistle is found in 94:8. Here the author directs his rebuke at those who have gained wealth on their own in sinful ways and in doing so they failed to remember the Most High (Deut 8:13–19; also Jer 22:16). Here the author writes, "Woe to you rich ones, for you have trusted in your wealth (bəʿlkəmu). However, you will have to depart from your wealth since in the days of your wealth you did not remember the Most High." In verse 8a, we find the contrasting idea of the individual relying on his or her riches and power and one's reliance on the justice, power, and mercy of God.[42] It is clear from this passage there is a contrast between just wealth and being mindful to God and unjust wealth and turning away from God (cf. Deut 8:17–18). Revelation 3:17 offers a near parallel to the idea in 94:8. The author writes in the letter to Laodicea, "For you say, 'I am rich, I have prospered, and I need nothing.' You do not realize that you are wretched, pitiable, poor, blind, and naked."[43] Here the context appears to suggest the members of the church have failed to remember the Lord is the one who has placed them in the positions they hold in the community, while at the same time it may be a critique of their aspirations to that kind of status (i.e. "rich" is being redefined by the risen Jesus).

1 Enoch 94:9, as part of the third woe, offers a firm eschatological warning to the rich which declares the coming day of bloodshed and the

---

42. For similar sentiments in the Old Testament, see Ps 49:6: "Why should I fear in times of trouble, when the iniquity of my persecutors surrounds me, those who trust in their wealth and boast of the abundance of their riches?" (Heb 49:6–7); Ps 52:7: "Behold the man who will not place his means of protection in God, but trusted in abundant riches, but strengthened (himself) in his wickedness" (Heb 52:9); and Prov 11:28: "The one who trusts in his riches will fall, But like a leaf, the righteous will flourish."

43. See 97:8; Jer 17:11. The author of Sirach 5:1 rebukes those who gain wealth by dishonesty—"do not depend on dishonest wealth"—μὴ ἔπεχε ἐπὶ χρήμασιν ἀδικοῖς. He also contends that wealth justly acquired and properly used—almsgiving—3:30; 17:22; 29:23; 40:17, 24—is acceptable—10:30–31; 11:14; 18:25; 40:13, 18.

"great day of judgment". The author writes, "and you have been prepared for the day of bloodshed (ʾəlätä kə ʿiwä däm), for the day of darkness (wä-ʾəlätä ṣəlmät), and for the great Day of Judgment (wä-ʾəlätä kʷənnene ʿabiy) (cf. Zeph 1:15).[44] We find a contrast in the verse between what has been prepared for the wicked and what has been prepared of the righteous. For the wicked, judgment; for the righteous, as we are told in 103:3, rewards are being prepared for them;[45] both of these outcomes will take place in the eschaton.

Another apocalyptic phrase "the day of bloodshed" is alluded to in Rev 14:20, which may be alluding to 1 Enoch 100:3 (also 99:6) or a similar tradition. The author of the Revelation passage writes, "And the wine press was trodden outside the city, and blood flowed from the wine press, as high as a horse's bridle, for a distance of about two hundred miles." Similarly the author of 1 Enoch 100.3 writes "a horse will wade up to its chest in the blood of sinners, and the chariot will sink up to its height."[46] Both passages refer to the eschatological judgment against sinners, which will bring about the outpouring of a massive amount of blood that will be shed through the sinners. Revelation 14:20 is set in the context of an angel reaping grapes from the vine (perhaps an allusion to Israel), i.e. sinners;[47] while the 1 Enoch passage is set in the context of the "spirit of anger" of the Lord is set to destroy you all (sinners) with the sword.

The phrase "the day of darkness" in 94:9 has its origins in the biblical tradition found in the prophets (see Amos 5:20; Joel 2:2; Zeph 1:15). This may simply be another way of describing the Day of YHWH or the Day of Judgment that follows.[48] In 92:5 the author writes, "And sin will be destroyed forever in darkness, and it will no longer be seen, then, from that day into

---

44. "That day will be a day of wrath, a day of distress and anguish, a day of ruin and devastation, a day of darkness and gloom, a day of clouds and thick darkness"—Gk. ἡμέρα ὀργῆς ἡ ἡμέρα ἐκείνη ἡμέρα θλίψεως καὶ ἀνάγκης ἡμέρα ἀωρίας καὶ ἀφανισμοῦ ἡμέρα σκότους καὶ γνόφου ἡμέρα νεφέλης καὶ ὁμίχλης. See also Job 3:4–5; Amos 5:18; Job 15:23; 1QS ii 8; Heb 12:18; 2 Pet 2:17; and Jude 13.

45. Cf. Mark 10:40, which suggests that places are being prepared in the heavenly realm for the righteous; 1 Cor 2:9, suggests that God has prepared a place in the heavenly realm for those who love him; and Heb 11:16, which states that God has prepared a city for the righteous.

46. 1 Enoch 99:6 perhaps offers an indication of the day of bloodshed to come: "And again I swear to you, O sinners, that sin is prepared for the day of unceasing blood."

47. We may also see an allusion to these events of vengeance against the sinners in Rev 19:2 in which God has avenged the blood of his servants (cf. 1 Enoch 95:2b). See discussion of vengeance in Stuckenbruck 2001:265–66.

48. Stuckenbruck 2001:266.

eternity." In addition, we are told in 103:7–8 that sinners will enter darkness when they come for the great judgment: "You yourselves know that they will bring your souls down to Hades, and there they will be in great stress, and in darkness and in a snare and in a burning flame, and into a great judgment your souls will enter during all the generations of eternity."[49] The author offers one occasion in the Apocalypse, 16:10, which describes the covering of evil with darkness; however, this episode is in the context of the fifth bowl being poured on the "throne of the beast" which causes darkness to fall on his kingdom: "The fifth angel poured his bowl on the throne of the beast, and its kingdom was plunged into darkness; people gnawed their tongues in agony." The phrase "the great day of judgment," found in 94:9, may be understood in the Apocalypse (Rev 14:7—"Fear God, and give Him glory, because the *hour of His judgment* has come; and worship Him who made the heaven and the earth and sea and springs of waters.") that the "hour of judgment" has come to those on the earth who will not repent before God (cf. 18:10—". . . standing at a distance because of the fear of her torment, saying, 'Woe, woe, the great city, Babylon, the strong city! For in one hour your judgment has come'").

Another passage to address is 1 Enoch 95:3–7 that speaks of the judgement of the wicked by the righteous. The reason for this is spelled out in 95:7, "Woe to you sinners because you *persecute the righteous* (lä-ṣadəqan təsäddədəwwomu), for you will be delivered over and persecuted by iniquity, and its yoke will be heavy on you."[50] This is a reversal of the roles spoken of in 99:2a and 103:11 in which the wicked place a heavy yoke on the widows, orphans, and poor (see Deut 28:48). First Enoch 95:5 also emphasizes the ways of the wicked and their coming punishment: "Woe to you who repay your neighbor with evil, for you [wicked] will be repaid according to your deeds."[51] The term "deeds" is language familiar to the apocalyptic worldview in the 2TP. Revelation 16:11 declares the sinners on the earth, at the pouring out of the fifth bowl, will be punished for their deeds ("and they blasphemed the God of heaven because of their pains and their sores; and they did not repent of their deeds."); this is the opposite of how the author depicts the

---

49. Cf. Rev 6:17 in which the author warns all that "the great day of their wrath has come, and who is able to stand?"

50. Cf. Rev 1:9; 1 Enoch 46:8; 108:7; *Jub.* 23:23–24; and *2 Bar.* 54.21. Also Pss 10:2; 119:84, 86, 150, 161; Judg 2:18; NT Matt 5:10–44; 10:23; Mark 13:9–13; Luke 1:49; 21:12; John 5:16; 15:20.

51. Punishment usually handed out by the Most High; see Sir 28:1—"the vengeful will face the Lord's vengeance"; 1QS x 18—"for with God is the judgment of every living being"; CD A ix 2–5, interpreting Lev 19:18. On the occasion in 95:9b God uses the righteous to "repay" the wicked for their deeds. The brackets in the verse are my own.

deeds of the righteous in Rev 19:8: "to her [Bride] it has been granted to be clothed with fine linen, bright and pure, for the fine linen is the righteous deeds of the saints." Again, in the Epistle we see the theme of "vengeance" against the wicked in the phrase "will be repaid."[52]

One final comparison of the apocalyptic nature of the Epistle and John's Apocalypse may be found in the "Woe" in 1 Enoch 98:15 and Rev 2:2, and 20. The "Woe" reads "Woe to you who write down false words and words of error (Gk. λόγους πλανήσεως; Eth. wä-nägärä räsi'an—"and words of the wicked") they themselves write, and lead many astray with their lies (Gk. καὶ πολλοὺς ἀποπλανήσουσιν τοῖς ψευδέσιν αὐτῶν; Eth. kämä yəsəm'əwwa wä-yərəs 'əwwo lä-ba'əd—"so that they will hear them and make others wicked"). Revelation 2:2 praises the church at Ephesus for testing "those who claim to be apostles but are not, and have found them to be false" (Gk. καὶ ἐπείρασας τοὺς λέγοντας ἑαυτοὺς ἀποστόλους καὶ οὐκ εἰσίν, καὶ εὗρες αὐτοὺς ψευδεῖς). In both passages the individuals in question are identified as false teachers. According to the author of Rev 2:2, these apostles/prophets were attempting to lead the members of church away from following after Christ. However, in Rev 2:20 we find the Church of Thyatira is rebuked for tolerating "that woman Jezebel, who calls herself a prophetess and is teaching and beguiling my servants to practice fornication and to eat food sacrificed to idols." Again, the implication is that this individual is a false teacher. In the Epistle these false prophets (see 98:15)[53] are condemned in 99:2 for attempting to alter the words of God's covenant: "Woe to you who alter the true words, and who pervert the eternal covenant and who reckon yourselves to be without sin; they will be trampled on in the earth."

One may also consider 1 Enoch 103:3 and Rev 5:1 as having some relationship. Both appear to be discussing a scroll/book of some sort in which good things are written (inscribed) for the spirits that have died in righteousness. Verse 103:3a in Ethiopic reads, "that everything good and joy and honor have been prepared and written down for their spirits which died in righteousness". One Ethiopic manuscript, BM 485a includes the addition of 'äsmatihomu—"their names." This may reveal a relationship with the names of individuals being written or not written in the Scroll/Book of Life in Rev 13:8; 17:8; 20:15 (all three speak of the wicked that are not written; however 20:15 suggests multiple books are opened, one that records the deeds of individuals, and the Book of Life which contains the names of the righteous), and 21:27, which speaks of those who are written

---

52. Stuckenbruck 2001:279-80.

53. "Woe to you who write down false words, and words of error they themselves write, and they lead many astray with their lies."

in the Lamb's Book of Life. The Greek manuscripts do not include the reading "their names," but does speak of "their spirits" [those of the righteous] being included in the Scroll. Both the Enochic text and Apocalypse place the events in a heavenly context.

Each of the illustrations demonstrates the measure of social and economic injustice that was occurring between the wealthy and powerful and the poor, i.e., one of oppression and persecution. Each author has explained in some detail the eschatological events that await both the wicked and the righteous. It may also be suggested that this injustice may be a result of sectarian disputes, although fairly clear this is the case in the Apocalypse, the Epistle does not offer a well-defined understanding of the disputes.

Conclusion

It is perhaps possible from the comparisons laid out above that the author of John's Apocalypse is familiar with the Epistle of Enoch or a common tradition that was circulating amongst "apocalyptic communities"; or as some might argue, what we see in both texts is the language of apocalypticism. We also find a similar depiction of the rich and poor in other NT writings; note for instance the Synoptic Gospels, 1 Timothy, and James among others; although, as some suggest, the NT communities could be considered "apocalyptic communities." Matt 19:23, 24 speaks of how difficult it is for a rich man to enter the Kingdom of Heaven (also Mark 10:25; Luke 18:25). Luke 6:24 states that the rich have received their reward in this life. Luke 16:19–31 is the story of the "wicked" rich man and Lazarus the beggar, which of course reveals the punishment of the rich who do not honor God. 1 Tim 6:9 and 10 (cf. 1QpHab viii 8–12) speak of the love of money and the temptation and destruction it can bring to individuals. And finally in James 2:6 we read of the rich oppressing the poor, and in 5:1, the author speaks of the punishment of the rich for their failure to honor God. These examples reveal the ongoing negative view of the wicked who are wealthy and powerful but do not honor God. One instance in Matt 27:57 suggests that it is acceptable for one to be rich, as is Joseph of Arimathaea, a disciple of Jesus, but one must honor God in all he possesses and his righteous acts. The presence of this particular view of the rich and poor in the NT suggests the author of these texts and their communities had connections, or a similar worldview, to early apocalyptic communities.[54]

One can gather from the Epistle and the Apocalypse that there are good things in store for the righteous poor, but only in the eschaton when

54. Matthews, "Riches, Poverty and the Faithful," 165.

the wicked and evil have been dealt with by God. First Enoch 104:2 states: "Take courage, then for formerly you were worn down by evils and oppression, but now you will shine like the luminaries of heaven; you will shine and appear, and the portals of heaven will be opened to you." Both our authors and others in the NT and other 2TP literature rebuke the wealthy for not accepting the responsibility that comes with wealth and power—taking care of the poor and powerless. As this examination has revealed, these views represent a change in the worldview concerning the reward for the righteous and the punishment of the wicked; they no longer take place in the earthly realm, but in the eschaton.

In examining this material, one must be careful not to get carried away with drawing too many parallels that are not clearly spelled out in the terminology used by the authors. Much more exegetical work is needed on the issue, but from this brief exercise hopefully one can recognize the continuing influence of the Enochic and other apocalyptic literature in the first century and early Christianity.

What Can We Learn?

From this examination, we can see that the idea of social injustice and economic inequality is not a modern phenomenon; rather it has been with humanity since early in its history. We have observed that the wealthy for the most part (although we are getting only a partial depiction of the larger picture within the communities in question) are considered wicked, greedy, and oppressive toward other members in their communities and apparently people groups outside of those communities. The poor, on the other hand (again, only a partial picture), are considered to be pious and are waiting for the change of their position in society (i.e., being blessed according to the dictate of the Deuteronomy passages discussed earlier). This reversal of roles is brought about in these particular texts by the God of early Judaism and the NT. So how does this relate to our current dilemma of a world of poverty-stricken people groups and the wealthy that hold power over them? According to our texts in question, the answer lies in the world of faith; in the broader scheme of things in the faith of the God of Abraham, Isaac, and Jacob and for those who are not of that faith, perhaps in the "spiritual leader/divine being" of their particular belief system.

6

The Political Theology of the Similitudes of Enoch in Its Ancient Context and Its Theological Implications

CRISPIN FLETCHER-LOUIS

Introduction: The Political Setting of the Similitudes of Enoch

The result of the 2015 UK general election was remarkable; for many reasons. During the campaign David Cameron seemed not to care very much for victory. Perhaps some of the British electorate do not like a leader who wants power too much. Cameron's unexpected victory was soon followed by another surprise: the sudden and meteoric rise of Jeremy Corbyn to the leadership of the British Labour party. Again, among the many virtues that have endeared Corbyn to his supporters there is a mild, unassuming manner. For many he has seemed to fulfil the dream of a new kind of politician characterised by integrity rather than a lust for power.

Among the political elite of the ancient world there were those who thought it the wisest course that a ruler should avoid the pursuit of power and its benefits. According to Cassius Dio, in 29 BCE Octavian was advised by his friend and counsellor Maecenas to avoid a self-aggrandising pursuit of honors that would have included the treatment of him as a god:

> So far as you yourself are concerned, permit no exceptional or prodigal distinction to be given you, through word or deed, either by the senate or by any one else. For whereas the honor which you confer upon others lends glory to them, yet nothing can be given to you that is greater than what you already possess . . .[1]

Maecenas' advice might seem like a straightforward anticipation of a modern British aversion to a vulgar grasping after power and honors. However, the rationale for his advice to Octavian has a logic that does not typically figure in our own political discourse. As one worthy to rule as an emperor, Octavian is already honorable and glorious; so he should not let himself be tempted by the flatteries of obsequious subjects. In practice, Greek and Roman rulers typically followed another, competing, ideal: that all should strive for honor and glory, even honours typically reserved for divine heroes and gods. However, as we shall see, the basis of Maecenas' appeal to Rome's new emperor perhaps has a parallel in the sphere of ancient Jewish political theology.

The Similitudes of Enoch was possibly written when Octavian was emperor.[2] I propose that, in its own distinctive way, the Similitudes contributes to a centuries-long Jewish debate about the nature of earthly rule and the problem of the human lust for power and prestige. From the margins of empire it prophesies a radical political theology to challenge the one at the centre. It articulates, *inter alia*, a theology that responds to the perceived failures of the nation's own religious establishment and the crisis of a new era of submission to a foreign rule and political culture.

My proposal builds on the argument of other publications, especially one inspired by Pierluigi Piovanelli's argument that the Similitudes was most likely composed somewhere in Palestine, in the late first century BCE, with an invective that has in view a Roman occupation of the land and Rome's client Herod with his cronies; the "kings and the mighty (and the exalted) (who possess the earth/the land)."[3] They are the enemies of God and his people.[4] If Piovanelli is right about the text's setting then that likely helps to

---

1. Cassius Dio, *Roman History* 52.35.1-2 (Cary 1914:170-71).

2. On the emerging consensus that the Similitudes is to be dated to the last decades of the first century BCE or the first decades of the first century CE, see Fletcher-Louis 2015:175, 201-2.

3. For this repeated formulaic description of the enemies of God and his people see 1 Enoch 38:4-5; 46:4-6; 48:8; 53:5; 54:2; 55:4; 62:1, 3, 6, 9; 63:1, 12; 67:8, 12; and Nickelsburg and VanderKam 2012a:103-6.

4. See Fletcher-Louis 2014 and Piovanelli 2007; cf. Charlesworth 2013 and Walck 2012. The lack of reference to actual sacrifices to the emperor in the text's imaginary

explain, I have argued, the distinctive pre-existent messianism of the text. In the Greek and Roman worlds, rulers gain power and glory through human endeavor; through military conquest, through great works that serve peoples (benefactions), through character and charisma (virtue).[5] They exalt themselves and they are exalted by their subjects through relationships in which there is a mutual exchange of glory and honor, even to the point that they receive "honors equal to the gods" (*isotheoi timai*) because of their benefactions. The gods themselves are divine because they are powerful. Men too may become divine if they can demonstrate great power. And for such men there are statues in temples fashioned in their likenesses that receive altars and sacrifices, there are festivals held in their honor, there is poetic praise and there are hymns that celebrate their *deeds* and their charisma—*their personality*.

Herod and his circle accommodated aspects of this political culture. Herod was willing to give such honors to Rome's rulers (in the building of three temples to Caesar: at Caesarea Maritima, Caesarea Philippi, and at Samaria-Sebaste). Even if Herod did not seek or receive *divine* honors for himself, Josephus says he rose to power on the back of his benefactions and the expectations of his supporters that in gratitude for their efforts they too would be exalted (*Ant.* 14.398; cf. *War* 1.293). His benefactions towards non-Jews were considerable (*Ant.* 16.24, 140, 146, 150). Even Josephus criticizes him for being a lover of honor (*Ant.* 16.156–158),[6] with the comment that the Jewish people are accustomed to justice not the pursuit of glory (*Ant.* 16.158). Herod also adopted an aggressive stance towards the established priestly families and the Jerusalem Sanhedrin in a way that might well be in view in the Similitudes' description of the behavior of the kings and the mighty of the earth (e.g. *Ant.* 14.168–176; cf. 17.304–310; *T. Mos.* 6.1–4).

The Similitudes has a two-pronged response to the new political realities under Herod and the Romans, I contend. On the one hand, there is direct criticism of the kings and the mighty who now possess or seize the land. Their "deeds" are unrighteous, lawless and come from idolatry. So, they are hardly the kind that warrant genuine human praise and glory (1 Enoch 46:7;

---

world might mean the Similitudes comes from the period before Herod built temples to Augustus at Caesarea Maritima, Caesarea Philippi and Samaria, that is, in the pre-27 BCE phase of Augustan rule.

5. For this see, for example, Quintilian (writing at the end of the first century CE): "some gods should be praised," he writes, "because . . . they earned immortality by virtue, a theme which the piety of our emperor has made the glory of the present age" (*Inst.* 3.7.9).

6. What Josephus says in *Ant.* 16.157–158 may mean that Herod wanted to receive the kind of cultic honors given to his Roman overlords, but the religious scruples of the Jewish people prevented him.

48:8; 53:2; 63:9, cf. 45:3; 52:5–9). Like the king of Babylon who exalted himself to a position of deity, the wicked have mounted an assault on the Most High that will end in their judgement and destruction (46:7, cf. Isa 14:4–20 and Dan. 8:10; 2 Macc 7:34; 9:5–12; Wis 4:20–5:15).

On the other hand, the Similitudes does not dismiss altogether the place for a God-appointed ruler. Neither does it utterly reject the widespread ancient view that an ideal or true ruler has a kind of divine identity. The Similitudes puts forward its own ruler whose peculiar divine identity is superior to the divinity that was typically claimed for rulers in the Hellenistic and Roman worlds. There is a coming Messiah (the Son of Man, the Chosen One) who will fulfill biblical prophecies of an ideal (Davidic) king: Isa 11:2–4 is applied to the coming Son of Man-Messiah in 1 Enoch 49:3; 62:2–3; and Psalm 2 is probably applied to him in 48:8, 10. He has the power, like Caesar, to judge and destroy his enemies. I have also argued that in various ways the Son of Man-Messiah is a priestly figure; at least much that is said about him finds a parallel in biblical and contemporary traditions surrounding the high priest.[7] The text applies the language of Daniel 7, especially 7:13, to the Messiah because that biblical text looks forward to the appearance of a (royal and angelic) high priestly figure. The Similitudes expands on and gives some fresh perspectives to a traditional, and prophetic, high priestly messianic hope. This too makes him Caesar's equal, inasmuch as (from 13 BCE onwards) the Caesars held the highest priestly office in the Roman state (*Pontifex Maximus*).[8] But in important ways he will be a ruler quite *unlike* Caesar or Herod.

The likes of Alexander the Great, the successors to whom Alexander's empire was parcelled out after his death, and then Octavian, all received divine honors during their reign and after their deaths *because of their deeds and character*. In effect, they were human beings who were "exalted" to heaven. And by their conduct and character they earned the divine honors that their contemporaries gave to them. The Similitudes says the one true God also has a ruler who will exercise great power, and who will have authority over the kings and peoples of the earth. He will condemn and destroy his enemies and will bless those who belong to him. But this ruler is never exalted, *because he has his origin in pre-mundane pre-existence—in heaven above*.[9] He already has divine glory. Like Maecenas' Octavian, he

---

7. Fletcher-Louis 2014:71–79.

8. For the ideal Hellenistic ruler as a priest, see Diotogenes in Stobaeus 4.7.61: the perfect king should be "a good general, judge and priest" (see Thesleff 1972:72).

9. It is possible that prior to the inclusion of the material that we now have in 1 Enoch 37–71 there was a version of the Book of Watchers that climaxed with the exaltation of Enoch to a position of glory and heavenly enthronement, and that that climax

does not need to become something by the people's praise that he is not already. Only, unlike Octavian, he has a glorious and divine identity *from heavenly pre-existence*. And unlike Octavian, he has no personal story; no story of deeds done, character developed or revealed, and of divine honors won. Nicolaus of Damascus wrote a biography of Octavian and late in Augustus' life an official record of his deeds (the Res Gestae) boasted of his achievements. The author of the Similitudes avoids anything that would warrant such literary forms for the divine ruler. Neither is there anything here that would justify the encomiastic form of the short hymn to Christ as cosmocrator in Phil 2:6–11.

The Son of Man–Messiah manifests something of God's own identity and he will receive human worship—praise, blessings, glorification, exaltation, *but not because of any deeds he has done*. If there is a focus on righteous deeds, it is those of the Lord of Spirits that are to be praised—1 Enoch 63:8. The absence of a personal biography helps ensure that the text remains monotheistic. The Son of Man messiah is a distinct figure. He is an agent of revelation (46:3), who will crush evil kings (46:4–5). He is one on whom the righteous will lean and in whom they will hope (48:4–6; 62:9). He judges the secret things (49:4) and the "word of his mouth will slay all the sinners." Nevertheless, in all these things he is an *agent* who simply acts on behalf of the Lord of Spirits, doing in the eschaton the kinds of things that God himself is typically expected to do in biblical and Jewish texts. He is the one-God-made-manifest, rather than a distinct divine person with his own developed set of relationships to God and the rest of reality. By contrast, it is the Lord of Spirits who is more clearly portrayed as a personal being in the Similitudes.[10] By denying the Son of Man Messiah a personal biography, the Similitudes minimizes the degree to which its theology threatens the boundaries of a simple belief in one God. The text does not speak of God (the Lord of Spirits) and *the god* Son of Man-Messiah. Rather it describes the one God, the Lord of Spirits, and his Messiah, the Son of Man (and Elect One), *who is his agent*, the unique bearer of his divine presence and action. But as his agent he is not a distinct person. And this is not a purely theological or abstract philosophical construction. It is in large part motivated, I

---

has been overlaid or replaced with the pre-existent messianism now in the Similitudes (see Fletcher-Louis 2014).

10. For this distinction between the personal character of the lord of spirits and the a-personal character of the Son of Man, compare the important discussion of the relationship between the Similitudes and Pauline Christology in Tilling 2012:207–33 in 1 Enoch 48 the Son of Man is given a name, however that name is most likely the divine name, *YHWH*, not a name that distinguishes the Enochic Messiah as a person in his own right. For this interpretation of the name bestowed in 1 Enoch 48, see Gieschen 2007; and Fletcher-Louis 2015:185.

propose, by a peculiarly Jewish critique of pagan patterns of ruler cult. It is both political and theological.

The Son of Man-Chosen One fulfils biblical royal prophecies. But he is not a king who goes out to battle, to win territory, to gather a people, reward his supporters, found new cities, provide military protection for peoples and lands, blessing his subject cities with great public works. There is no echo in the portrayal of him of stories from the life of David or Solomon that one would expect for a typical Roman-era ruler (contrast *Pss. Sol.* 17–18). This is deliberate, I have proposed. *The distinctive pre-existence messianism of the Similitudes is a direct response to the structure of a pagan political culture.*[11] Where pagan kings work their way up, from below; the messiah of the Similitudes simply comes—already fully armed with God's own wisdom, life, power and authority—from above. In the former deeds produce an identity (or status), in the latter deeds express an identity (or ontology). *The Son of Man is what he is from before the creation of the world. He acts* (in the eschatological future) because he *is* (in pre-existence); he does not *become* something on the basis of his actions. Deeds do not maketh this *divine* figure.

If these observations are anywhere near the mark then the Similitudes' political theology may help us interpret Son of Man texts in the New Testament.[12] The fact that there are passages in the NT that express a belief in Christ's pre-existence is sometimes explained as the result of an attempt to be theologically consistent: if Christ is divine he must be eternally so. If the pre-existent messianism of the Similitudes expresses a distinctive *political* theology then it may shed new light on similar patterns in early (Jewish) Christian views of Christ. I will offer some reflections on that possibility at the end of this essay. But first, I would like to look backwards and make

11. Though it also has parallels in the pagan world. For example, Dio's Maecenas speech (cited above) has a remarkable echo of the Similitudes (and of Phil 2:6–11) when it says that the true divine ruler already has within himself all the honor he needs. He does not need to receive anything from his subjects.

12. A fuller examination of this interpretation of the Similitudes has to address the identification of Enoch with the Son of Man Messiah in 1 Enoch 71:14–17. That identification does not undermine the foregoing observations on the Enochic Son of Man's lack of a distinct personality, but it does require explanation given the ways in which the early Enochic material recounts experiences and events in the life of the pre-lapsarian hero. Although biographical stories of the kind that would typically be ascribed to a ruler are lacking, there is a limited interest in Enoch's own person and his individual history. This suggests that the point of 1 Enoch 71:14–17 is to say that, at that point in his visionary career, Enoch became the Son of Man Messiah in a way analogous to an Aaronid entering into the high priestly office. For that explanation of 1 Enoch 71:14–17 we can compare the relationship between Enoch's visionary journey in the early chapters of 2 *Enoch* 1–21 and his installation into a high priestly position in 2 *Enoch* 22–67.

some further suggestions about the origins of a pre-existent messianism in relation to the biblical text and mainstream Jewish politics *prior* to the Herodian age.

In summary, *I propose the Similitudes' pre-existent messianism is conceptually indebted to the biblical distinction between the high priestly office and the person of the king. In the last decades of the Hasmoneans that distinction was eroded. The Similitudes' solution to the failure of the Hasmoneans, to the Roman occupation and to the rise of Herod is a radical intensification of the distinction between the royal person and the high priestly office, with the parameters of the latter transposed to a new position that utterly transcends all contingent personal human interests and aspirations. A biblical distinction between the office of the high priest and the person (of the king, for example) is transposed to the eschatological scenario.*

A Biblical Distinction between Office and Person

The challenges of an oppressive Herodian and Roman rule were not new. The nation had suffered oppressive royal rule from within and without before, and many passages in Israel's scriptures speak to such a situation. Israel's scriptures do not set out a neat, tidy and comprehensive political theology that would forever solve such problems. However, among the many threads woven by the Primary History (Genesis to 2 Kings) one stands out: a thoroughgoing critique of kingship and the promulgation of a constitution in which, from Sinai onwards, monarchy is subordinate to priesthood. The issues surrounding kingship and its relationship to other institutions are complex. What follows is a simplification that highlights one, dominant, strand of political and religious thought in Israel's scriptures. It is a strand that provides a conceptual framework that helps to explain the origins of the distinctive shape of the messianism of the Similitudes.

God's purpose was always that royal power be distributed among God's people. Insofar as God's people need leadership, Torah provides a priestly office to mediate divine presence, revelation and instruction (Exodus 25—Deuteronomy 33). The God-given Mosaic constitution also allows the people to have a king, on the proviso that royal power should be constrained by the regulations of Torah and royal persons should be subordinate to a priestly office (that is defined by, and exercises judgement in accordance with, Torah) (Deuteronomy 17).

God did not intend that his people should be ruled by a king. Israel asked for that model of government because they were envious of their neighbors who had kings (1 Samuel 8–12, esp. 8:5, 10–20). God was not utterly opposed to kingship and all that it entailed. But Genesis says that, from the beginning, his intention was that *all humanity* should exercise royal dominion in creation (Gen 1:26–28; Ps 8:5–8). Neither is God, in principal, against a delegated rule, the distribution of authority and divine presence in and through those whom he chooses.[13] But Israel's three founding kings— Saul, David and Solomon—are problematic characters. And nearly four-hundred years of bad kings come after Solomon, who started well (1 Kings 3–8), but ended badly (1 Kings 10–11)—even as a new Pharaoh-within (in 1 Kgs 9:10—14:20).[14]

Solomon's fall exemplifies the inherent problems of kingship. In 1 Kings 10–11 Solomon's "regime is noted for its egregious tyranny, and his wisdom is directed toward his own self-aggrandizement."[15] In effect, he exalts his heart over of his people, against the deuteronomic law of the king (Deut 17:20). With the arrival of the Queen of Sheba (in 1 Kings 10) he has an opportunity to bring in something of the nations' wealth and glory to Yahweh and to his house (cf. Isa 60:1–14). Instead Solomon takes it for his own house (1 Kings 10). He strengthens his own hand—economically and militarily—in a way that contrasts sharply with the earlier years of his reign when newly created prosperity accrued to the benefit of his people as much as it did to his own benefit (1 Kgs 10:26–29, cf. 1 Kings 4). Torah stipulates that the king shall not multiply for himself wives, silver and gold (Deut 17:16–17). According to the Deuteronomistic History, these are the very things that Solomon multiplies for himself in the later years of his reign (1 Kgs 10:14—11:8).

In the overarching sweep of the Primary History the period of the monarchy is a phase subsequent to, and a declension from, the ideal constitution given to Moses at Sinai. In the constitution that comes from that golden age there is no king—at least, not one quite like Saul, David and Solomon. From Sinai onwards Israel has a figure with royal attributes; but he is an office, not a person. He is the great priest (*kohen gadol*). His garments (Exodus 29, 39) signify royalty, but in other ways he is a poor candidate for the role of an ancient Near Eastern king.[16]

---

13. On the distribution of powers in biblical law see, e.g., McConville 2006b:88, 187 n. 11.

14. For Solomon like Pharaoh see e.g. Sweeney 2010:179–89. Already in the earlier phase of his life Solomon's character is flawed in ways that anticipate his later fall (cf., e.g., 3:1–2 with 11:1–8).

15. Parker 1992:86.

16. For the high priest a royal figure see Davies 2004:157–61 and Propp 2006:524–25, 732.

All that the high priest does is carefully prescribed by Torah. He is not his own man. He is purely an office. An actor on a stage, fulfilling a script. In the case of the king, according to Deut 17:14–20, Torah *pro*scribes some behavior. But it recognizes, implicitly, that kings like to act independently; that they can be men of initiative and enterprise.[17] By putting a high priestly office at its head, Torah protects the nation from the evil inclination that sometimes led kings to exalt themselves over others, taking advantage of their position for their own personal benefit. A king's personal freedom and power often meant that his own interests competed with God's and the peoples' interests. Kings typically want the power too much. The priestly office is designed to prevent that problem. For the priesthood the script is already written. It just has to be acted out.

The office is a gift to the chosen one (of the chosen tribe and family): it cannot be earned, won or bought. It cannot be wanted too much. Any who try to exalt themselves to enjoy the office's privileges—a Korah or an Uzziah, for example—are swiftly judged (Leviticus 10; 2 Chr 26:16–21; cf. 1 Sam 13:7–14). By clothing the high priest in garments of dense symbolic significance Torah empties the office holder of his own personality. The rituals of consecration are probably intended to achieve the same effect, by marking, or effecting, a transfer from one identity (the holder's own) to another (the office) (esp. Exodus 29).[18] The high priest is virtuous. But his moral qualities inhere in the garments of the office (so *T. Levi* 8), once he and the garments have been consecrated with special oil.[19] The distinction between the office and the person also means that the high priest may prophesy without knowing that he is doing so: Caiaphas prophesied "not from himself, but being high priest" (John 11:51–52). And the person cannot wear the garments that define the office outside the Temple. The office is divine within the Temple because that place is a microcosm of a perfected heaven and earth. So the high priest's role is also analogous to the one played by an actor in a theatre. All this means that *the office transcends the space-time contingencies of its individual holders*. It is the same, yesterday, today and forever. *In effect, the office pre-exists (and post-exists) the individuals who serve within it*.

---

17. In terms of a modern analysis of personality types, the king has a high dominance score on a DISC test, the high priest is to have a high compliance score. Aaron's compliant behavior in response to the people's requests in Exodus 32 shows that, in a way, he was perfectly suited to the high priestly office.

18. Cf. the discussion of the ordination of the priest in Propp 2006:528–31.

19. His ministry is effective *ex opere operantis*—"by the work of the working one" (not just *ex opere operato*—"by the work worked"), but only because the personal (transient, flawed, sinful) identity of the person who holds the office has been occluded.

98   THE BLESSING OF ENOCH

Probably Israel was not alone in thinking about models of leadership in terms of a distinction between an office and persons in this way. It has been suggested that aspects of Assyrian kingship can be explained along similar lines.[20] In any case, with this careful distinction in mind, some Jews believed it was possible, or right, to say, without slipping into a ditheism, that the high priest is "divine": he is God's living image-idol (Exodus 28).[21] He is clothed in God's own divine glory and beauty (Exod 28:2, 40). He is God's mouthpiece—his angel (Mal 2:7; Hecataeus of Abdera 40.3.5; cf. 1QSb 4:25; *T. Mos.* 10.2; LXX Exod 23:20-23). It may be best, then, to say, that it is the office that is divine, not the person who holds the office.

Extra-biblical texts near to the time of the Similitudes further illustrate how this works in a way that helps to explain what is going on in our Enoch text.

Ben Sira's Praise of the High Priest

In Sirach 50, at the climax of the hymn begun in 44:1, there is a hymn in praise of the (late third / early second century BCE) high priest Simon son of Onias. Although *generically* quite different, I propose it is a text that stands somewhere upstream in the same conceptual river that produces the Similitudes.[22] Some reasons to see a connection are obvious, other points of contact need a little explanation.

Both texts are interested in Enoch and give him a position of prominence (see Sir 44:19; 49:14; 1 Enoch 37-71 *passim*, esp. ch. 71). Both envisage the worshipful praise of a human or human-like figure (Sir 50:1-21 as a whole, esp. v. 21 and 1 Enoch 46:5; 48:5; 62:3, 9). In both, the figure is identified with God's own glory—especially *the* Glory that Ezekiel saw by the river Chebar (Ezek 1:26-28; cf. Sir 50:7; 1 Enoch 45:3; 46:1; 51:3; 55:4; 61:8; 62:2-3, 5). In both, the figure is closely identified with Wisdom (though the identification is stronger in Sirach).[23]

20. See Winter 1997:374; and Machinist 2006:187-88.

21. See Meyers 2005:242-44; Propp 2006:525-26; Fletcher-Louis 2004a, 2004b, and 2007.

22. Sirach has often been viewed as anti-apocalyptic. For an important critique of that view see Maston 2012.

23. For the high priest actualizing the presence on earth of Wisdom (as she is described in Ben Sira/Sirach) see Sir 24:10 and the carefully developed thematic and structural correspondences between 24:1-23 and 50:1-21 laid out in Fletcher-Louis 2004c. (A slightly revised and updated version of this article is available here: http://bit.ly/CFLCollectedWorks1). The main points of that article are summarized in Fletcher-Louis 2002:73-81.

As with the Similitudes, Sirach also combines royal and priestly characteristics in the one figure. The opening verses of chapter 50 pick up portions of the preceding chapters to say that Simon is royal. Like Hezekiah (48:17–21), he fortifies the walls of Jerusalem and develops its water supply (50:2–3).[24] Both texts, I propose, are testimony to a debate about the ideals of rulership (a subject that was widely discussed in the Hellenistic and Roman eras) and discussions about how best the covenant people should respond to Hellenistic and Romans ideas and practices surrounding "divine" rulers.[25] Ben Sira's response to that world is to put forward the high priestly office over against the deification of the king's person. Writing more than a hundred years later, the Similitudes develops the theology evident in Ben Sira and transposes the office-person distinction to an altogether new level.

Ben Sira goes well beyond the occasional intimations of a worshipful praise of kings in the Hebrew Bible (e.g. Psalm 45; cf. 1 Chr 29:20) to produce a text that conforms in some respects to the new religious fashions of the Hellenistic age. In form and in content, Sir 50:1–21 can be compared with contemporary hymns to divine rulers.[26] Amongst Israel's neighbors rulers received divine honors for their great public works and because they provided military protection to city-states.[27] Honors equal to the gods were given to a ruler in thanks for past benefactions and protection, and in the expectation that those honors would be reciprocated with future military and economic help.[28] So it is remarkable that the hymn in Sirach 50 begins (in vv. 1–4) by praising Simon for his great works of civil engineering—for the benefit of Jerusalem and its Temple—and, above all, because he "took care of his people" to preserve them from attack (Sir 50:4). Simon is, in effect, Jerusalem's "savior" (*sōtēr*).[29] In the hymns to divine rulers—and in

---

24. On the Hezekiah allusions in 50:1–4 see esp. Aitken 2000:197. Aitken also makes helpful observations on the relationship between Simon's building and engineering works and the activities of Hellenistic kings (205–207).

25. For Sirach's concern with Hellenistic politics see Aitken 2000.

26. For evidence of the content and form of Greek hymns to divine rulers see the Athenian hymn to Demetrius I Poliorcetes (337–283 BCE) (in Athenaeus *Deip.* 6.253e), Theocritus' "hymn" (line 8) to Ptolemy II Philadelphus (309–246 BCE) (text and commentary in Hunter 2003) and the fragmentary record of the hymnic praise of Seleucus I Nicator (c. 358–281 BCE) in *I.Erythrai* 205.74–6 (Engelmann and Merkelbach 1972:2:340). That inscription refers to poetic hymnody to the ruler during a libation offering (cf. the Greek at Sirach 50:15).

27. See e.g. Chaniotis 2003:433.

28. I have collected texts describing honors equal to the gods given to human beings, especially to rulers, at http://bit.ly/isotheos.

29. Compare, for example, Callimachus' fourth hymn (from the first half of the third century BCE) that describes Ptolemy Philadelphus II (309–246 BCE) as "another

other expressions of ruler cult—rulers were typically compared to, or identified with, one or more of the gods. In the famous third-century BCE Hymn to Demetrius Poliorcetes (337–283 BCE), the savior of Athens is likened both to the goddess Demeter and to the god Poseidon. Similarly, in Sirach 50, Simon is described as the visible manifestation of *YHWH*; "wrapped" in light-giving "garments of glory" (Sir 50:5–7, 11), just as the Creator is "wrapped in light as with a garment" (Ps 104:1–2). And point-by-point, his activities and character recapitulate those of Lady Wisdom in Sir 24:1–23.[30]

But Sirach 50 should not be viewed as a complete sell-out to the new ways of the Hellenistic world. Sirach does not present Simon as "Simon Soter I" (as if he were a rival to "Ptolemy Soter I, the founder of the Ptolemaic kingdom and royal dynasty—323–283 BCE). Sirach 50:1–21 has sometimes been labeled an encomium. But as Burton Mack has pointed out, that is an inadequate label because the praise of Simon does not celebrate his *personal* biography and achievements.[31] There is no interest in Simon's birth or origins, and Sir 50:1–21 is carefully structured so as to say that everything Simon does fulfils a high priestly script. So the carefully structured praise of Simon is *sui generis*. It is *a hymn in praise of the ideal-ruler-as-office*.

It might be objected that, on a casual reading, much of what Simon is praised for in Sirach 50, especially the opening verses, is precisely what we would expect of a hymn focused on the personal achievements of a national ruler or figure-head. Everything in verses 5–21—the Temple procession, with Simon dressed in his rich multi-coloured garments, surrounded by priests and people, ministering at the altar—is done in fulfilment of a *cultic* office (cf. the description of Aaron in 45:6–22). But the civil actions in vv. 1–4 describe Simon repairing and fortifying the Temple, digging a water cistern (a great public work), and protecting the capital from siege. These are precisely the kinds of actions we expect to find in an encomium (or encomiastic hymn) to a virtuous and praiseworthy person.[32] On closer inspection, however, these actions are also set within the conceptual framework of the *representative* function and activities of the high priestly *office*. In this hymn they are *not* included to celebrate Simon's person, so much as to say that Simon conducted himself according to the expectations of the high priestly *office*. This can be seen when we recall that the high priestly

---

god" "from the lineage of the Saviors" (lines 165–166) (Mair and Mair 1921:98–99).

30. For the details of the correspondence between Wisdom and the high priest see the references in n. 23 (above).

31. Mack 1985:135–36: instead of Simon's "personage . . . it is rather his office that is in focus."

32. For Simon's fortification and defense of the city, a commonplace in the encomiastic tradition, see Mack 1985:133.

office is a representative one, in that (1) it brings the people to God and (2) it makes God present to the people.

(1) In Exodus, the high priest is a representative of Israel: he wears the names of the tribes on his garments of glory and beauty (Exod 28:2, 9–12, 21, 29, 40). So, too, in Sirach he is the "beauty of his people" (50:1). In doing what Hezekiah did before him (50:1–4—see above), Simon incorporates royal functions within his priestly portfolio: he does not claim to be a king himself. Rather he does these things as one who represents Israel's kings (of old) and their activities. In turn these activities are tied to the whole nation's call to embody the "beauty of Adam" over all things (49:16) and to fulfil the vision for a glorious, royal (and "crowned") humanity in Ps 8:6–8 (see Sir 49:16–50:1; 50:4, 11–13).

(2) As I have attempted to show in another longer study, what Simon does in 50:1–4 represents the first three parts of a seven-part sequence in which the high priest's duties are aligned to the seven days of creation.[33] The whole hymn makes the priest's actions a sacramental actualisation of God's work as Creator: in 50:3 he imitates God's work on Day 3 when he creates a *miqvah* like the "sea" (cf. Gen 1:9: "God gathered (*yiqqavu*)" the waters to create "the sea"). In 50:2 his engineering works evoke the separation of the upper and lower waters (Day 2). In 50:5–7 he brings forth the light of the sun and moon from the sanctuary-that-is-heaven: Day 4. And so on.

Everything Simon does conforms to a pre-defined script. *It is not personal to Simon.* The primary purpose of all he does is to glorify (and to actualize the presence of) God the Creator. In the foregoing chapters there is criticism of some in Israel, including king Solomon (47:19) because they strayed from Torah and allowed their personal interests to distract them from their God-assigned task and Torah piety (47:23–25; 48:15–16; 49:4, cf. 46:19). Implicitly then, Simon is praised in 50:1–4 because in these things (not just in his liturgical duties), he did not let his own personal interests get in the way of his duty, as high priest, to represent: to represent the people (and the world) to God and to make present God to the people (and to the world). Throughout his career, says the text, he was an actor who faithfully performed the script given to him.

It is tempting to ascribe to Ben Sira an over-realized eschatology. Certainly, he makes some strong claims for the world under Simon's leadership. But he still looks forward to a further fulfilment of biblical promises (see 36:1–22) and chapter 50 is best taken as a witness to the mainstream liturgical theology of the Second Temple period, *in which Temple and priesthood provide an ever-present access to creation perfected; to the end of history within*

---

33. See the references in n. 23 (above).

history. There is, perhaps unavoidably, it should be admitted, a little focus on the individual Simon inasmuch as he performed his duties so perfectly. But Ben Sira paints this picture because the author thinks this is the way the job should be done by all those who would serve, as high priest, after Simon. Simon is the model, precisely because his own personal interests—and glory and fame—never got in the way of his duties as a public and sacral servant.

The Similitudes Radicalises the Office-Person Distinction

If we put ourselves in the shoes of the author of the Similitudes—given what now seems his likely situation and perspective—we can understand why he adopts a radically new hope for a pre-existent messiah. Wisdom has departed (1 Enoch 42). In other words, Wisdom can no longer be found in the Jerusalem Temple and the priests who currently serve there (as Sirach 24 and 50 had claimed). The old ideals represented by Ben Sira were not wrong, they just did not go far enough. Probably, our author is reacting to two features of recent history.

The Hasmoneans, with increasing confidence in their power and position, took a direction that Ben Sira had avoided. In the pro-Roman 1 Maccabees (written sometime between 134 and 63 BCE) we find poetic praise of Judas Maccabeus (d. 160 BCE) (1 Macc 3:3–9) and Simon Maccabeus (d. 135) (14:4–15). In a way typical of Hellenistic honorific texts, the Hasmoneans Judas and Simon are praised *for their deeds and benefactions*.[34] In these texts there is no attempt to contain the achievements of the nation's (priestly) leaders within the framework of their priestly office. *It is the Maccabean ruler's own name that goes out to the ends of the earth* (1 Macc 3:9; 14:10), not Israel's God's name.[35]

In these passages, 1 Maccabees celebrates the *person* of the ruler.[36] Not long after Judas and Simon, the Hasmoneans took the next logical step and

---

34. See the discussions in van Henten 2001 and 2007.

35. There is talk of the praiseworthy and memorable name of the righteous in the hymn in Sirach 44–50 (see 44:8, 14; 46:12; 47:16). But that is balanced by the way the righteous magnifying the name of God (47:10; 47:13, 18; 50:20). In the schema of the historically structured narrative in Sirach 44–50 individuals appear briefly to exemplify the virtues of a particular office. But in the grand sweep of the historical procession, all faces are turned to the figure of the high priest, who gathers up the virtues and glories of the men of old in his one representative performance (50:1–21). There is a muted interest in individuals and personhood, but it is firmly subordinate to the idealized identity manifest in the priesthood.

36. For these texts, I use the word person in the sense it was used in Greek and

claimed the title "king" (from Aristobulus I, 104–103 BCE, onwards). But then the glories of the Hasmoneans faded in the course of the first century BCE. Their wealth may have grown, but their energies were increasingly absorbed by infighting between dynastic rivals (and between competing religious factions). Ben Sira's unequivocal subordination of the person to the office seems to have been replaced by a newfound confidence in personal power and achievement. Judging by Josephus' two accounts of the way that the Hasmoneans conducted themselves (*War* 1.70–357; *Ant.* 13.301—14.491), there was less interest in the fulfilment of religious duties, and a greater focus on the pursuit of personal ambition.

In the end, the Hasmonean high priests were not able to do what Simon ben Onias had done according to Ben Sira's praise of him. They were not able to protect the city from the thieving, conquering enemy. Pompey stormed the Temple in 63 BCE and Herod, along with a new political order, filled the power vacuum created by Hasmonean disunity (Josephus, *Ant.* 14:490–91). The older priestly dynasty continued for a while, but only by conceding to the greater Roman and Herodian might.

In response, the nation's thought-leaders and visionaries dreamt of new and better models of government. Some—and surely the Qumran community exemplify the phenomenon—responded to the inadequacies and failures of the Hasomonean model by adopting a radical separation of priestly office and royal person, with the king or, rather, a "prince" firmly subordinate to the priesthood (e.g., 1QSb 4–5; 11QTemple Scroll 56.12–59.21). The author(s) of the *Psalms of Solomon*, on the other hand, called for a full-bloodied royal messianic hope, with the priesthood's authority diminished, though not entirely removed (see *Pss. Sol.* 17–18).

The Similitudes of Enoch offers a third strategy and its distinctive messianic hope is best understood when it is set in the context of competing political theologies all responding to the nation's experience of a variety of models of government. For the Similitudes a merely human king will not do: the royal messiah of the *Psalms of Solomon*, who would emulate the exploits of David and of Hellenistic and Roman kings, would not do. Neither, says the Similitudes, can the nation afford to jettison, or downplay, the exalted, divine, identity of the priestly office. The military strength of a new David will not be enough to remove the idolaters—the kings and the mighty who now possess the land. But for the Similitudes the combination of a separate transcendent, "divine," high priestly office alongside an enterprising,

---

Roman antiquity, as it is defined, for example, by Cicero: "We hold the following to be the attributes of persons (*personis has res adtributas putamus*): name, nature, manner of life, fortune, habit, feeling, interests, purposes, achievements, accidents, speeches made" (*De Inventione Rhetorica* 1.24 [34]).

task-focused, royal prince (the model advocated at Qumran in, for example, 1QSb 4–5) will not do either. The Similitudes agrees with the mainstream pre-Herodian position that priestly and royal functions should be combined in the one messianic figure. What is still needed, for the author of 1 Enoch 37–71, is a *combination* in the one messiah of a royal executive power and the divine identity of the priesthood that is not susceptible to the temptations that had lately bedevilled the Hasmoneans.

For the Similitudes there is nothing wrong with the notion that the priesthood is only an office and that its holders' personal lives must be screened out of view. It is simply that that subordination of the person to the office has not gone far enough. Better to eradicate the personal identity of the messiah altogether. That is achieved, I propose, by the Similitudes' *transposition of the essential features of the office to the reality beyond ordinary space and time; to heaven above and to the eschaton.* The high priestly office was always susceptible to a trans-historical interpretation. The office pre-exists and post-exists the life of each incumbent to the office. It is designed to transcend the ravages of time and the vicissitudes of history; to be effective regardless of the character of its holder. And because the high priest plays out a cosmic drama, the office transcends historical realities. What he does recapitulates the actions of the Creator at the beginning.[37] Of course, from one perspective the priestly office was first instituted at Sinai—*at a point in Israel's history.* However, from another, it transcends even that historical moment. So it is only a small step for the Similitudes to say that there is a Son of Man-Chosen One, with some priestly (and royal) credentials, who has been waiting, above and beyond the vicissitudes of sinful human history, since before the world. Where the priestly office is played out on a stage that is the temple-as-microcosm, now there is no microcosm. All the world—the whole cosmos—is the Enochic Messiah's stage.

The Similitudes and Christian Theology

Although there has been little scholarly discussion of the relationship between the Similitudes of Enoch and Christian theology, the use of the expression "Son of Man" for the Elect One–Messiah likely has some bearing on the shape of New Testament Christology since the same expression is

---

37. In turn, there are ways in which the priestly service anticipates the end of all history. It brings about a manifestation within the cult-as-microcosm of the divine and human sovereignty that God had always intended with the creation of Adam to be his image and likeness, ruling and reigning in creation For the achievement of divine and human sovereignty and true Sabbath rest in the temple see esp. Sir 50:11–19 and the discussion of that and related texts in Fletcher-Louis 2017/2018 forthcoming.

also used for Jesus in the Gospels. So there is a *prima facie* case for thinking its distinctive messianic hope would have some significance for Christian theology. Nevertheless, scholarship has, broadly speaking, adopted one of two positions on the Similitudes and the shape of New Testament Christology, both of them leading to negative conclusions about any possible constructive contribution the Enochic text might make to Christian theology. To understand and appreciate these two positions each has to be set in the context of developing scholarly views on the date and life setting of the Enochic text.

Firstly, there are those who have argued that the Enochic Son of Man figure stands behind the use of the Son of Man expression in the Gospels. The Similitudes is judged a pre-Christian text, closely related in some way to Daniel 7. On this, so-called apocalyptic Son of Man theory, the messianism of the Similitudes is a radical departure from the earthly, royal and Davidic messianism of the Old Testament. So, the Son of Man Christology of the Gospels has to be explained historically as the product of the influence of (one idiosyncratic strand of?) post-biblical Judaism. Either that influence impacted the historical Jesus himself (who imagined that a heavenly, transcendent Son of Man would soon come, but not that he himself was that Son of Man) or it influenced the creative tradents of the post-Easter gospel tradition who came to identify Jesus with the apocalyptic Son of Man of Jewish hope. Whilst some form of an apocalyptic Son of Man theory in Gospel scholarship has weighty literary-critical, that is to say historical, arguments in its favor (and is now enjoying a revival among specialists), its implications for Christian theology have seemed to be largely negative.

If the Gospels' Christology is largely indebted to a distinctive Jewish and post-biblical messianic hope that has developed beyond, or departed from, the messianism of Israel's scriptures, their contribution to a Christian theology is problematic. On this historical account of things, the central claims that are made for Jesus' identity appear heavily indebted not to scriptural revelation, but to the contingencies of Jesus', or the early church's, situation in first century Judaism. A prominent and distinctive feature of the Gospel's Christology comes from an "intertestamental," that is non-canonical, text. Unless the theologian follows the Ethiopic church's inclusion of 1 Enoch in the canon (a move which is problematic on other grounds), any historical conclusion that the Gospel's central Christological vision comes from the Similitudes problematizes the Gospels' claim to divine revelation.

In addition, there are problems that have to do with the usual view that, as a text that exemplifies the apocalyptic worldview, the messianism of the Similitudes sits within a dualistic conceptual framework. According to this reading of the text, the Enochic Son of Man messiah is an utterly transcendent (angelic or divine) figure. And that means it has proved hard to make historical and, therefore, theological sense of Jesus' recorded use of the title. The dominant twentieth century view has been that, assuming the apocalyptic Son of Man theory, no first century would-be messiah—an historical Jesus of Nazareth, for example—could possibly have talked about the apocalyptic Son of Man figure in all of the ways that the Gospels claim Jesus did. Scholars then disagree about which of those Son of Man sayings come from Jesus and the likely source of those sayings that are not his *ipsissima verba*. Whichever way we slice up the sayings, the result is a cracked or fragmented story of Jesus that provides no secure basis for clear theological claims about the man of Nazareth and his relationship to the divine Christology of Christian theology. Down the road of the apocalyptic Son of Man there lies a dirty great ditch, between the Jesus of history and the Christ of faith. Safer, the wise theologian concludes, to do Christian theology from Pauline texts and the works of the Church Fathers. In no way does the Similitudes make a positive contribution to the theological enterprise, rather it is a hindrance.

Since the 1970s many have been drawn to an historical account of the Christology of the Gospels that dismisses the apocalyptic Son of Man theory altogether. In the wake of the conclusion that the Qumran Library apparently did not include the Similitudes in its Enochic corpus, there have seemed cogent reasons to reject the near consensus that the gospel Son of Man expression comes from an apocalyptic world of thought exemplified by the Similitudes.[38] On this view, 1 Enoch 37–71 is almost certainly post-Christian, possibly even composed as a Jewish reaction to the earliest Christian beliefs about Jesus.[39] We can dispense with it. This has seemed a necessary conclusion historically. It has also been a boon to those confessionally-oriented NT scholars who have a stake in the defense of a traditional Christian theology.

Whilst this second understanding of the life setting of the Similitudes allows for a simpler reading of the Gospels, it has its own problems. Most importantly, there is now a consensus, as we have seen, that the Similitudes are actually pre-Christian and the fact that there are so many points of conceptual and linguistic connection between the Similitudes' Son of Man material and gospel Son of Man sayings surely means that the Christian material is somehow related to the Enochic text.

---

38. For this phase of scholarship see Fletcher-Louis 2015:174–75.
39. See, e.g., Dunn 1980:77–82 and compare Hurtado 2003:296.

I consider the conclusion that there is some kind of connection between the two unavoidable.[40] There is no avoiding some form of an apocalyptic Son of Man theory to account for the Gospel sayings (and the Son of Man passages in Acts and Revelation—Acts 7:56; Rev 1:13; 14:14). However, the approach to the distinctive messianism of the Similitudes that I have taken in this essay points to a new, third, way to explain the historical relationship between the Similitudes and the Gospel Son of Man sayings; one that allows the pre-Christian text to make a fresh and positive contribution to the quest for a coherent theological account of the Christ event and its claims for the identity of Jesus Christ.

Firstly, the argument of the main body of this essay diminishes the supposed distance between the Similitudes and the "Old Testament." To be sure, 1 Enoch 37–71 has a distinctive theology and messianology. But, if it displays the kinds of connections to an older biblical understanding of the priestly office that I have drawn, then the Similitudes' hope for a divine and heavenly Son of Man bears witness to a transcendent or divine messianism that is essentially biblical. The otherworldly messianic hope of the Enochic text is not the product of a strange new worldview that has replaced the politically- and this-worldy-oriented eschatology of the scriptures with a world-denying and dualistic apocalypticism.[41] The distinctive pre-existent messianism of the Similitudes is witness to a traditional, Israelite, political theology that critiques the tyrannical, power-hungry and self- aggrandising behavior of kings with an alternative, priestly, model of government. That theology, I contend, is a major theme of Israel's scriptures and may therefore be judged a central part of its "revelation". So, the Similitudes can enter the conversation between theology and the scriptures (Israel's and the church's), without it having a full canonical status because, like other ancient sources, it is witness to the original meaning of scriptural texts. The *Similitudes* has a legitimate voice in the theological conversation because it is, *inter alia*, reception history to the Old Testament.

Secondly, if there is a political theology in the *Similitudes* that critiques the prevailing Greco-Roman models of divine rulership, then the text challenges a common assumption of New Testament scholarship. Typically, debates about Christology play off against one another two perspectives on Jesus' identity. Either texts are deemed to be theological and concerned with a high or divine Christology and so they are not political, or they are found

40. For my reasons, see Fletcher-Louis 2015:171–205.

41. For the prevailing twentieth century view that "apocalypticism" as a whole, and the Son of Man tradition in particular, represents a major theological departure from the theology of the Hebrew Bible, see the survey and critique of scholarship in Fletcher-Louis 2011.

to present a Jesus Christ who is politically engaged, but not at all the kind of divine person that occupies the attention of later Christian faith. The Christ of faith is apolitical, otherworldly; the Jesus of history is a model of radical socio-political concern. The Similitudes suggests that, for (biblically faithful) first century Jews, a high or divine messianism was every bit as much a politically critical and engaged hope as was the traditional royal expectations of classic biblical prophecy.

Perhaps, then, we should not be surprised to find that in the Gospel of Mark one of the few verses that can plausibly claim a Christology of pre-existence appears in a passage in which Jesus contrasts his own movement's values with the ideals and the values of the culture surrounding pagan rulers. In Mark 10:45 the Son of Man "has come" to give his life as a ransom. Arguably, in this passage Jesus speaks of himself as a figure who has come to earth from heavenly pre-existence.[42] He is certainly a figure whose pattern of life brings under judgement the culture of power-grabbing, tyrannical rule that Jesus says characterizes pagan politics (Mark 10:35–44). Similarly, in Phil 2:6–11 we find that one of the clearest articulations of a pre-existent, incarnational, Christology appears in a passage that, simultaneously, critiques the grasping, self-exulting, pagan culture of honor that manifests itself most starkly in the claims of soi-disant divine kings and emperors.[43] In texts such as these there is evidence, then, that the pre-existent, incarnational Christology that is central to classic Christian orthodoxy is deeply indebted to the kind of creative Jewish reflection on the relationship between messianism—that is, a biblical theology of the God-ordained ruler—and pagan models of kingship that we find in the Similitudes. Again, it may not be that the authors of Mark 10:35–45 and Phil 2:6–11 knew the Similitudes. But at least now the Similitudes can be invited to the witness box to speak for the case for thinking that both these NT passages represent (a Christian form of) a distinctive Jewish, and biblical, political theology.

Thirdly, there is the issue of the use of the word "person" in discussions of New Testament theology. Most biblical specialists would say that it is anachronistic and inappropriate to use that word in the exegesis of Christological texts in the New Testament. The word has a well-defined (though still hotly debated) meaning in later patristic Trinitarian debates and creeds. I agree that the word should not be used to describe the earliest beliefs about Jesus without due recognition that it carries a set of meanings which may not necessarily apply to New Testament texts. However,

---

42. For this interpretation of Mark 10:45, see Gathercole 2006:167–68.

43. For this interpretation of Phil 2:6–11, see Hellerman 2005; and Fletcher-Louis, 2017 forthcoming.

I suggest that the word may, in some cases, be an historically appropriate one for the discussion of Jewish, and early Christian, messianic (and, therefore, of Christological) beliefs. This essay on the Similitudes can serve as a case study for thinking that both Israel's scriptures and first century Jews worked with a careful distinction between the categories "divine person" and "a divine office." That being so, it is striking that the earliest Christians expressed their messianic beliefs in terms of Jesus Christ's strongly personal identity. They wrote gospel accounts of his life that are generically much like ancient biographies—a literary form appropriate to the description of persons. Similarly, they employed encomia, the form used for the praise of persons (and places or things), to recite and honor him for his personal story (e.g., Phil 2:6–11).[44] Any first century reader or hearer who was familiar with the centuries-old rhetorical conventions of the Greek and Roman worlds, would be bound to hear in a piece like Phil 2:6–11 the claim that this Jewish messiah is a divine *person*, not simply one who has faithfully acted out a divine office. He is pre-existent, but not because his appearance at the eschaton represents the transposition of a liturgical and cosmic drama that transcends the exigencies of quotidian reality. He comes to live out his own, unique personal story (of humility and shameful death that turns to universal fame through the intervention of God the Father). For those Jews who cherished the Similitudes the messiah whom Paul praises in Phil 2:6–11 is a shockingly individuated divine person, whose story is generically the kind that might be penned in praise of a pagan ruler; the kind of story denied to the Son of Man-Elect One in 1 Enoch 37–71.

Lastly, I would like to comment on that dirty great ditch that theologians fear lies down the road marked Similitudes of Enoch. If, in fact, the transcendent and divine Son of Man messianism of the Similitudes is witness to contemporary Jewish beliefs about Israel's high priest, perhaps it is not so incredible after all that the Gospels should have Jesus use an apocalyptic Son of Man title to claim that he is the fulfillment of Dan 7:13. Perhaps it is entirely to be expected that Jesus' identity as Son of Man would span the ontological spectrum of divine and human (and angelic) identities, with some sayings designating him a human being (e.g., Luke 9:58) and others giving him the glory and position of Israel's one God (e.g., Mark 8:38; Matt 25:31). If, that is, the historical Jesus did in fact believe he was Israel's long awaited eschatological high priest (albeit as a distinct individual person, not as the holder of an office or the mythological end-time counterpart to the high priest) then it would make plausible historical sense that he

---

44. Among the several studies that have argued Phil 2:6–11 is an encomium; see Berger 1984:1178–89; and Martin and Nash 2015.

would use the Son of Man title in the way that the Gospels say he did. On such an historical account of Jesus' life and Christian origins we should also conclude that the ditch between the Jesus of history and the Christ of Faith is not as deep or wide as has been thought until now.

7

Words from the Book of Enoch on the Environment

LOREN T. STUCKENBRUCK

Ever since Lynn White provocatively blamed Christianity, including the Bible which it holds sacred, for contributing to the modern ecological crisis,[1] biblical researchers and theologians have felt with growing urgency the need to have something from within the Christian tradition to say about human responsibility in relation to the environment. However oversimplified White's claims may have been,[2] his challenge remains. It remains because some theologians have deliberately appealed to non-Christian frameworks in order to say something constructive about the environment.[3] It also remains because perception of a crisis has not abated. It is taken for granted in the twenty-first century that the "environment" of which we are a part[4] continues to face *unprecedented*

---

1. White 1967.

2. See, e.g., the critique and comments by Roszak 1992:99–101, who balances out White's criticism with the observation that logical positivists' view of the cosmos as a "meaningless universe" stands alongside Christianity. For a helpful and more sustained critique, see Vonnahme 2012.

3. So the influential process approach by Cobb 1976; the ecospirituality advocated by Berry and Swimme 1992; and ecofeminist framework offered by Ruether 1992:61–173; and Sally McFague 1993.

4. Whereas early on, the "environment" was understood as the world that surrounds and stands apart from us as human beings who adopt attitudes towards it, it has acquired a more relational connotation, so that it actually *includes* all humans who inhabit it; cf. Bilen 2008:114–15; Jahn and Dunne 2007:333; and the notion of "deep

challenges from the second half of the twentieth century until the present. These challenges, which to greater or lesser degrees affect people in virtually all parts of the globe, have many dimensions. Without trying to list all the problems, we can together imagine some of them that have different degrees of impact, depending on where one lives: the partial loss of the protective ozone layer in the earth's atmosphere, the extinction or endangerment of many animal species, the pollution of both the air we breathe and the water we use, the removal of land used to produce food, and, of course related to this, climate change (often referred to as "global warming"). Whether or not one agrees with the severity or uniqueness of these conditions within the world as we now know it, it is at least clear that the problems faced by the natural world often have their origin in things that people do. It is people who manufacture and use of products that release nitrates or other toxic fumes; it is people who overuse of land for farming with the irretrievable loss of top soil; it is people who engage in warfare with often disastrous and long-term consequences (whether this involves the use of conventional weapons or, more acutely, chemical weapons, not to mention the threat of nuclear warfare); it is people who commit themselves to economic competition for use of natural resources; it is people who become embroiled in ethnic and socio-political conflict; it is people who invest in larger industries that produce non-biodegradable products; and it is people, often the well-to-do, who encourage the overconsumption of animal meat and of by-products while many remain without sufficient food. Individually, some of these problems might be the sort that can be managed. However, taken together, they present our contemporary world with a unique and growing challenge. We do not live in a world that offers endless sources of supply through seasonal replenishment; the rate of population growth in some parts of the world, combined with insatiable appetites among those who have power and control over resources, resulting large-scale starvation and undernourishment, and the real possibility of nuclear conflict along with the use of chemical weapons, threaten the survival—that is, the sustainability—of our planet.

Though this scenario has been variously described many times over, there is some disagreement within the larger Christian community on how to address it, especially if Judeo-Christian tradition is supposed to play a role. Responses are huge and varied, and for purposes of this discussion we cannot review many or even most of them. Allow me, however, to

---

ecology" as initially proposed by Naess 1973:96.

describe two overarching approaches that have attempted to draw on biblical tradition.

First, there are those who believe that, essentially, Christian faith is about the salvation of souls and is heavenly in orientation. Though giving care to how one treats the environment is not necessarily seen as a bad thing, it is not held as central to the gospel. An extreme version of this view can be found in appeals to biblical texts such as 2 Pet 3:10–13:

> (10) But the day of the Lord will come like a thief. *The heavens will disappear with a roar;*
>
> *the elements will be destroyed by fire, and the earth and everything*
>
> *done in it will be laid bare.* (11) Since *everything will be destroyed* in this way,
>
> what kind of people ought you to be? *You ought to live holy and godly lives*
>
> (12) as you look forward to the day of God and speed its coming.
>
> That day will bring about the destruction of the heavens by fire, and the elements will melt in the heat.
>
> (13) But in keeping with his promise *we are looking forward to a new heaven and a new earth,*
>
> where righteousness dwells. (NIV)

We do not have to look very far to find Christian leaders and groups who use this text to dismiss ecological "alarmism" as unnecessary hype. Any emphasis on the environment, they maintain, should not distract us from what is really important; our eyes should "stay focused on being ready for the Day of God's Judgment."[5] Since the world is temporary and will someday come to an end, why should it be so vital to include care for the environment within the ambit of Christian responsibility? When looking for biblical instruction

---

5. So "Ecological or Theological Nightmare? 2 Peter 3:10–13" (Chatham, NJ; March 9, 2008, AM), in www.chathamchurchofchrist.org/podcasts/030908_Ecological_or_Theological.pdf; or, in response to Al Gore's film *An Inconvenient Truth* (2006), note numerous responses such as Jim Grove, "Hellfire is the real global warming," in www.ydr.inyork.com/ci_11103726, cited in Horrell 2010:17–18; Gene Gregory, "Don't Sweat Global Warming," www.sermoncentral.com/sermons/dont-sweat-global-warming-gene-gregory-sermon-on-evangelism-urgency-109542.asp?page=3; David Palmer, "Global Warming, Nuclear War, or the Hand of God?," in http://blog.itsgodsword.org/2011/08/01/global-warming-nuclear-war-or-the-hand-of-god/; and Dianne Smith, "Global Warming, the Environment, and the Christian Response," in http://diannesmith.suite101.com/global-warming-the-environment—the-christian-response-a341128.

on what to do in relation to the world, those adopting this perspective frequently find the well-known text of Genesis 1:26-28 to be useful. Here, in Genesis 1, humans are commissioned by God to "subdue" and "dominate" the earth (the meaning of the Hebrew verbs כבש and רדה do not envision a timid use of the earth's resources). In this reading, the text functions as a warrant for regarding the earth's resources as *belonging* to humans during their time on earth and destined to be used for *their* benefit because they *stand apart, stand over*, and *stand above* creation. Thus a commitment to the Bible as authoritative has meant for many that one resist (or at least marginalize) calls for Christians to engage actively with the environment.[6]

Second, the way of interpreting the Bible just outlined stands in contrast with other strategies that insist that the reading of the Bible in relation to the natural world should be more constructive. Interpreters who adopt this approach look for biblical passages and ways of receiving them that uphold the integrity of creation as something of value in its own right. Here, the reading of Genesis 1 has also played a role, with regard to God's declaration on each day that what God made is "good" (Gen 1:4, 10, 12, 18, 21, 25, 31). Significantly, attention is drawn to the phrase *"very* good" in the divine pronouncement at the end of Genesis 1 (v. 31); it does not merely describe humans, but "everything" that God made. In other words, everything that God created on the six days was, in the words of Gerhard von Rad, "completely perfect" in the sense of the "wonderful properness and harmony" of everything in the world.[7] The natural world, including humanity made in God's likeness, is "good for achieving its purpose."[8] Human beings may have responsibility in relation to the earth (Gen 1:26-28); however, they are also *part* of the earth because God made Adam "from the dust of the earth" (Gen 2:7). There are also texts that sideline the place of humans within creation. Examples of this are Job 38:1-40:2 (creation runs with or without human beings) and Psalm 104 (which emphasizes throughout the praise of God by creation as a whole: "make a joyful noise to the Lord, all the earth!"). Moreover, the Day of the Lord is described as a time when the ground will mourn because it has been laid waste (Joel 1:2-2:17). Jesus is seen to have illustrated the kingdom of God by nothing less than ways animals behave and how the agricultural cycle works (e.g. Mark 4 par. Matt 13; Matt 6:25-34). Creation is said to groan and hope for redemption in which the faith of

---

6. Significantly, one does not have to be a Protestant conservative to hold such a view; cf., e.g., Bultmann 1956:20: "Man is a creature. But this does not mean that he is just a part of nature or its processes. He is not a part of the objective world, but stands over against it ... The real sphere where God rules is in History."

7. Von Rad 1972:62.

8. Rogerson 1991:61.

humans in the gospel plays a key role (Rom 8:19-23). The work of Christ is not simply for the peoples of the earth, but embraces all creation itself (Col 1:15-20). And the future in the Book of Revelation is envisioned, not so much as a getting rid of heaven and earth, but in creating a new heaven and a new earth presumed to involve a material existence (Rev 21:1—22:5).[9]

Although these biblical texts have all played a significant role for those who advocate an eco-friendly form of Christian faith, it is recognized that they cannot simply ignore the reality that the biblical tradition is in many ways very human-centered (e.g. the doctrine, so important within Protestant circles, of "justification by faith" which, as understood by Luther, placed humans at the center of the universe as the primary object of God's salvific activity). Even Christian theologians who advocate a just handling of the environment understand that one does not necessarily arrive at such a view by a straightforward reading of the Bible. As David Horrell has stated in his recent book, a survey "of biblical texts and their various interpretations" yields a predominantly negative picture; "the Bible ... is ambivalent and ambiguous in terms of its ecological implications ... This finding raises difficult questions about the role and contribution of the Bible in shaping Christian thinking about the environment and human responsibility towards it."[10] In particular, the notions of human rule over creation (Gen 1:26-28) and the anticipation of future cosmic destruction (which reinforces the world's so-called temporary nature; Mark 13 par.; 2 Pet 3:10-13; Rev 21:1—22:5) make it difficult to recover a constructive "biblical" voice. If we felt like being provocative, we could speak of a "broken relationship" between biblical texts and contemporary theological reflection. However, if the Bible is to remain important in developing a caring understanding of our world, reading strategies need to be devised that engage *critically* with the biblical tradition.[11] Horrell calls this an "ecological hermeneutic"[12] in which we as readers become aware of the doctrinal lenses that shape our reading of biblical texts and, however correct such faith positions might be, that we

---

9. These texts are discussed by Horrell 2010:21-103. Horrell, in addition, devotes a chapter (104-14) to "Apocalyptic Visions of Cosmic Catastrophe" in which he admits interpretive challenges for those who wish to take into account passages such as Joel 2:28-3:21 and 2 Pet 3:10-13.

10. Horrell 2010:117.

11. The ambiguity of the Bible in relation to the natural order has driven many theologians, philosophers and intellectuals to advocate perspectives outside the Christian tradition. In fact, some eco-theologians actually *blame* the biblical narrative and the worldview it espouses as the primary reason we are facing the current global ecological crisis in the first place. Influential in this regard (as noted above) have been White 1967, and Ruether 1992:61-173.

12. Horrell 2010:117. See esp. earlier work of Santmire 1985.

realize that cherished convictions not infrequently blind us from seeing or discovering aspects of God's word to and *for* us.

So, if one adopts an "ecological hermeneutic," is it merely a matter of making the Bible say what we want it to say? If so, we would not be the first to do so. It is naïve to think that the Bible can be read and interpreted in a way that recovers its truth in a pristine, pure form that we can recognize in all its fullness.

Rather than going through theological gymnastics by focusing on how we might develop a more eco-friendly reading strategy for the Old and New Testaments, I would like to introduce a voice into the discussion that has been largely lost. It comes from a book—or better, a collection of books—which R. H. Charles once argued shaped the world of Jesus and earliest Christian thought more than any other book.[13] We are referring to 1 Enoch, variously called The Book of Enoch or Ethiopic Enoch since it is only fully preserved in Geʿez. The work, which contains traditions composed during a period of 400 years from the late fourth century BCE until the end of the first century CE), is considered scripture only in the Ethiopian Orthodox Church. The voice that we recover here not only offers a reading of tradition we know from the Bible, it also engages that tradition in a way that is suggestive for a Judeo-Christian worldview and puts us in a position of reading familiar texts with new eyes.

What we are talking about here is a storyline that interweaves with the tradition known to us from Genesis chapter 6. In Genesis 6, the story we have in mind is very short, telling us only in three verses (6:1–2, 4) that the sons of God mated with the beautiful daughters of humanity to produce a race of "mighty men," also called "Nephilim" and "men of renown" (v. 4). Although these verses occur between the mention of Noah's birth (5:28–32) and the story of Great Flood (6:5–8:22), there is no transparent attempt in Genesis to link what the sons of God have done with the sending of the Flood. The Flood, according to Genesis, was sent because of uncontrolled human violence and sin (6:5, 11–12); God's decision to do this happens when God "was sorry he created man upon the earth" (6:6).

Now, let us allow ourselves to hear a summary of this story, taken from 1 Enoch chapters 6–11, which begins with events that occur before the time of the Great Flood of Noah. As humanity multiplies upon the face of the earth, the sons of God (who are angelic beings in heaven) look upon the daughters of humanity and recognize how beautiful they are (1 Enoch. 6:1–2; cf. Gen. 6:1–2). The noticing the beauty of women by the heavenly beings leads the latter to engage in an act of rebellion against God. On account of

---

13. Charles 1912:xcv (cf. further pp. ix–xii): "The influence of 1 Enoch on the New Testament has been greater than that of all the other apocryphal and pseudepigraphal books taken together."

their attraction to the human women, these sons of God, some two hundred in number, make a pact to take them as sexual partners (1 Enoch 6:3-6; it is not clear whether the women actually become their wives). The women bear for them a race of gigantic offspring who, according to the tradition, reach a height of up to 3000 cubits (7:3a). In addition to fathering the giants, the angels teach all sorts of bad ideas and practices to humanity, both men and women (8:1-3).

For our present purposes it is what the giants are described as doing that is of interest. According to the Ethiopic version of 1 Enoch 7:3-5, the 3000 cubit giants had appetites that could not be satisfied. First, they "consumed all the toil of humanity, until humans were unable to sustain them" (7:3b). This is a reference to the agricultural produce, and the texts assume that humans were enslaved and forced by the giants to grow food that, in the end, could not supply their insatiable needs. Second, presumably when the agricultural produce was not enough, the text states that, "the giants turned against them in order to eat men" (7:4). Here, beyond being enslaved through hard labor, the bodies of humans become victims as the giants turned to cannibalism. Third, the text goes on to emphasize that humans were not the only victims. The giants "began to sin (or: to do violence) against birds, and against animals, and against reptiles and against fish" (7:5a). So far, the victimization or overconsumption of agricultural resources, the killing of humans, and the annihilation of animal species in the air, on land, and in the sea amounts to a destruction of what God created on the third, fifth, and sixth days in the creation account of Genesis 1 (vv. 11-13, 20-22, 24-30). The very creation that according to the biblical tradition God had declared to be "good," even "very good" (Gen 1:31), is being turned upside down. Fourth, the text states that the giants even began to eat "one another's flesh" and to drink "the blood from it" (7:5b). The "drinking of blood" amounts to an ultimate insult against life.[14] The Aramaic text from the Dead Sea Scrolls (4Q201 I iii 19-21) is even longer and more descriptive at this point.[15] What does all this destruction of the vegetation, humans, and

14. See Nickelsburg 2001:186. For a fuller treatment of this element in the tradition, see Goff 2010.

15. The *Book of Giants*, another Enochic work preserved in many Aramaic fragments from 10 mss. in the Dead Sea Scrolls, is even more detailed when describing the giants' activities. The fragmentary text from 4Q531 may include the moon among their victims and alludes more clearly to language from Genesis 1 (reference to "plants yielding seeds" and mention of "all" and "all kinds"; cf. Gen 1:11-12, 21, 24-25). The text reads as follows:

]the moon[
everything that the] earth produced [

animals lead to? According to 1 Enoch 7:6, "the earth complained against the violently wicked ones (ሰከየቶሙ ለአማፅያን)." Note here that it is *the earth* (ምድር), and not simply humans, that utters a lament. A few verses later, after a catalogue of bad things which the angels taught humanity, the cries of humans who were killed reaches heaven (8:4) where the four archangels angels—Michael, Gabriel, Suriel and Uriel—receive and relay them to God (9:1). Just before conveying to God the lament, the angels say to one another, "Let the devastated *earth* cry out with the sound of their cries unto the gate of heaven" (9:2). Although the killed humans are complaining to heaven, they are doing so together with the earth of which they are a part.

It is in response to these laments from the suffering earth and humanity that God sends punishment through both the Flood and the giants' cannibalism of one another (10:1–3, 9). Although humans are described as having been taught bad things by the angels, the primary blame for these catastrophic events is assigned to the angels and their offspring. How different from the Genesis story, where the blame is ultimately assigned to the humans themselves and in which it is God, through the Flood, who even destroys many animals and plants (without, of course, eradicating the species)!

So, what we have from this part of the Enochic tradition—it is taken from the so-called Book of Watchers composed sometime during the third century BCE—is nothing short of an environmental catastrophe that involves land, animals, and humans. By assigning such cosmic destruction to the sacred past (i.e. before the Flood), the text does something that no text in either the Protestant or Roman Catholic Bible does. Whereas cosmic destruction in the Protestant and Catholic canons is envisioned as a prelude to God's judgment in the end of history, here in the Enoch tradition cosmic destruction, i.e. a time when the earth is ravaged beyond its means to survive, is given a place in the sacred story.

To the Book of Watchers we may add a story about the beginnings of evil that comes to us from a different part of 1 Enoch, namely, the Astronomical Book at chapter 80. Here, the patriarch Enoch is given a vision that anticipates what "the days of the sinners" will be like (probably referring to the days just before the Flood in his time or perhaps the days when history

---

the hea]ven[and all] the great fish [
]and all the birds of the sky with all that grew[
and with] plants yielding seeds of the earth and all kinds of grain and all the trees[
and with] sheep; small cattle, with [
al]l creeping things of the earth and after everything[

For a convenient bi-lingual (Aramaic and English) presentation of the *Book of Giants* fragments, see Parry and Tov 2005:6:472–513.

runs out at the end of time). In the Ethiopic form of the book, Enoch has been observing the times and places of the sun's rising, the phases of the moon, and the movements of the stars (1 Enoch 72–79). Now, however, Enoch is told that something will go wrong with the heavenly bodies. The text of 1 Enoch 80:2-6, which only survives in Ge'ez, states:[16]

> (2) But in the days of the sinners the years will become shorter, and their seed will be late on their land and on their fields, and all things on the earth will change, and will not appear at their proper time. And the rain will be withheld, and heaven will retain (it). (3) And in those times the fruits of the earth will be late and will not grow at their proper time, and the fruits of the trees will be withheld at their proper time. (4) And the moon will change its customary practice, and will not appear at its proper time ... (5) ... it will appear in heaven and come ... and shine with more than normal brightness. (6) And many heads of the stars in command will go astray, and these will change their courses and their activities, and will not appear at the times which have been prescribed for them. (7) And the entire law of the stars will be closed to the sinners, and the thoughts of those who dwell upon the earth will go astray over them, and they will turn from all their ways, and will go astray, and will think them gods. (8) And many evils will overtake them, and punishment will come upon them to destroy them all.

The description here is of a universe that is no longer running according to the way God created it to be. Humans are seen to live in a world that is profoundly out of sync with itself. Seasons do not happen when they are supposed to; excessive heat occurs at the wrong times; harvest is delayed; and the universe operates according to a scheme that is intrinsically evil. Here, of course, we have a different story than the one reviewed above regarding the rebellious angels. The stars, which are regarded as living beings (of an angelic order) are disobedient, so that the calendar of the world runs according to 365¼ days per year rather than the 364-day calendar that God created the world for (an ideal calendar exactly divisible by 7, which honors the Sabbath and means that feast days every year fall on the same day of the week; cf. 1 Enoch 84:4–7). Although the parallels to today should not be pressed too far, the Astronomical Book envisions something of a climate change of cosmic, not local or regional, proportions. The writer attributes the dysfunctional climate to disobedience and to sin, in

---

16. Despite text-critical considerations not yet worked out in the Ge'ez manuscript tradition, I follow here for convenience the excellent English translation of Knibb 2:185–86.

which stars and humans who follow them have not respected the created order. Again, the narrative of a world going out of sync is assigned to the sacred past and, again, there is no real parallel for this in the Protestant or Roman Catholic Bible.

The early Enochic literature, then, provides us with material about a protological destruction of the environment. Since it has happened in the past, it can happen again as people, under the sway of disobedient powers, act out of step with the ways of God. This is not all. We also learn that rebellion against God, whoever the perpetrators of that rebellion might be, manifests itself in the *cosmic* destruction of land, vegetation, animals, and humans. If we include the Astronomical Book, the disobedience manifests itself in a universe that is profoundly out of step with God's design. Whereas the Protestant and Roman Catholic Bibles assign such cosmic catastrophes to the eschatological future, thus opening up the possibility that readers can relativize the created order as a temporary phenomenon, the Enoch tradition also assigns this to the past and makes clear that *any* violent and insatiable use of the earth's resources, including human beings, is a blatant act of rebellion.

So far, we have looked at the negative side of the story that comes from the sacred past. In the Book of Watchers, however, eschatological future is envisioned as well. The future is described by drawing on images associated with the destruction and restoration related to Noah's Flood, though the imagery is developed beyond this. Once evil has been held to account and is decisively punished by God, the world will be a place in which "every evil work will cease" (1 Enoch 10:16). In concrete terms, what will this world look like? First, those who are righteous (i.e. obedient to God) "will plant righteousness and truth in joy forever" (10:16). They "will be humble, and will live until they beget thousands" (10:17; cf. 6:1). Significantly, such replenishment and flourishing is anticipated for agriculture as well: "the entire earth will be tilled *in righteousness*, and all of it will be planted with tress, and it will be filled with blessing" (1 Enoch 10:18). The bounty of farming "in righteousness" suggests that the text contemplates that abundant crop yields in themselves are not necessarily the mark of faithfulness to God and can be the result of activity done at the expense of others. Trees will flourish, and vines planted by the righteous "will produce fruit in abundance"; "every seed that is sown upon it (the earth), each measure will produce a thousand and each measure of olives will produce ten baths of oil" (10:19).[17] Reading in the context of 1 Enoch chapters 6–11, this is a reversal of the

---

17. Again, in the Enochic *Book of Giants*, the eschatological flourishing of creation is more developed and, according the fragmentary text of 1Q23, includes animal reproduction as well.

undoing of creation that has taken place when the giants raped and ravaged the resources of the earth (1 Enoch 7:3–5). The multiplication of the earth's resources, in which the natural world functions once again as God intended, draws on the divine command to "be fruitful and multiply upon the face of the earth" (Gen 1:28; 9:1) which, the first time it is given, includes the animals as well. Not only the fertility of the earth reverses that catastrophic ruin of the giants, the agricultural "toil" among humanity will be blessed as well. According to the conclusion of our story, in 1 Enoch 11:1 (which borrows imagery from Isa 65:21–22), God will pour out the storehouses of heaven "upon the earth, upon the work and upon the toil of humanity." Hard agricultural work is not done away when God has God's way with the world. Unlike the time of the giants, however, human labor has a purpose and will be rewarded, as "peace and truth become companions for all the days of eternity and for all the generations of eternity" (11:2).

What, if anything, does the human community of faith have to do with the fertility of the earth? We have already seen the text's reference to agricultural activity "in righteousness" (10:18). A further statement, however, develops the possibility that human agency even more. The flourishing of the created world is coordinated with an amazing statement in 1 Enoch 10:21–22 that, "all humanity will be righteous, and all the nations shall serve and bless me, and all shall worship me," while the earth is cleansed from all corruption, wrath, and torment. Whereas the unjust destruction of the earth's resources belies rebellion and disobedience, its flourishing in the eschatological future is an index of the proper worship of God. It does not matter to the writer of this text whether or not "ecological alarmism" (as it is sometimes negatively called today) is scientifically justified. People of the earth—not just Jews (we have to remember that this is a Jewish composition!)—are not the center of the cosmos, but have a vital role to play as they are subject to punishment, on the one hand, and participate in fertility, on the other, of the world. The responsibility of the human community is primarily to worship God; this worship is not understood simply in terms of gaining salvation for the human soul but also in terms of giving place and integrity to the world in which humans live.

Although the link between human faithfulness to God and the fertility of creation is located by the Enochic tradition to the eschatological future, we are not to infer that the text advocates for inactivity in the meantime. More explicitly than in the Protestant and Catholic biblical tradition, the Book of Watchers links future blessing to the agency of righteous humans. As the divine defeat of evil has been inaugurated in the past through the Flood and the self-destruction of the giants, so also the present is marked by activity that anticipates a future as God wants it to be can. The protology of the environmental destruction as an act of rebellion defines a trajectory that, by contrast, defines faithfulness in relation to the earth's well-being. Given the link between protology and eschatology, it would be strange were the Enochic text to envision anything else than the faithful as active contributors to the well-being of the natural world.

The value of the Enoch tradition for us today does not consist in whether or not we call it "Scripture" or whether or not it provides exact parallels to challenges that we face in the modern and post-modern world. I submit that what is important is the theological conviction that the "worship of God" not only involves acts of piety and praise towards God in the gathered community of faith, but also relates to responsibility for the upkeep and flourishing of the world and its resources. In this respect, the Enochic vision, which draws its meaning within the context of a wider biblical narrative we know from Genesis, leaves us with a message: the welfare of the created world falls within the sphere of concern addressed by the worship of God.

David Horrell and others may be justified that the Protestant Bible at least is ambiguous when it comes to how humanity and the environment are related. Our straightforward reading of the Enoch tradition, however, does not require as much critical engagement to make the tradition useful for theological reflection. The Westminster Catechism of 1647 declared that "Man's chief and highest end is to glorify God, and fully to enjoy him forever." If the Enoch tradition comes into the equation, we need less hermeneutical strategies than applied by Horrell and others in order to reformulate the Catechism with him as follows: "Creation's chief and highest end is to glorify God, and fully to enjoy God forever."[18] Embracing the importance of creation may not be distinctively Christian; other faith traditions and even non-religious people of the world today can engage in ecological activities. However, Christian communities can be called to do this in a particular way, that is, as an expression of their Christian witness, not least if Christ is thought to have been an agent in creation itself and in the establishment of a new world order that involves the world (Col 1:15–20). Although the church affirms life after death and embraces an eternal life, the next world, "the new heaven and new earth" envisioned near the end of the Book of Revelation in the New Testament may be regarded in the texts as more "earthy" and tangible than many are led to believe. Just as post-mortem existence is in continuation of the way people have lived out their lives, so also we are invited to consider whether the next world may not be so completely non-materially "other." More importantly, we are invited by a tradition such

---

18. Horrell 2010:135.

as 1 Enoch 6–11 to question any attempts to drive a wedge between the Church's commission to proclaim "the Gospel," on the one hand, and the Church's living witness to respect and help sustain the "very good" world, on the other.

8

The Cry of the Earth in 1 Enoch and Environmental Theology

Daniel Assefa

In 1 Enoch the earth suffers much because of the enormous disaster brought about by the offspring of the fallen angels, because of violence, injustice and sin. The flora and fauna, including human life, is seriously threatened. The earth responds to these crises by "crying." Now the same expression of "the cry of the earth" appears in some of today's theological conversations on the environment. In his *Bible and Ecology*, Richard Bauckham refers to biblical citations where the whole creation mourns and laments.[1] *Laudato Si'*, the recent encyclical of Pope Francis, uses this expression repeatedly. There is a burgeoning theological literature on the environmental crisis that cannot be addressed in detail here.[2] Can we make some analogy between the two reactions of the earth despite the fact that the causes of the environmental crisis are not the same? It is true that electric power, technological devices, electronic gadgets, wastage, chemicals, greenhouse effect, noise pollution, overpopulation and the like were unknown to the author of 1 Enoch. What does, after all, the expression "cry of the earth" mean in 1 Enoch? What kind of cry is it? Is it a cry of despair or a plea for help? If it is a plea to whom would it be addressed? Does the expression have the same meaning today in

1. Bauckham 2010:92–102.
2. But as a sample, see Haffner 2008; Feehan 2010; Delio 2013; Northcott 2013; and Johnson 2014.

connection with environmental crisis? By showing that 1 Enoch reflects a universal concern that surpasses the interests of a given territory, this essay proposes to draw attention to its significance for modern theological discussion on the environment.

The Earth in 1 Enoch

The Frequent Occurrence of the Term Earth

The term *mədr*,[3] which stands for the earth, is among the most frequently used nouns in the whole of 1 Enoch. Out of 218 occurrences, 210 are in the nominative form, whereas 5 are in the accusative[4] and 3 in the construct form[5] (*mədrä*). As for *yäbs*, signifying dry land or ground, it is found 49 times in the nominative form and 3 times in the accusative[6] form (*yäbsä*). There are, as a consequence, 270 references to the earth in 1 Enoch.[7] The "earth", according to scholars, is the fourth most frequently used word in the Hebrew Bible. Like in 1 Enoch, the term earth is one of the most frequent words in the Hebrew Bible. Yet it is in the book of Genesis and the book of Jeremiah that we find the highest number of occurrences. While the book

---

3. For the statistics on the words and expressions, I have based my work on Flemming's critical edition (1902). Whenever it appears to be relevant, other editions or variants of newly discovered manuscripts will be taken into consideration. Examples of the term ארעא ("earth") in Aramaic, see 1 Enoch 2:3 (4Q201, frg.1 Col.ii, line three), but also 1 Enoch 10:12; 32:2; 106:15, 16; 107:1. The Greek term γῆ, besides its presence in all these verses, is more attested, given that the data set is larger than the Aramaic one. Milik (1976). Since then other authors have published their works on the Aramaic fragments of 1 Enoch. See Beyer 1984:225–60. Stuckenbruck has revised Milik's Aramaic-Greek, Greek-Aramaic glossary; see Stuckenbruck 1990. Also see Stuckenbruck 2000. Also see Parry and Tov 2005 and Langlois 2008.

4. In the following references, the term "earth" is a direct object: 1 Enoch 21:2; 39: 12; we have a case of the "Accusative of Place" in 45:2 ("they shall not come to the earth"; see Dillmann 1907: §174b); 101:8; 65:1

5. 1 Enoch 53:2 (expressing possession; "his earth"); 56:6 (2x) ("the land of his elect"; lit. the earth of his elect).

6. 1 Enoch 55:4 "who dwell in the dry land"; see Dillmann 1907: §174b; Knibb translates "dry ground", see Knibb1978:2:139; the other two references are 1 Enoch 60:9; 65:6.

7. A brief comparison with some important terms in 1 Enoch would be helpful. The Divine is expressed 221 times by the term "Lord" and 12 times by the term "God". Human beings are directly referred to 134 times: man (44 x), woman (5x) and men (85x). Whereas there are 122 occurrences of the word Angel or angels, the words Time and life are less frequent: Time (40x) life (36x). In the decreasing order of frequency we have the following nouns: earth (269 x), Lord (221), Heaven (194 x), Human beings (134 x), Angels (122 x).

of Genesis, with 311 occurrences, surpasses 1 Enoch, the book of Jeremiah, with 271 occurrences, is quite close to it,[8] provided that we include the dry land (*yäbs*) in 1 Enoch.

Various Meanings

In 1 Enoch, the earth may mean simply the ground (or the dry ground), a piece of land, the underworld (Abyss), a territory (land of Egypt) and a totality, that is, the earth in its entirety. The theme of inheriting the earth (cf. the Book of Watchers and the Book of Parables) and the question of the heavenly or new Jerusalem (Animal Apocalypse) should remind us that the concept of land, in its restricted sense, is also dealt with in 1 Enoch.[9]

Piece of Land

Earth can signify a piece of land as in 1 Enoch 27:1 "... this blessed land"; *zäti mədr burəkt*. Similarly, in 1 Enoch 80:2, the Ethiopic *bämədromu* refers to a piece of land while the expression "on their land," instead of the literal translation "on their earth", makes more sense. In the Book of Parables, where most of the references to the dry land (*yäbs*) are found, "those who possess the earth" (*əlä yə'əḥazəwa lä mədr*; 1 Enoch 38:4), are those who own a piece of land.

Territory, Land

Earth can also stand for a given territory like in 1 Enoch 56:6 "the land of my chosen ones" (*mədrä ḥeruyanä*). It is interesting to note that *mədra* is replaced by *hagärä* in the immediately following verse (56:7) through the expression *hagärä ḥeruyanä* which is parallel to *mədra ḥeruyanä*. Both have the same meaning. Among the numerous biblical examples for earth as territory, it might suffice to quote from Gen 15:18; "To your descendants I give this land," *läzärə'kä əhuba läzati mədr*. Quite unlike the Hebrew Bible which uses frequently expressions like "The land of Egypt" (*'ĕreṣ miṣrayim*;[10]

---

8. See H. H. Schmid on *'ereṣ* earth, land, in Jenni 1997:1:172–79 at 173.

9. In her book entitled *The Other Lands of Israel*, Lied proposes to explore the significance of the land for the righteous Israel in 2 Baruch, well beyond the material land of Palestine. According to Lied (2008), the rarity of references to the physical land of Israel in apocalyptic literature, far from being a lack of interest in the land, should be seen in terms of hoping for a new land in the other world, created for the sake of Israel.

10. *Passim* from Gen 13:10 onwards.

mədrä gəbṣ in Geʿez), names of a given land are absent from 1 Enoch. Neither Israel, nor Egypt, nor Syria or other lands of neighbouring peoples are mentioned there. Even when the Parthians and the Medes are referred to in 1 Enoch 56:5, the text does not speak about their land.

The land is promised by God and given to his people: "the land that I gave to Abraham and Isaac I will give to you, and I will give the land to your offspring after you" (Gen 35:12 NRSV). It is a land "flowing with milk and honey" (Exod 33:3) that God has given to Israel for a "possession" (Lev 14:34). Yet, the land can also be dispossessed when it is defiled: "Thus the land became defiled; and I punished it for its iniquity, and the land vomited out its inhabitants" (Lev 18:25 NRSV).

When we look at 1 Enoch, we do not find many references to the motif of the land belonging to a given people, be it Egypt or Israel. It is, in fact, in the Animal Apocalypse (1 Enoch 85–90)[11] that we find a widespread reference to the land of Israel. There, Jerusalem is called a pleasant and glorious land (*wäbämədr ḥawaz*; 1 Enoch 89:40). And in 1 Enoch 90.20 it is stated: "And I looked until a throne was set up in the pleasant land; *bämədr ḥawaz*"). In 1 Enoch 90:28 the temple will be removed and put aside at the south of the land (*bäyämanä mədr*), that is at the south of Jerusalem.

Land versus the Earth

What should we learn from 1 Enoch's focus on the earth in its entirety? The concern of a global disaster makes it relevant indeed. In a modern context, there seems to be a conflict between two visions of the earth. People and governments speak in the first place of their land, their mother-land. The focus on one's land may not allow a person to see the earth in its entirety. The competitions, the fight for resources and the idea of exclusively working for one's land implies a neglect of "other lands" within the globe of the earth. Such an attitude would compromise the call for ecological concern. First Enoch here shows a remarkable worry for the whole earth as the home of human beings.

Earth in its Entirety and the Ecosystem

The Enochian focus on the earth in its entirety fits well within the presentation of scientific theories about the globe. It also makes good sense inside

---

11. The Apocalypse of Weeks (1 Enoch 93:1–10; 91:11–17) makes a clear allusion to the land but we cannot say that it is extensive.

the discourse of environmental philosophy and theology. More than ever, scientists, philosophers and theologians recognize the interrelatedness of localities as well as the flora and the fauna. From this point of view, with its universalistic concern for the earth and with its emphasis on the relevance of all created things or all nature, 1 Enoch does indeed show an interesting approach.

Complaints of the Earth

Complaint against Violence

Different characters cry in 1 Enoch. Crying for the loss of a beloved is mentioned in 1 Enoch 85:8, when Eve cries for Abel. In 1 Enoch 89:38 the Israelites mourn the death of Moses. They cry for the loss of their prophet. Yet, the loss of Abel is caused by violence whereas Moses, one may say, dies naturally. Would the cry at the death of Abel enlighten our understanding of the cry of the earth? Both the Earth and Eve have lost their beloved as a consequence of violence. The cry of Enoch at the suffering and death of the Israelites seems to reflect something analogous.

In 1 Enoch 7:5-6, the earth cries like a person, complaining about the lawless ones who devoured one another and drink other's blood. In the Book of Watchers, the earth, filled with blood and iniquity (1 Enoch 9:1; 9:9) is more victim than guilty. The earth is a place where evil is perpetrated. The motif of the earth's complaint is continued in 8:4 and 1 Enoch 9:2 where human beings cry and where the angels express their desire to hear its grieving: "And they said to one another; "Let the devastated earth cry out with the sound of their cries towards the gate of heaven."[12] The cry of the earth, mentioned above (1 Enoch 9:2), is also reported in the Animal Apocalypse (87:1).

Noah cries when he foresees the flood in the Book of Parables (65:5) and Enoch cries for the same reasons in the Book of Dreams (83:5). Yet, the cry of Enoch, unlike the cry of the earth and the poor, is unheeded in the Animal Apocalypse (1 Enoch 89:57ff). Cry meaning complaint and plea is attested in 1 Enoch 22:5 where the spirit of Abel cries out against Cain and in 1 Enoch 89:15-16, where it refers to the Israelites who cry to God because of their slavery in Egypt. In 1 Enoch 9:10 the souls of the dead that cry towards heaven.

---

12. See Nickelsburg 2001:186-87 for the links between 7:6; 8:4; and 9:1-2.

God, the Earth and Human Beings

The connection between God and the earth is not limited to the fact that the latter has been created by God or that it is the footstool of the divine. According to 1 Enoch, the earth is capable of receiving righteousness, especially when God comes down on Sinai (1 Enoch 1:4),[13] or when He comes to visit the earth with goodness (1 Enoch 25:3). Now these two verses (1 Enoch 1:4 and 25:3) are so close that we may infer that the precise place through which God comes to visit the earth is Sinai even if other mountains of sacred manifestations like Mount Hermon (1 Enoch 6:6) and Mount Zion (1 Enoch 26:2) are not excluded.[14]

That the earth needs inhabitants is implied in 1 Enoch 67:2:

> ... I will put my hand on it, and keep it safe, and from it will come the seed of life, and a change shall take place that the earth may not remain empty.

God will cause a change so that the earth may not remain empty after the flood. He will comfort the earth after all the destruction (1 Enoch 107:3). Similarly, after his first dream, Enoch prays so that posterity may be left on earth after the flood (1 Enoch 84:5). Yet, Enoch does not implore on behalf the posterity of those who provoked God's anger but rather for righteous ones (1 Enoch 84:6). The concern is both in 1 Enoch and in the Book of Genesis in the sense that human beings should continue to live. This is parallel to God's decision to restart life in Gen 9:15: "... and the waters shall never again become a flood to destroy all flesh."[15] Yet, 1 Enoch betrays an apprehension for the righteous, not expressed in Genesis 7–9.

Since the earth is the dwelling place of human beings, a strong link is made between the two, expressed in parental image. In effect, human beings are called children of the earth (*wəludä mədr*; 1 Enoch 15:3) by God in contrast to the angels who are called "children of heaven" (*wəludä sämayat*; 1 Enoch 6:2). Angels left the "high heaven" and defiled themselves with women by behaving like "children of earth" (1 Enoch 12:4; 15:3).[16] In 1 Enoch 85:3, the earth, from which humans emerge, has children (*wəludä*

---

13. His coming down, implying also judgment, is not beneficial to all.

14. The word Zion is not explicitly mentioned, but it is possible to identify it through the context of the concerned verses.

15. On the importance of Genesis for literature from the second Temple period, see Stuckenbruck 2002.

16. For a sample of some of the copious literature on this subject, see Delcor 1976; Hanson 1977; Dimant 1978; Newsom 1980.

mədr) who tremble (1 Enoch 86:6; 88:2; "all the sons of the earth began to tremble").

However, *wəludä mədr* is not the only expression used to designate human beings in 1 Enoch. "Sons of men" (*wəludä säb*';[17] *huioi tōn anthrōpōn*) is an even more frequent appellation (1 Enoch 6:1; 10:7(2), 21; 11:1; 12:1, 4; 13:2; 15:12; 22:3, 5; 39:1, 5; 40:9; 42:2; 64:1(2); 69:6(2), 8, 12, 14). In 1 Enoch 15:3, 86:6; 88:2 and 102:3 "children of the earth" seem to refer to all humanity.[18] On the other hand, in 1 Enoch 100:6 they appear to form a separate group distinct from the righteous.[19]

Presenting human beings as "children of the earth" is not so common in today's world. These references to God are difficult to transfer to a secular society.

Predicting an Ecological Disaster

Today, those concerned with the ecological crisis either predict a disaster, or promise an acceptable future depending on the behaviour of nations and individuals. The latter group look like the prophets of the Old Testament who call to repentance lest a disaster should happen. Unfortunately, those ancient Israelite oracles of doom were not given enough attention. Most of the time, neither the political leaders nor the people were ready to repent and return to righteousness. One may, for instance, think of the Assyrian and Babylonian invasions that were understood in the Bible as consequences of disregarding the prophets' critique.

Are we in a better position today with regard to the danger of ignoring the need to care for the environment? People tend to be more concerned with the immediate needs and future than with the remote consequences.

---

17. The Ethiopic term *säb*' is generic and thus does not refer to a particular gender.

18. See Stuckenbruck 2007:491.

19. See Stuckenbruck 2007:443-44. Stuckenbruck even thinks of three possible meanings behind the expression "children of the earth." His following statement regarding 1 Enoch 102:1-3ff illustrates well the ambiguity concerning the expression "children of the earth": "The passage clearly distinguishes between 'the children of the earth' and 'the sinners'. Whereas the former are caught up in the fearful response of creation to the activity of divine judgment, the latter are the targets of God's wrath. This distinction does not, however, make it possible to conclude that the term 'sinners' here (v. 3) specifically refers to the opponents of the author's community or is a broader description that includes them. A similar problem surfaces through the expression "the children of the earth": (a) are they those who will eventually comprise the righteous in the eschaton, (b) are they the same group as the "sinners" who will be judged", or (c) are they the mass of humanity who the author does profile in relation to the socio-religious conflict underlying many of the invectives in the Epistle . . ." (2007:487).

Yet, it is said that the consequences of the degradation of the environment can no longer be considered as remote. Can human beings avoid and prevent the danger before it is too late or it becomes irreversible?

Resignation

The situation in the modern world shows great progress paralleled with fragility. Human beings are at the same time beneficiaries and victims of advanced technology. In front of the benefits of innovativeness, can one speak of unavoidable side effects? In front of such a complex and ambiguous situation, human beings may adopt an attitude of resignation. This human vulnerability, surely caused also by greed and arrogance in the case of modernity, is also visible in the Book of Enoch. Human beings are unable to solve the problem of the disasters that affects the flora and fauna. In 1 Enoch, human beings are hopeless in front of the death of animals caused by the giants. They themselves are not spared. Humanity would have disappeared if it were not for the intervention from above. Similarly, today's environmental disaster does not concern the planet only; it is the survival of human beings too which is at stake.

Different Causes for Disaster

There is an important difference between 1 Enoch and our age with regard to the root cause of the ecological disaster. In 1 Enoch human beings have not triggered the horrific situation. The initiative came from angels, children of heaven, but the consequences became terrible for children of the earth. Even the act of leading wars and bloodshed through killing is attributed to the seducing teaching of the angel Azazel. In the case of Azazel, the influence passes through the teaching of skills and hidden knowledge. The consequences then reach all humanity in war, adultery and idolatry. Human beings are less cause and more instruments and victims of the disaster. It is not so with the role of human beings today. The rapid degradation we see is attributed to imprudent human action that has taken place during the last two hundred years or so.

Conclusion

Some analogy between the situation described in 1 Enoch and today's situation may be drawn here. In both cases there are few responsible and many victims. The side effects of modern technology affect all humanity. Yet not all are innovators. Those who innovate and possess the skills are by and large a minority. The consequences, on the other hand, affect everybody. No one may be spared, even if the disaster does not reach all regions at the same time. Sooner or later all will be victims. This therefore touches the question of responsibility and accountability. In the case of 1 Enoch, God held accountable those responsible for the disaster, imprisoned the perpetrators or the fallen angels and eliminated their offspring, that is, the giants. And there was chance to renew the earth and life on earth.

What would be said about today's situation? Who can be symbolized by the fallen angels? The meaning of the story in 1 Enoch can indeed be relevant for our contemporary discussion. First Enoch reflects a response to difficulties and crises that took place over two thousand years ago. Various scholars have proposed the situations that may have caused the crisis. Among these, one may mention challenges that have come from Hellenistic culture that dominated and threatened the Jewish worldview.

The danger of pretentious human wisdom, seen as threat, is criticized through the story of the fallen angels. Are we not also today in an analogous situation where the seductive and partially beneficial progress bears at the same time unexpected and unwanted side effects? If lust, murder and idolatry are behind evil according to 1 Enoch, are these vices still not a challenge today? Do not consumerism and pride and greed constitute some of the causes of the complicated situation concerning environmental degradation?

The authors of 1 Enoch tried to understand their situation in the light of their Israelite faith. Why is their violence and injustice? Why are we dominated by Greek culture? Is our faith relevant in the face of a dominant and threatening foreign culture? One also finds social injustice denounced. The condemnation of social injustice shows the interaction and the interrelation that exists between cosmological and social issues. If theology is faith seeking understanding, it needs to help believers to understand today's environmental crisis and human beings questionable relationship vis-à-vis the earth, the common home of various creatures.

9

The Identity of the Son of Man

Messianism and Participation in the Book of (1) Enoch

GRANT MACASKILL

In this chapter I will explore the complex identity of the Son of Man in the Book of (1) Enoch,[1] particularly in the section that we refer to as the Parables (chapters 37–71 in the standard scholarly divisions). This name clearly identifies a particular individual using a title that is associated in the Christian tradition, especially in the New Testament, with the person of Jesus Christ. By this and other titles, that individual is not merely identified, but is represented in ways that establish a *correspondence* between his identity and the identity of the redeemed community. As well as being called the Son of Man, he is also named as "the Chosen One" and, as such, his identity corresponds in some sense to the identity of the community repeatedly designated as "the chosen (ones)." With the title Son of Man, however, a particular correspondence is established between this individual and Enoch himself, the narrator, who is himself

---

1. In historical critical scholarship, the text that we here consider is typically labeled 1 Enoch, with the numeral distinguishing this body of writing from the distinctive work preserved in Slavonic (2 Enoch) and the later Rabbinic material about Enoch (3 Enoch). Scholars further identify a number of distinct units within this (The Book of the Watchers, The Parables of Enoch, The Astronomical Book, The Dream Visions, and The Epistle of Enoch. Within the traditions that consider this work to be scriptural, however, it is simply the Book of Enoch, or some variant of this. Much of my previous work has been focused on the Slavonic Enoch material and because of my sensitivity to the existence of those texts, I will generally use the label "1 Enoch" in what follows.

identified as (and addressed as) "that Son of Man" (71:14). Historical critics and text scholars argue over the originality of this identification, but this has little bearing on the theological truth found in the final form of the text: that a human being can, in the end, be identified so closely with the person of the Son of Man that the identity of that heavenly person becomes superimposed onto—or realized within—that of the earthly individual. As I will highlight later in the essay, this is a key element in biblical teaching and is a key element in some theological traditions, but it is one that is often difficult for those from the modern West, or from the global North, to comprehend, not least because of the concepts of "personhood" that have dominated our thinking since the Enlightenment. The theological value of this element in the Book of Enoch, then, lies in its particular rendering of Christian identity as derived from and constituted by the living identity of the Messiah, the Son of Man. Such a "reading" of the text is distinctively Christian, and this should be no more problematic in relation to this particular Jewish text than it is in relation to the texts of the Old Testament.

In order to explore this reading, I will begin by highlighting the solidarity or correspondence between the Son of Man and the community that he represents: the Chosen. Once I have done this, I will look at the particular correspondence established with Enoch, who becomes thereby a model of Christian "ascent," one of the common traditional paradigms of Christian life.

Preliminary Comments

Before turning to this, I need to offer some clarifications about the way that I am using 1 Enoch in my own constructive theological reflection. As someone who operates within the Western theological tradition and, more specifically, within the Reformed theological tradition, I do not approach the books of Enoch as part of the canon of Scripture. They are, for me, works outside of the canon. That, however, does not make them by necessity theologically problematic or theologically insignificant. One of the problems that has afflicted twentieth and now twenty-first century discussions of the concept of canon is the assumption that canonicity determines the authority that is ascribed to a particular book or designates the recognition of its "inspired" origin. Neither, however, were historically determinative for the canonical status of particular works: some books were not deemed canonical, despite being taken as genuine prophecy, and others were seen as authoritative (*Didache*, *Shepherd of Hermas*, etc.), despite not being seen as canonical. What lay behind the formation of the canon was, rather, whether texts were deemed to belong to a unique category of writings in which the church considered itself to hear "the Word of God"; this was as much a response to those texts and their perceived effects as it was a decision about their credibility.[2] We need not allow ourselves to be too bogged down in the fine detail of this, and we have to admit that the criteria by which canon decisions were made were complex and controversial.[3] All that we need to recognize is that the non-canonical status of a work in a given tradition does not necessarily mean that representatives of that tradition must consider it uninspired and without authority.

Once we have recognized this, the fact that the text has operated with a particular authority within one branch of the Church becomes important. Within that branch of the church, what scholars today classify as 1 Enoch has indeed been read as Scripture and this means that it is taken as a reliable and constructive source for the development of theology. While unable to affirm the conviction that 1 Enoch belongs among the Scriptures, on the basis of decisions taken by forerunners in my own tradition, I can nevertheless acknowledge the function of the book within the Ethiopian tradition and can see it as an authoritative text in its own right, while stopping short of ascribing it the *distinctive* authority that goes with canonical status in my own tradition. That distinctive authority is associated with the *normative* status of the canon and that last word may allow for a helpful point of dialogue: for me, and for others who do not see 1 Enoch as canonical, it will never be normative for Christian theology, in the way that Paul or Isaiah may be. Nevertheless, it may an important and authoritative resource for Christian theology, provided it is properly subordinated to the canon. Authority and normativity are two different, if connected, things. This allows constructive engagement with the text and with theological positions developed by fellow believers in the Ethiopian or Eritrean traditions, while also candidly acknowledging the differences between those traditions and my own, in terms of the extent of Holy Scripture.

This involves a recognition that, whatever its authorship and origins, 1 Enoch functions as part of Christian tradition. This is true of a number of works that were authored in the context of Judaism but that went on to be vibrant parts of the Christian theological traditions in which they were (often exclusively) transmitted. The comment is not intended to detract

---

2. For a sensitive theological reflection on this, see Childs 1970 (Chapter 6) and Webster 2003 in toto.

3. The best historical discussion remains von Campenhausen 1968.

from the Jewishness of the work or to steal the work from its place in Jewish heritage; rather, it is intended to highlight the fact that just as the Hebrew Bible becomes Christian scripture when it functions as the Old Testament, so 1 Enoch and various other works become part of Christian tradition when they are circulated in that context.[4] The identification of the author, then, is less important than the fact that these texts have functioned as part of the Christian theological tradition.

The Son of Man, the Righteous, and the Chosen One(s)

It is generally recognized that a complex of titles is used of the figure of the Son of Man in the book of the Parables. In addition to this principal designation, he is also the Righteous One, the Messiah, and the Chosen One.[5] As has been noted elsewhere, the combination of titles is closely connected to Isaiah's prophecies concerning the figure of "the Servant."[6] This detail is important for what follows, since one of the observations made about the figure of the Servant in Isaiah is that his individual identity (and narrative) is constitutive of the corporate identity (and narrative) of a community: those designated as "the Servants." This element in the Isaianic material has been seen as influential on Paul's theology of Christian identity and experience.[7]

When the Son is first introduced to us in the book of the Parables, it is as the Righteous One, but it is important to note that this identification is made in the context of the introduction of the community of believers as "the congregation of the righteous" (38:1). When the Righteous One appears, it is precisely "in the presence of the righteous" (38:2). It is clearly important that this is part of a strict schema that distinguishes the righteous from "the sinners," but the striking detail for our purposes is the direct nominal correspondence between the figure of the Righteous One and the community with which he is present. The term "chosen," as a designation

---

4. See my discussion of 2 Enoch in Macaskill 2007.

5. VanderKam, in his essay "Righteous One, Messiah, Chosen One and Son of Man in 1 *Enoch* 37–71," examines the interchangeability of the terms (2000:432–33). Older scholarship tended to fixate on the possibility that the variety of titles was to be explained by source criticism: see Charles 1912:64–65 and Beer 1900:227. Such approaches are critiqued by Sjöberg 1945:24–33. Also important as discussions of the relationship between the Chosen One and Son of Man traditions are the following: Theisohn 1975:47–52, 203; Coppens 1982:125–34. While such discussions are interesting in their own right, they typically neglect the potential that the multiplicity of titles has to contribute to the complex theological identification of the figure in question, when encountered in the final form of the text.

6. See my article, Macaskill 2013b.

7. See Wagner 2002; and Gignilliat 2007.

for the community of believers on earth, also begins to be used in 38:2, anticipating its wider use throughout the Parables.

This close identification of the Righteous One and the righteous ones is continued in 39:4–8, where Enoch sees (in clear parallel), the dwelling and resting places of the righteous ones and the Chosen One respectively. Interestingly, from a narrative point of view, his description of the dwelling of the Chosen One ends with an expression of his own desire to dwell in that particular place, a desire that will ultimately be fulfilled in the identification of Enoch as the Son of Man in 71:14.

The Chosen One is the object of arch-angelic blessing in 40:5, and it is interesting to note the pattern of which this is part. The first two of the four angels (identified in 40:9) respectively bless the Lord of Spirits and the Chosen One/chosen ones, with the third interceding for righteous who dwell on earth, and the fourth angel protecting them from the accusing satans. The chain of blessing, or perhaps the concentricity of the blessing, is important. God, the Lord of Spirits, is blessed above all. The blessing of the Chosen One/chosen ones is specified as being directed to "those who depend on the Lord of Spirits," emphasizing its participation in the first blessing. The ministry for those who dwell on earth, vulnerable to evil, itself proceeds from these central blessings. Thus, the figure of the Chosen One—named ahead of his counterparts—takes on an important mediatorial role: his participation in the divine blessing makes possible the participation of others. Crucially, though, this participation depends on the correspondence of his identity with theirs, the sharing of the status, "Chosen." It is, perhaps, important to note that this designation has covenantal overtones, made more explicit if we translate the word as "elect."

The mediatorial role of the Son of Man is further associated with the divine throne.[8] The Parables explicitly parallel what we find in Matt 25:31, with the throne being designated as "the throne of *his* glory" (62:5; paralleled without this specific ascription in 45:1). The throne is thus represented as that of the Son, even though it is also identified as God's own throne (cf. 51:3, where it is "my throne"), establishing a close link between the identity of the Son and God himself, one that is further developed by the use of the term "glory." The Son is thus depicted as divine, not in any partial sense, but in the full sense that he occupies the divine throne and manifests the divine glory. He does so, however, as one who is also a human being, who is a "Son of Man," and as a consequence of this, his occupancy of the divine throne has a distinctive potential for participation. For his person is represented

---

8. For further exploration of the representative dimension of mediation, see Collins 1980:112–16.

with what we might call a "dual solidarity": a solidarity with God, on whose throne he sits and whose glory he manifests, and a solidarity with human beings, at least those who share in his specific human identity as "chosen."[9]

It is, then, striking that the enthronement of the Chosen One coincides with, or corresponds to, the eschatological reversal of the fortunes of the chosen (cf. also 50:1), but also to a transformation of the earthly and heavenly worlds:

> On that day, my Chosen One will sit on the throne of glory...
> On that day I shall make my Chosen One dwell among them,
> and I shall transform heaven and make it a blessing and a light forever; and I will transform the earth and make it a blessing, and my chosen ones I will make to dwell on it. (45:3-5)

The transformation that is here described involves all of the realms and identities that participate in the being of the Chosen One: the development of his personal narrative, his enthronement, therefore bears on all of these.

What I am isolating here is a consistent feature of the Parables (numerous further texts could be cited within the book), namely, a close identification of the singular figure of the Son of Man with the community of the righteous, an identification that is achieved by means of nominal or epithetic parallelism. What I have traced up to this point is simply a surface feature of the text, a consistent juxtaposing of the parallel titles as they are attached to the Son of Man and to the community and a close identification of his narrative with their fortunes.

Taken by itself, this feature would not necessarily lead us to the conclusion that the Son of Man's identity is *constitutive* of that of the community: he could be seen as a representative figure of some kind, or as first among equals. If we push deeper, however, and read this text in relation to both the New Testament and the later Christian theological tradition, a merely representational account is seen to be inadequate: it is certainly part of what we encounter, but there is clearly a further participatory dimension. I have already noted the connection between the Enochic representation of the Son of Man and the Isaianic Servant, whose identity is also linked to that of a community (the servants). I have also noted that this play of identities is taken up in the New Testament, where it is exploited by Paul, in particular, to articulate the relationship between Jesus and his people.[10]

---

9. For the overlap of the titles of the Son of Man with those applied to God, and hence his "divine solidarity," see the brief discussion in Nickelsburg and VanderKam 2012a:40–44.

10. See, for example, Romans 6–8; 12:1-3; Ephesians 1–2; 2 Corinthians 1. Outside of the Pauline (or deutero-Pauline) corpus, see 1 Pet 2:4-10; Revelation 11. These are

What is striking there is that the identification of Jesus and his followers is particularly developed in narrative terms: they share in his story, with their own narrative identity and experience (particularly in terms of suffering, martyrdom and glorification) re-actualizing his, through the work of the Holy Spirit in uniting them to Jesus.

The Patristic traditions develop this even further, but there the ontological dimension of this becomes more prominent. The possibility of Jesus' human followers participating in his story rests on their shared human ontology, on the fact that he is indeed a Son of Man; but the significance of that participation lies in the fact that he is also Son of God and that by participating in his humanity by means of the dynamic presence of the Spirit, they are also thereby brought into union with his participation in the Godhead. This becomes the ontological foundation for the concept of "deification" in the Christian tradition and the key to this is the unique ontology of the figure of Jesus. As the one who unites in himself the nature of God and the nature of created man, he makes possible the participation of the creature in the Creator, without the two ontologies being collapsed in the way that they may be in idealism, pantheism or panentheism.[11]

What we have seen in the Parables can fruitfully be read in such terms, with the necessary coincidence of the human and divine identity of the Son of Man, the Chosen One. It is perhaps worth reflecting, however, on the distinctive development of such theology in the Ethiopic traditions, particularly in the *andəmta* commentaries, something that I leave to others better versed in those traditions. Such discussion may highlight some significant distinctions between the ways that solidarity with Jesus is understood in the different traditions of theology. Within the Patristic traditions of the Greek Orthodox traditions, particularly from the period of the Cappadocian Fathers, and subsequently in both Greek and Latin traditions, and the early modern theology of both Catholic and Reformed churches, the coincidence of Jesus' divinity and humanity was understood in terms of what tends to be labeled as "two natures Christology," the doctrine of the hypostatic union: in the singular person of Jesus Christ are united two distinct natures, one divine, the other human. As I have indicated already, this did not (as is commonly held) arise from an abstract Greek interest in substance metaphysics, but rather from soteriology, from reflection on what it meant for human beings to participate in the life of God, and hence to be saved from evil. In fact, in the Reformed accounts (anticipated in the medieval period by Franciscan

---

just a brief selection of the relevant texts. For a fuller discussion, see Macaskill 2013a in toto.

11. For full discussion of this, including the complex relationship between Christian (particularly Alexandrian) theology and Platonism, see Russell 2004.

theology),[12] this was developed in a thoroughgoing way in relation to covenant theology, with Jesus occupying the unique role of covenant mediator on account of his divine and human natures. Later modern theology, at least in the West and North, has widely forsaken such a configuration of Christology, although it has seen a resurgence of popularity in recent years as the problems of the alternatives have been exposed.[13] The representation of the Son of Man in the Parables can certainly be read through this lens, and his relationship to the chosen ones explicated thereby, but this may be quite different from the kind of readings that arise in a *tewahedo* context[14] and that are reflected in the *andəmta* commentaries. Based on my prior work in this area,[15] I would suggest that a fruitful focal point for such discussions may be around the theme of "covenant," and its relationship to the concept of "adoption."

"You are that Son of Man": Enoch's Participation in the Messianic Identity

What we have seen to this point is a broad identification of community and individual, but there is also a narrower identification of individual and individual. What I am speaking of here is the identification of Enoch himself as the Son of Man in 71:14. It is, I think, important that we pay close attention to the features of the narrative description that lead up to this identification. First, it is important that the Enoch's identity and that of the Son of Man are actually differentiated in 70:1.

> After that, while he was living, his name was lifted up into the presence of the Son of Man.

Enoch and the Son of Man are two different and distinguishable identities here and the narrative requires us to recognize this fact. In the verses that intervene between this differentiation and the subsequent identification

---

12. See the discussion of Franciscan covenant theology (and its relationship to nominalism) in Oberman 2003.

13. As two excellent examples of this, see Davidson 2005; and John Webster, "Incarnation," in Webster 2001:113–50.

14. *Tewahedo* is a Ge'ez word meaning "being made one" or "unified." It forms part of the name of the Ethiopian and Eritrean Orthodox Churches and refers to their belief that in Christ there is one single, unified nature, that is, a complete union of his divine and human elements. In Western theology, where this view is called "monophysite," the usually accepted position, dating from the Council of Chalcedon in 451 CE, is that Christ has "two natures," human and divine, existing in "hypostatic union."

15. Macaskill 2013a:297–304.

what is described is the ascension of Enoch through heaven and into the heaven of heavens. As he ascends, Enoch sees both heavenly and cosmic realities (in an account with a number of quite striking parallels to the detailed description of the ascension found in the Slavonic Book of Enoch). Perhaps importantly, Enoch's journey is not one made through his own effort or strength: he is carried upward by Michael. Specifically, his "spirit" is lifted (passively, as it were) and is eventually set in the heaven of heavens. The identity of the spirit thus passively elevated as being that of Enoch himself is further stressed in 70:5. Crucially, the final event before the identification of Enoch with the Son of Man is a thoroughgoing transformation:

> I fell on my face and all my flesh melted and my spirit was transformed. And I cried out with a loud voice, with a spirit of power, and I blessed and praised and exalted. And those blessings that went forth from my mouth were acceptable in the presence of that Head of Days.

Enoch is here transformed into a being fit for the presence of the Lord of Spirits. There is a tendency to describe such transformations in Jewish and Christian literature using the language of "angelomorphism," whereby Enoch is seen as being transformed into an angelic or angel-like figure. That language is, I think, problematic, since only in some cases do the texts in question specify a similarity to the angels. The key point is rather that Enoch is now able to stand in the presence of the Lord, his physical transformation paralleling a spiritual and moral transformation: with a spirit of power, he now speaks words that are acceptable in the presence of the Head of Days.

It is only now that this physically and spiritually transmogrified Enoch is fully assimilated to the identity of the Son of Man, an identification that is represented as a matter of disclosing the true identity of both individuals. This, in fact, is a development of the theme of the naming of the Son of Man that has been encountered already in Chapter 48, notably verses 2–3. That chapter is interesting because of how it represents the Son of Man as a pre-existent figure. His name was named before the creation of the stars (48:3) and he himself was chosen and hidden before the foundation of the world in the presence of the Lord of Spirits (48:6). Not only so, of course, but he is the recipient of worship from all who dwell on the earth (48:5). Taken together, I would suggest that these elements place some important restrictions on how we understand the relationship of Enoch to the Son of Man. The Son of Man cannot *simply* be Enoch, since Enoch was not hidden with God from before the creation of the world. Neither can it simply be a matter of typology (of Enoch being a type of the later incarnation), since a type anticipates and in certain senses informs the reality to which it corresponds, where here it is the identity of the Son of Man that is constitutive for Enoch's identity, and not the other way round, even though it is Enoch's name that is attached to the Son. Moreover, the identification is possible only after Enoch has ascended and been transformed.

Instead, then, I would suggest that this should be read in terms of the broadly found Christian theological tradition that utilizes the imagery of ascent into heaven and identification with Jesus in relation to the *telos* of Christian life. This is encountered throughout the history of the church and across the various traditions (examples are found in Irenaeus, Gregory of Nyssa, Augustine, Bonaventure and Calvin, to name but a few). The goal of Christian life is to attain maturity, which is equated with being conformed to the likeness of the Son (Rom 12:2): our fallen selves and their fleshly elements share in his death and we are raised as new selves, whose moral identity is shaped like (or after) that of Jesus Christ. Across the Christian traditions, the imagery of ascent into heaven has been used in relation to the pursuit of such maturity, and typically in close connection to the theme of knowledge. The one who ascends does so as his or her mind comes to know God better: they are no longer conformed to this earthly world, but are transformed by the renewing of their minds (Rom 12:2, again) into those who can discern the will of God, who can, like Enoch, speak and act in a way that is acceptable in the heavenly presence of God. That theme of renewed knowledge and heavenly ascent is, in turn, associated with the practices of Christian discipline, particularly the ascetic practices central to monastic life but also practiced more widely in the Christian traditions.

Obviously, we must be careful if we are to read Enoch in this way. Such an approach requires us to bring a number of theological and interpretative decisions to the text *in advance*, decisions about Christology and its relationship to discipleship and pneumatology. This requires us to treat with some generosity those parts of the text that we consider to lack what we would like to see present. But all theological interpretation requires such a process of dialogue, whereby we bring some kind of "rule of faith" to the text and then allow a hermeneutical spiral of conversation to develop, one in which Scripture and doctrine speak to each other. What this allows us to do is to see Enoch as a paradigmatic representation of the individual within the community, morally and spiritually conformed to the likeness of our heavenly *archegos* ("forerunner" or "author," Heb 12:2) to an extent that he himself can be addressed as the Son of Man. If we do indeed read the text this way, then a particular significance can be ascribed to the use of the title, Son of Man, rather than the use of a proper name. The title has a generic quality that allows it to designate the correspondence between the believer and Christ without effacing the distinctive identities of each. Enoch remains Enoch as he is identified as the Son: he does not become, simply, Jesus.

Contributions to Contemporary Theology

Why, though, might this be a particularly significant contribution to contemporary theology? Let me suggest two reasons, both concerned particularly with what would probably be labeled modern Western theology (although there is a growing sensitivity to its distinctively "northern" features). The first is simply that modern thought struggles with the concept that "I" could be so identified with another person that I would see myself as actually corresponding to that person. I might see myself as "like" that person, or even as a "beneficiary" of that person, and hence in some attenuated sense as determined by that person and his or her work; modern theologies, then, have frequently reduced the *correspondence* (to use Barth's favored term) between believers and Jesus to one of moral example (for example, in modern liberal theology) or one of passive beneficiary (in modern evangelical theology). The idea that my whole identity, the entirety of myself, might be constituted by the personhood of another is an alien one, though, and the roots of this arguably lie in what happened to the notions of personhood at the Enlightenment, with the shift to thinking of personhood as a self-subsistent concept, rather than as a necessarily dynamic and social one.[16] The imagery of 1 Enoch 71:14 simply slices across this and does so by means of an identification that cannot be rationalized into these modern categories. Enoch is the Son of Man, the Son of Man is Enoch. Once we read this in relation to some of Paul's language, it begins to open up new-yet-old ways of understanding Christian discipleship as true and utter identification with Christ, yet one that does not cause the elision of the basic distinction between Jesus and the believer:

> "I died to the law. I have been crucified with Christ. I live, yet not I: Christ lives in me" (Gal 2:20)
>
> "For me to live is Christ" (Phil 1:21)
>
> "For his sake I have suffered the loss of all things and count them as rubbish, in order that I may gain Christ and be found in him" (Phil 3:8–9)

---

16. See David Kelsey 2009:357–71, for analysis of this and further theological discussion. In philosophy, the problems associated with modern treatments of selfhood are thoroughly evaluated by Taylor 1992.

This begins to expose the inadequacy of some of the modern western accounts of identification and to lead us back to older accounts, which in turn takes us back to Christology and its ontological elements.

The second distinctive contribution concerns what we might call salvation history. The figure who participates in the identity of the Son of Man is Enoch, the seventh from Adam, and his participation is thoroughgoing, despite the fact that his life begins long before what might be referred to as "the Christ event," the period of earthly Incarnation. This is quite intelligible in many theological accounts of the relationship of earthly time to the work of God, whereby the timelessness of the triune God and of the *Logos* that took human flesh mean that the work accomplished in the Incarnation at once slices through and encapsulates all created time. Irenaeus and Athanasius, for example, have no difficulty in seeing Adam as made according to the likeness of the human Jesus,[17] and Paul sees nothing problematic in the ideas that Moses and the Israelites drink from the Rock that is Christ (1 Cor 10:4).

It is, however, less easy to accommodate such a reading in the modern accounts of "salvation history" that emerged particularly in evangelical theology in the twentieth century and continue to dominate much of what is labeled "biblical theology." These approaches seek to defend the coherence of the biblical texts by recourse to a history behind those texts, to which they commonly point. God's mighty acts are consecutive, they are part of an unfolding plan and events are to be understood as taking place at particular stages in that process.[18] Those who themselves pre-date the Christ event can only anticipate its fullness; they cannot enjoy it. Hence, while in the pre-modern period (and still today in interpretative communities less affected by modernity, such as my own Scottish Gaelic tradition) one commonly encounters figural readings of the Old Testament/Hebrew Bible that see the various characters participating in some ways in Christocentric salvation, in the modern period such readings typically vanish, even from evangelical theologies that take seriously the coherence of Scripture.

Again, what I would suggest is that the Enochic account cannot be squeezed into those categories. If it is to be read Christianly, it demands that a different set of categories be brought to the discussion, a set of categories at home in older readings of Scripture but alien to much modern discourse, one that starts with the being of God, now understood in terms of the Incarnation, and understands all in this light. This is truly "apocalyptic" but, unlike the approach that is popular in some contemporary Paul scholarship,

---

17. E.g., Irenaeus, *Adv. Haer.* 4.33.4.
18. See Childs 1970:13–87.

which sees itself as a sensitive theological approach,[19] this one affirms the coherence of scripture and the significance of God's dealings with Israel.[20]

Conclusions

Since the last section really constituted a set of conclusions, I will close with a reflection on how the Book of Enoch contributes to my own understanding of contemporary theology. This may or may not be considered acceptable to all readers but it should spark some further constructive reflection about how 1 Enoch might be approached theologically.

As noted at the beginning of this chapter, I personally do not consider the Books of Enoch to be part of the canon of Scripture, and therefore I read them in a way that will differ from others who do. Yet, I recognize that they have functioned as authoritative theological texts for those who belong to another part of the Body of Christ and my solidarity with that community allows me to engage with 1 Enoch as part of Christian tradition, even if its authorship is pre-Christian. Such engagement has two dimensions, and I hope that these have both emerged in this chapter. One is simply a matter of dialogue across the traditional boundaries. I am a representative of a particular theological tradition and, in order for me to dialogue with those of another tradition, the Ethiopian one, I must read and engage with the Enochic writings that are important to it. As with any dialogue, though, this is a two-way experience, and the Ethiopian tradition must be allowed to speak back to my modern, Western, Northern, Reformed tradition. This is the second dimension of this paper. Within this, 1 Enoch functions as part of a deliberate exercise of *ressourcement*, within which it does not operate alone, but is read in relation to other ancient sources, particularly the Patristic texts. Its own relationship to those sources is complex, of course, but clearly some read the Enochic books (some of them, at least) as sources for theology and this further warrants my own approach. This task is of particular value in exposing the deficiencies of many distinctively modern theological approaches to the personhood of Jesus Christ and the significance of this for church and discipleship, as well as to Christian reflection on how one reads the Old Testament. As always, I think it leaves more questions than answers, but it is always better to have the right questions than the wrong answers.

---

19. E.g., Campbell 2010, a work that is explicitly set forth as a response to the interpretative weaknesses left by western forensic modes of thought. See, especially, "Introduction—Common Problems and a Complex Culprit," 1–9.

20. Note John Barclay's comment that Campbell's argument uses precisely the same categories of the perfection of grace as Marcion's (2015:171–73).

And there is the key point: we modern Westerners are often like teenagers, ditching the old fashioned ways of our parents, and convinced that our own ways are better, but frequently lacking any real ability to get to grips with the world. When one comes up against a text like 1 Enoch, one realizes the emptiness of those decisions and is forced back to older worlds, seeking to rediscover those things we thought we did not need.

10

Suffering and *Anawim* Identity in 1 Enoch 108

Towards a Theology of Persecution

SOFANIT T. ABEBE

Introduction

By constructing a narrative worldview of God's action in the world, Chapter 108 in Mäṣḥafä Henok ("the Book of Enoch"), the Eschatological Admonition,[1] seeks to provide a theological framework for interpreting the adverse circumstances of its addressees. Faced with the threat that his addressees would succumb to pressure to conform or retaliate, the author of 1 Enoch 108 strives to outline ways of coping with persecution while maintaining fidelity to YHWH. In this essay I aim to explore the impact the voice of this Enochic author might have on contemporary Christian experience and the attempt to formulate a theology of persecution. This finds legitimation in Philip Esler's "socio-theological" model that places the interpretive task within the theological framework of persons in communion and dialogue. Noting that the model engages the historical interpretation of texts within a "theologically and socially constructed framework of persons in communion," Esler distinguishes

1. This is the title given to this section by Stuckenbruck 2007:91–108.

147

his methodology from traditional approaches that first interpret texts historically and then "hand . . . over [the results] to systematic theologians as a component in a larger ordered theological structure."[2] Nevertheless, according to this approach, the first step in the theological appropriation of a given text, out of respect for its alterity, is the historical interpretation of the text.[3]

To this end, I will explore 1 Enoch 108 and its narrative world in its ancient social context, as well as the situational strategy and theological agenda of its author. In so doing, I will look at the ways in which 1 Enoch 108 responds to the problem of its readers' suffering by constructing sectarian and liminal identities based on the Jewish *anawim* tradition. It is hoped that the analysis of the text's situational strategy and theological agenda will serve to demonstrate the potential that 1 Enoch 108 has for making a positive contribution to formulating a theology of persecution.

The Character of 1 Enoch 108

Attested only in the Ethiopic tradition, 1 Enoch 108, which is purported to be "a final book by Enoch" (v. 1), is an editorial "appendix" that has rich theological motifs. The chapter serves as a conclusion to the corpus and reflects the previous Enochic account of the material as a revelation to Enoch. Although 1 Enoch 108 is not ascribed to a specific author, it is clear from the document's description of the work as "another book, which Enoch wrote for his son Methuselah" (v. 1) that the author belongs to an Enochic group which received and interpreted earlier Enochic traditions.[4]

The content of 1 Enoch 108 can be structured as:

A. Introduction

    (1) Title, Superscription, Addressees (v. 1)

    (2) Opening Exhortation to the Righteous (vv. 2-3)

B. Apocalypse

    (1) Vision of a Cloud (vv. 4-5)

    (2) The Angel's Explanation (vv. 6-10)

---

2. Esler 2005:276.

3. Esler 2005:38-66, 276. On the importance of respecting the alterity of the text within a New Testament hermeneutics built on dialogue, see also Luz 2014:19 and throughout.

4. Nickelsburg 2001:554.

(a) The Wicked to be Punished (vv. 6–7)

(b) The Righteous to be Rewarded (vv. 8–10)

(3) The Reward of the Righteous through Divine Words of Promise (vv. 11–12)

(4) Conclusion (vv. 13–15)[5]

One way to characterise the content of 1 Enoch 108 is in terms of its "narrative world." This narrative analysis derives from the approach proposed by Richard Hays which views Pauline epistles as "reflective discourse" based on a story.[6] This story, alluded to in Paul's discourse, provides the 'narrative substructure' for Paul's theology. Employing such an approach to 1 Enoch 108 has the benefit of giving us a glimpse of the already existing language, culturally conditioned perspectives and ancient traditions of Israel that the Enochic author inevitably draws upon to formulate his situational strategy.

The table below communicates key events in the narrative world of 1 Enoch 108. In its dramatic depiction of time or chronology (denoted below as a "plotted series"), the narrative world projected by 1 Enoch 108 relates events that can be arranged in the order of real chronology (represented by "referential series").[7]

Table 1. The Narrative World of 1 Enoch 108

Referential Series	Plotted Series	Event/Action
1	v. 9a, b	The addressees are righteous, "from the time they came into existence, they lived for God."[8]
	v. 8	They love God more than the world
	v. 1	They obey the law
2	vv. 10c, 8b	Their faith is reviled by the wicked

5. Stuckenbruck 2007:690–91.

6 Hays 2002. For an analysis of the narrative world of 1 Peter, Boring 1999: 183–201 and 2007.

7. See a similar approach taken by Esler in Chapter 12 of this volume.

8. That the addressees are also pious is evident from verse 7 which reads: "For writings and inscriptions about them were found to be upon heaven, so that angels may read them and know what will befall sinners and the spirits of the lowly and those who afflicted their flesh and were compensated by God and those who were humiliated by evil men."

Referential Series	Plotted Series	Event/Action
3	v. 9c	Their faith is tested by God
4	vv. 7c, 10a	They are persecuted by evil men
	v. 8	They abase their bodies[9]
5	vv. 10c, 7b	The righteous continue to bless God despite their persecution and show piety by depriving their body
6	v. 7a	Heavenly inscription about the fate that awaits the righteous and the wicked is revealed to Enoch
		Punishment awaits the wicked persecutors
7	vv. 10–14	Reward awaits the righteous
8	vv. 5–6, 15	The wicked will be punished in the immediate afterlife
9	vv. 2–3	Readers are urged to wait for "these days" until evil men are destroyed and "sin passes away"

Various aspects of this outline will be discussed below.

Understanding 1 Enoch 108 in Its Social Context

The Enochic corpus is a composite pseudepigraphic work written under the name of the ante-diluvian patriarch "Enoch" from Gen 5:21–24. The various parts of the work do not share the same socio-historical or theological settings, which is significant given insights from the sociology of knowledge that posits that knowledge is conditioned by social settings and is perspectival. The Eschatological Admonition (1 Enoch 108) has a particular socio-religious context that is distinct from the rest of the Enochic corpus and reflects that context.

---

9. They abase their bodies in ways that recall Levitical ordinances about afflicting oneself which is described there as the pious act of fasting on a feast day or Sabbath (Lev 16:29, 31; 23:27, 32; and Num 29:7). For a discussion of text critical issues involved in this verse, see Stuckenbruck 2001:711–16.

Date of Composition and Addressees

Stuckenbruck argues that the work was composed "sometime during the late Second Temple period, perhaps around the latter part of the 1st century CE."[10] Although the geographical location of the chapter's particular audience is not explicitly mentioned, the chapter's thematic similarity to other works of Hellenistic Judaism (such as the Wisdom of Solomon and Testament of Job)[11] indicates an intention on the part of the author to address Israelites even outside of Palestine. The multi-religious and perhaps multi-ethnic setting of the addressees is indicated by the work's characterization of its addressees as those who are being persecuted for their faithfulness (108:4–5, 11).

Although the chapter lacks explicit allusions to historical events, the document contains the rather revealing motif of religious persecution.[12] Taking this cue, Nickelsburg suggests a historical circumstance similar to that reflected in 2 Maccabees 6–7, so that the chapter is seen as speaking to those who find themselves in the same suffering and persecution as that of the Maccabean period.[13]

The addressees, those who "keep the law in the last days" (108:1), are further described as the "lowly" (*təḥḥutan*) (1 Enoch 108:7). The term frequently occurs alongside "poor ones" to designate groups behind Dead Sea community documents (CD A vi 21; CD B xix 9; 1QM xiv 7; 1QHa vi 3–4; x 34; xiii 13–14, 20–22; xix 25; 4QpIs^a 8–10 iii 3; 4QpPs^a 1–2 ii 8–10, 16–20; 4Q501 i 5–9).[14] Besides indicating a state of poverty, the term *teḥutan* (ተሕታን) denotes a "quality that is receptive to (and therefore predisposes) divine favor; see, for example, Job 5:11; Psalm 37:11; 82[81]:3; 138[137]:6; Proverbs 16:19; 29:23; Zephaniah 3:12; Sirach 10:14; 11:12; Jdth 9:11; Greek Esther 11:11; 4 *Ezra* 14.13; 1QHa xxiii 14 (in the NT, cf. Luke 1:52; Jas 1:9)."[15]

Furthermore, the addressees are characterized as the righteous "who love God" more than the world (vv. 9, 11, 13) and "still bless [his] name"

---

10. Stuckenbruck 2007:694; Nickelsburg 2001:554 reaches the same view on the date.

11. Nickelsburg 2001:553.

12. Nickelsburg 2001:554.

13. Nickelsburg 2001:554; However, how the text of Chapter 108 may have functioned as a response to the general ideological and social situations described for the corpus or what specific social context it reflects has not been dealt with in Nickelsburg's commentary (2001:57–64).

14. Stuckenbruck 2007:715.

15. Stuckenbruck 2007:715.

despite being crushed by evil men ("put to shame" [v. 8]; verbally and physically abused [v. 11]). It is clear from this description and the reversal of their social status promised in vv. 11-15 that the addressees currently "experience poverty and undergo persecution and social hardship."[16] But in all this they can hope for divine justice and are assured that their present suffering will be rewarded.

Regarding the characterization of the evil-doers who persecute the righteous, Stuckenbruck notes that "while the references to them as 'sinners' [ḫaṭəʾan] and 'godless' [ṣərufan] and as doers of evil [ʾəll ä yəgäbbəru ʾəkuy ä] are generic, the accusation that they have 'altered' or 'changed' the revelation associated with 'the prophets' is more specific."[17] This accusation of changing what has been revealed through the prophets is similarly brought against the opponents in the Epistle (92:2; 104:10-11) that draws on the fallen angels tradition and the cosmic order they trespassed (1 Enoch 5:4-6; 1 Enoch 80:4-6).[18] The persecutors' specific accusation against altering divine revelation is the only instance "the prophets" are mentioned in the Enochic corpus.[19]

It makes good sense to interpret the addressees of 1 Enoch 108 as *anawim* within the ancient traditions of Israel. According to Martin Dibelius, following the Exile a religious and social development took place that associated the state of being poor with piety. He notes as follows:

> on the one hand, the opposition of the great prophets to the proud authorities who were all too sure of their power and resources; on the other hand, the prophets' social injunctions, which then in Deuteronomy were partially accomplished by way of the Law—all these ideas received new impetus because of the catastrophe. The rich had estranged the people from God, so it must be the poor to whom the divine favour belonged. The more piety was understood as humbling oneself before God's will, the more poverty could function as intrinsically fertile soil for piety.[20]

This appears to be the context for texts that assume the "poor" are pious and the rich are enemies of God (cf. Pss 37:10-11; 86:1; 89:11; 109:31; 132:15; 138:6; cf. 82:3; 131:2). In the prophetic tradition, *anawim* are identified as the remnant of Israel (Zeph 2:3; 3:11-12; Isa 10:1-2; 57:15; 66:2; see

16. Stuckenbruck 2007:4.
17. Stuckenbruck 2007:711.
18. Stuckenbruck 2007:711.
19. Stuckenbruck 2007:711.
20. Dibelius 1976:40.

also Sir 35:21–26; Jdth 9:11; Greek Esther 11.6–12; 4 Ezra 9.45; 14.13–15; CD A vi 14–21; CD B xix 9–10). Reflecting this tradition, in instances where the New Testament writers mention the poor, it is often in contrast to the rich: Matt 5:3; 6:1–4; 11:5; 19:21; 23:1–36; 26:9; Mark 10:21; 12:42–43; 14:5, 7; Luke 14:13, 21; 16:20, 22; 19:8; Jas 1:9–11; 2:5–12; 5:1–6.[21]

All this is also true for 1 Enoch 108 where, piety is associated with lowliness and suffering in affliction as is made clear from v. 7: "For writings and inscriptions about them were found to be upon heaven, so that angels read them and know what will befall sinners and the spirits of the lowly and those who afflicted their flesh and were compensated by God and those who were humiliated by evil men." In speaking of the readers' piety in terms of the deprivation of the body, the author thus seems to echo the *anawim* tradition. An allusion to such a tradition is also evident from the characterization of the readers as "the lowly" (v. 8); "generation of light,, and "those born in darkness" in vv. 11–15 that is unique to the Enochic corpus. This can be taken to indicate a group behind the text that understands itself as standing in the Jewish tradition of the *anawim*, that is, the tradition of the "pious," who are socially oppressed and await redress from God alone. That the oppressors in 1 Enoch 108 are other less pious Jews or Hellenizers is clear from the specific charge the author brings against the oppressors as the powerful ones who "alter everything that the Lord has done through the mouth of the prophets (about) all the things which will happen" (v. 6).[22] Not only do the persecutors fail to observe the law, they also fail to interpret the prophets correctly.

The addressees, in contrast, are those who suffer for their faithfulness at the hands of the rich who have little regard for divine revelation. Although they love God, faithfully observe the law and the prophets and shun the world and its riches, they nevertheless suffer reproach, insult and abuse at the hands of the wicked more powerful than they.

Situation and Strategy: An Emic Perspective

The problem directly addressed by the Eschatological Admonition is that of adverse social relations between the *teḥutan* and their rich oppressors. As shown by our earlier treatment of the characterization of the addressees, the latter group has caused the innocent suffering of the former. I will begin the discussion with the emic dimension to understanding this situation namely,

21. See Roth 1997. For the argument that 1 Peter and 1 Enoch 108 reflect an *anawim* tradition, see Abebe 2015.

22 Stuckenbruck 2001:697.

the insider or indigenous perspective. Later I will propose etic (outsider and social-scientific) perspectives for interpreting it.

The picture of the strained social relations between *teḥutan* (the *anawim*) and other contemporary faithless or Hellenizing groups can be corroborated and supplemented by evidence from the Hebrew Bible and the Dead Sea Scrolls as shown above. In order to address the devastating effects of such external opposition on the group cohesion of his community, the author of the Eschatological Admonition extols their present sufferings which is really the testing of their spirits by the Lord—whereupon they were found pure (v. 9).

Their characterization as *teḥutan* indicates their special status as a group favored by God—they are YHWH's poor whose status in post-exilic Israel "became virtually synonymous with the just, the faithful remnant with the right to call upon the Lord."[23] Furthermore the author begins his work with a description of its addressees as "those who . . . will keep the law in the last days" (v.1). This affirmation of the group behind the text as law-abiding "stands in antithesis with the sinners . . . who are unfaithful to the Torah—that is, other Jews, contemporaries, who the writer thinks should be."[24] The text likely presents a critique of the wicked oppressors who "proclaim the law but not actually observe it faithfully or correctly (see 108:2)."[25] Not only do they fail to observe the law, they also fail to interpret the prophets correctly (v. 6).

This reference to the prophets is significant in relation to our concern for the social context of the Eschatological Admonition. Firstly, the prophetic tradition implied by the term is important for both the author's addressees and their opponents. This indicates that both the group behind the text and their persecutors share an interest in the prophets in contrast to other Jewish groups for whom only the Torah was valued.[26]

Secondly, as noted earlier, given the association of the author's descriptions of the opponents in terms that indirectly allude to the fallen angels tradition and their transgression of the cosmic order, the author of the Eschatological Admonition sees the opponents as lacking the authority correctly to interpret the prophetic tradition.

Thirdly, given the designation of the righteous group as *teḥutan* who suffer at the hands of evil-doers, the socio-religious implication might indicate a conflict between the powerful rich and the poor where the former

---

23. Brown 1996:233.
24. Stuckenbruck 2007:697.
25. Stuckenbruck 2007:697.
26. Stuckenbruck 2007:712.

oppress the latter—a social evil the prophetic tradition decried. The wicked rich shame the righteous poor (cf. the honor/shame language in vv. 7, 11, 12 and an allusion to the "power of wrong doers" in v. 2). The Geʻez word for lowly, *teḥutan* in the sense of "being socially or economically disadvantaged or physically destitute" also appears in 1 Enoch 96:5 which portrays the humiliation of the righteous poor by the wicked who are wealthy.

In sum, the addressees are Jewish groups associated with the Enochic tradition and concerned with the keeping of the law and what they deem to be the faithful interpretation of the prophets. They see themselves as disadvantaged sufferers who are facing persecution for their faithfulness at the hands of the rich who have little regard for divine revelation through the prophets. This is the conflict situation the addressees face for being faithful. Although they love God, faithfully observe the law and the prophets and shun the world and its riches, they nevertheless suffer reproach, insult and abuse at the hand of the wicked who are more powerful than they. It is this situation, which is referred to in the text as the testing of their spirits, which the author mentions in v. 9.

In light of the adverse socio-religious context of his addressees, the author of Eschatological Admonition seeks to exhort his group to remain faithful even in the face of persecution by assuring them of the final calamities that await their oppressors. This is achieved through the notion of punishment for the wicked in the immediate afterlife, an idea that is not paralleled elsewhere in the Enochic corpus.[27] For their sinfulness and their persecution of the righteous, the wicked will be punished in the immediate afterlife in the following ways:

1. their names will removed from the "book of life and "books of the holy ones";[28]

2. their seed will be destroyed which, although it might refer to the ultimate destruction of sin, seems to echo the destruction of the fallen angels' progeny within the Enochic corpus (10:9, 12; 12:6; 22:7; 99:5); and

3. their spirits will be killed (v. 3).

Unique to this chapter, the killing of human spirits will not, however, result in their complete or final destruction, since the *ḥaṭəʼan* ("the sinners")

---

27. Stuckenbruck 2007:692.

28. Regarding textual difficulties associated with "the book of life" see Nickelsburg 2001:553 n.3a. The theme of removing sinful names from a heavenly book is found in various places with the Hebrew Bible (Ps 69:29 and Dan 12:1), in 1 Enoch (103:2), as well as the New Testament (Rev 3:5).

will continue to "cry out and lament in a deserted place that is invisible and burn in fire." Verses 4–6 go on to describe the fiery place of punishment as filled with weeping, groaning and pain. This is the final place of punishment of the spirits of the "godless." Knowing their ultimate vindication in the definite promise of deliverance, the addressees are encouraged to remain faithful in the face of persecution.

Two Social-Scientific Perspectives: Sectarianism and Liminality

A construal of the specific social situation and strategy of 1 Enoch 108 can be greatly assisted by the use of etic (that is informed outsider, or social-scientific) models. Two etic/social-scientific perspectives, in particular, are helpful in seeking to understand the situation of the addressees of 1 Enoch 108: sectarianism and liminality.

Sectarianism

Social-scientific perspectives on sectarianism have proved useful in the analysis of biblical and extra-biblical texts since Wayne Meeks inaugurated the enterprise in 1972.[29] The (mainly sociological) theory of sectarianism has been explained and applied by John Elliott and Philip Esler.[30] Elliott has written on the movement of a group from a "faction" to a sect and Esler on the movement from "reform movement" to sect.[31] In either case, we witness increasing tension between the group and the particular body from which it sprang or with the world at large.

Bryan Wilson usefully developed the idea that a sect's tension with the wider world could be theorised into seven types.[32] It should be remembered that typologies are not sets of pigeon-holes into which data is slotted, but tools for comparison, so that any given phenomenon may be comparable with more than one type. Nevertheless, one of Wilson's types, "introversionism,"[33] is easily comparable with the situation in 1 Enoch 108. Here the world is seen as irredeemably evil and salvation is to be attained by the fullest possible withdrawal from it. As a social response, this might

---

29. Meeks 1972.
30. Elliott 2005; and 1987.
31. Elliott 1995; and Esler 1987:65–70.
32. Wilson 1975:9–30.
33. Wilson 1975:23–24.

entail the establishment of "a separated community preoccupied with its own means of insulation from wider society."[34] Associated with a separate life can be "the quiet fulfillment of religious obligations."[35] Its proponents see salvation as a present endeavor, while also looking forward to its realization in the future. This salvation is only for those who belong to the ingroup. Social-scientific research indicates the context of tension and even conflict with the world as a typical feature of the emergence of sects.[36] Although the data of 1 Enoch 108 does not support a complete dissociation of the *teḥutan* group from other Jews, the initial stage of a protest group in tension with those who exhibit lax attitudes to the Torah and the prophets and moral behavior and that views itself as an elite community favored with special revelation reveals the initial stages of sect formation in an introversionist mode.

As shown in the previous section, the picture portrayed by 1 Enoch 108 is that of a pious ingroup loyal to the Torah and the prophets. The indication that their opponents are also cognizant of the prophets and the general description of them indicates an overarching Jewish identity embracing ingroup and outgroup. Therefore, the pious group can be viewed as a late mid/late first century faction (Elliott) or reform movement (Esler) within the Jewish people who are persecuted for fidelity to YHWH by other Jewish groups and who seem to channel divine revelation through the prophetic tradition—perhaps indicating the beginnings of the pious group's ideological separation.

That the group is in the process of religious or ideological dissociation from its parent body comes out in the text's treatment of the judgment of the wicked oppressors. In contrast to the prophetic literature of the Hebrew Bible, the sinners are no longer covenanters of YHWH's salvation—their destruction is not conditional but emphatically certain. By stating that their "spirits will be killed" (v. 2), the author draws a vivid image of their destruction in terms that echo the destruction of the fallen angels. The honors, divine favour, and tradition associated with the remnant of Israel are attributed to the addressees. In light of these observations, this group can be understood as a nascent Jewish sect of the *anawim* associated with the Enoch tradition in the first century CE.

Writing of 1 Peter, where the sectarian status of the group addressed is well-developed, Elliott has suggested that to maintain the separatist attitude exhibited by the group against the world, the author attempts to assure

---

34. Wilson 1975:24.
35. Wilson 1975:396.
36. Elliott 2005:80.

"collective identity, internal social cohesion and ideological commitment."[37] These are also present in 1 Enoch 108. The first of these, collective identity, is affirmed through the identification of the group as *teḥutan* who were found to be pure in spirit and therefore morally superior over outgroups identified as sinners. Their privileged status is further alluded to in the eschatological reward that awaits them.

Secondly, to equip their respective addressees to face the persecution they are suffering in the society, the author skillfully encourages internal solidarity through a call to shun evil, implicitly, by using the sinners as a negative example; and an acceptance of their socially ascribed status. Furthermore, images such as "*teḥutan*" or "righteous" in 1 Enoch 108, like the words "holy" or "elect of God" in 1 Peter that inform identity, serve as "interpretive grids through which [the group] sees reality and through which [members] contemplate responsibilities and actions."[38] For example, the Enochic author's implicit paraenetic agenda, which serves to promote internal solidarity via a common ethical aim, can be gleaned from the use of identity-informing images of his addressees as the generation of light, righteous, and faithful. Such an agenda is comparable with the "the quiet fulfillment of religious obligations" that, as noted above, Wilson points out can characterize introversionist groups.

Thirdly, the author of 1 Enoch 108 encourages his addressees' ideological commitment to God in the face of persecution by providing: (1) a rational for suffering as a necessary "testing" by God so as to ascertain the necessary in-group quality of purity, that is, suffering as a test of fidelity (v. 9); and (2) an assurance of salvation and reward for those who will persevere.

Therefore, in the Eschatological Admonition, the unfortunate condition the pious find themselves in has a silver lining—they are poor and rejected but poor they are to remain for it is those who reject this world and are rejected by the world for the sake of purity that will find favor and acceptance by God.

In sum, in line with Bryan Wilson's sociology of sectarianism, the Eschatological Admonition is intelligible as having an "introversionist" approach of a nascent sect to outgroups which is evident from the document's strong focus on withdrawal from the world and its riches and encouragement of a separate way of life as well as fulfillment of ethical and religious obligations where the certainty of salvation is posited.[39]

---

37. Elliott 2005:80.

38. Dryden 2006:140.

39. Wilson 1975:23–24, 396, quoted in Esler 1994:114 and 2014:128.

Liminality

My second social-scientific/etic perspective for interpreting the emic data of 1 Enoch 108 is that of liminality. The notion of liminality stems from Arnold van Gennep's *The Rites of Passage*, first published in 1909. Put simply, Van Gennep divided rites of passage into three stages: preliminary, liminal and post-liminal. This theory was actively taken up in a number of works by anthropologist Victor Turner, who showed particular interest in the liminal or threshold stage, when the participants were "on the threshold" (*limen*), betwixt and between their old way of life and the one they were about to enter.[40] Also important for Turner were the relationships between participants during the transitional stage, when hierarchical structures, for example, tended to break down and they have no status, property or insignia and their behavior is passive and humble. They must accept arbitrary punishment without complaint.[41] He described this condition as *communitas*, where they "develop an intense comradeship and egalitarianism."[42] *Communitas* can be also described as a state of "social relationship or sentiment arising between people who experience certain crucial events—for example, moments of liminality or pilgrimage—together. This bond temporarily unites them in a way that is outside normal social structure."[43] Liminal phenomena are characterized by "the blend they offer of lowliness and sacredness, of homogeneity and comradeship."[44]

This social-scientific model is relevant to 1 Enoch 108 in the following way. The author's response to this situation assumes specific social dynamics and a social aim that are presupposed by the document.[45] On the one hand, the picture portrayed by 1 Enoch 108 is that of a lowly group that is not yet dissociated from its oppressors. Significant here is the lack of

---

40. Turner 1967:93–111; and Turner 1969.
41. Turner 1969:95.
42. Turner 1969:95.
43. See Morris 2012:45.
44. Turner 1969:96.

45. To access this presupposition in a more detailed analysis than this essay can offer and expressed in relation to 1 Peter but with equal relevance to 1 Enoch 108, see Elliott 1986. Elliott notes elsewhere (1993:79) that one would need to "examine further social and cultural features of the environment that are encoded in the text [including the social conditions of Jews in piety movements in Palestine and the diaspora]; conventional concerns regarding social order, status and roles; the social scripts regulating relations in the civic, public sphere (in-groups and out-groups); . . . modes of social interaction; . . . modes of internal group governance; . . . and encoded aspects of the culture, including the values and scripts concerning honour and shame; [as well as] attitudes toward suffering and physical discipline."

evidence in the text for understanding itself as religiously or ideologically separated from the group that opposes it. The lack of a theological manifesto or a deliberation on points of ideological difference with outgroups thus indicates that this pious group has not completely dissociated itself from the parent group.

On the other hand, though not complete, what seem to be the beginnings of the pious group's social as well as ideological dissociation is indicated, for example, in the critique against the oppressors' religiosity, that is, lax attitude towards the Torah and a charge that they misappropriate divine revelation through the prophets.

Taking both of these features of the group behind 1 Enoch 108 into account, one can surmise that the process of identity distinction has begun. And the group is at an "in-between" or a "neither here nor there" state that can be referred to as one of liminality following Turner.[46]

Although it is not described in detail or fully embraced precisely because of the group's liminal phase, the group's changed worldview is oriented around Torah observance, faithful appropriation of the prophetic tradition, and a novel eschatological view of reward and punishment that draws upon earlier Enochic traditions. The initial stage of a liminal group that no longer identifies itself with the status quo is also evident from the group's critique of lax attitudes to moral behavior. The new religious reality on whose threshold the *anawim* stand, is implicitly described in antithesis to the charges brought against the wicked.

Furthermore, this *anawim* group's liminal phase is indicated by the author's identification of the addressees as those favored with special revelation because they are pure in spirit and therefore morally superior to outgroups which are in contrast identified as sinners. Their position is further underlined in the eschatological reward that awaits the addressees.

In order to help his addressees face their persecution, the author of 1 Enoch 108 skillfully encourages his liminal group to persist in piety and overcome the temptation of retaliation by urging them to shun evil. This is done implicitly by using the sinners as a negative example to be avoided. The writer does this positively by employing constructions of a communal self-identity for his addressees through identity-informing images such as *teḥutan*, *ṣadəḳan* ("righteous"), generation of light, etc. (vv. 1b-2 and 7-9). These serve as the "interpretive grids through which [the group] sees reality and through which [members] contemplate responsibilities and actions."[47] This is also made clear in the narrator's implicit paraenesis for his liminal

---

46. Turner 1967:93–111; and Turner 1969:94–130.
47. Dryden 2006:140.

group which are hidden in characterizations for the righteous, which "taken together, . . . function implicitly as exhortations to readers who, if they are pious, should recognize themselves in them and embrace them within their self-understanding."[48]

The Enochic *andəmta*[49] picks up on this implicit situational strategy used by the author of 1 Enoch 108 to urge his readers against a response of retaliation or conformity:

> Those who are faithful will receive the ultimate reward of their faith. The faithful congregation will receive compensation for good character and faith in the Kingdom of God, in heaven, should they continue in works of righteousness and in keeping the Ten Commandments. God's justice is righteous; they will shine. (42:14)[50]

In sum, the author of Eschatological Admonition encourages his addressees' ideological commitment to God in the face of persecution by placing his addressees in the long tradition of YHWH's pious poor and constructing for them a liminal identity that sees suffering and oppression as a transient reality through which they must live before being glorified in the immediate afterlife. First Enoch 108 thus encourages the addressees' ideological commitment to God while living in this liminal phase marked by suffering and persecution by providing: (1) the *anawim* framework as the basis for their honored status before God (thereby countering their shameful status as the reviled and humiliated), (2) a rationale for suffering as a necessary "testing" by God, that is, suffering as a test of fidelity, (3) an assurance of salvation and reward, and (4) hope of vindication.[51]

Liminality for Turner extends well beyond the bounds of ritual "to any condition outside, or on the peripheries of, everyday life."[52] This is to say, for Turner, this transition phase is a pervasive aspect of life, affecting not

---

48. Stuckenbruck 2007:719.

49. The *andəmta* denotes the Amharic Ethiopian commentary tradition; see Chapter 3 in this volume, by Ralph Lee, in this volume for an explanation.

50. My translation from Anonymous 2003 EC.

51. These four points can also be said to apply to the addressees of the epistle of 1 Peter which begins its response to the situation of suffering and persecution by identifying the liminal nature of Christ-movement identity. The author then proceeds to prescribe how the oppressed liminal community—composed of both neophytes and veterans—is to live out its identity among its oppressors from outside the movement. Resolution is achieved when Christ is depicted as the sufferer *par excellence* who suffered for a little while but was later glorified.

52. Turner 1969:132–34.

only individuals but also groups.⁵³ Persons in the liminal phase are "neither here nor there; they are betwixt and between the positions assigned and arrayed by law, custom, convention, and ceremonial," they are paradoxically characterised as "being *both* this *and* that."⁵⁴

While literal liminality signifies actual transition from one social condition to another, metaphoric liminality indicates the representation of liminality through, for example, imagery of birth or death. Liminality, both literal and metaphoric, can be institutionalized by employing symbols of marginalization, outsider-hood and social inferiority to construct an *communitas*-type identity for a given community and to characterize internal and external relations for that community.⁵⁵

Summary of Sectarian and Liminal Approaches

Both of these social-scientific approaches, sectarianism and liminality, offer comparative, etic perspectives that help us make sense of the emic data to be found in 1 Enoch 108. They do this by allowing us to interrogate the data in comparable frameworks of meaning, which is a heuristic exercise, and also by assisting us to make sense of the answers the text provides to such questioning. The latter aspect may be described as "drawing lines between the dots." The time has now come to move from this historical dimension of this essay, its concern with the alterity of 1 Enoch 108, to consider what it might have to say to us, theologically, in the present.

Towards a Theology of Persecution

In 1 Enoch 108 persecution is identified by: (1) social/cultural estrangement (vv. 7, 10); (2) verbal and physical abuse (v. 10); (3) unjust treatment (vv. 3, 6) and (4) its occurrence because of a new way of life or as a result of loving God (vv. 8, 10, 12). In helping his addressees cope with persecution, the author describes suffering as something meted out by God for the testing of faith (v. 9) and therefore inherently beneficial.

---

53. Turner 1969:133.

54. Turner 1969:95.

55. Turner 1969:133–46. In 1 Peter "the directives for intracommunity relations presuppose acceptance of the letter's construction of Christian communal self-identity" just as institutionalized liminality leads to normative communities; so Bechtler 1998: 125.

The conflictual situation of the addressees corresponds with the reality many Christians face today.[56] In Nigeria, for example, Christians are routinely beaten or killed by militant Muslims.[57] Christians are also increasingly being persecuted in the Middle East by ISIS and other radical Muslims as well as in countries such as China and Eritrea.[58] Interacting with the thoughts of our Enochic author and attempting to hear his voice for our present situation accords with the idea that human persons should be understood relationally as beings in communication and communion. As Catherine LaCugna notes, the human person can be understood as being "created in the image of the relational God and gradually . . . being perfected in that image (*theōsis*), making more and more real the communion of all creations with one another."[59] In communion with the author, we are thus justified in attempting to discern his wisdom for the persecuted Body of Christ.

Regarding the author of 1 Enoch 108 as being in communion with present day Christians finds further legitimation when one takes into account the canonical or at least quasi-canonical status of 1 Enoch within the Ethiopian Orthodox *Tewahǝdo* Church,[60] and within the living tradition of its nearly 32 million members.[61] Recognizing this entails respect for the other, the Enochic author and the tradition of brothers and sisters in Christ, which becomes an important notion with ethical implications. In this sense we can conceive of the author of 1 Enoch 108, though long dead, as founding a legacy that continues to inform the identity of Orthodox Christians in Ethiopia. The author of the text can also be considered as being present in the collective memory and life of a particular Christian community and nourishing its identity.[62] According to Esler, this memorialization route will enable us to "experience the shock of unexpected meanings that may be applicable to our own situations or which we must decide, exercising critical discernment, have little or no place" among our own Christian traditions or twenty-first century contexts.[63] Thus, in fellowship with Christian brothers and sisters for whom 1 Enoch embodies the Word of God, we read chapter 108 in its first century context within the framework of communion and dialogue with its author.

---

56. See Marshall 1998 and 200.
57. See for example Boer 2003; Minchakpu 2004; and Nyberg 2004.
58. See Marlin 2015; and Rubin 2014.
59. LaCugna 1992:292; Esler 2005:38–66, 276.
60. See Baynes 2012 and Stuckenbruck 2013.
61. Federal Democratic Republic of Ethiopia Population Census Commission 2008:17.
62. Esler 2005:278.
63. Esler 2005:278.

In crafting a contemporary theology of persecution that seeks to understand and respond to contemporary incidents of religious persecution, the specific socio-cultural, historical and theological contexts of persecution texts will need to be investigated. In our case, the *anawim* ideology, understood in both sectarian and liminal terms, can serve to provide the setting within which we can evaluate the Enochic author's interpretation of persecution. Such a comparison of past and modern contexts enables us to proceed to the task of appropriating the author's concern to our present situation.[64] When it comes to 1 Enoch 108, the author's central concern with placing his addressees in the religious community of sufferers and reinterpreting persecution as an occasion for growth can provide insights to contemporary theories of post-traumatic growth and mechanisms for coping with persecution.

The response to persecution outlined in 1 Enoch 108 does indeed mesh with what social scientists have identified as styles of religious coping with persecution such as the mechanism of "surrender,"[65] where the persecuted actively relinquishes her will to the outworking of God's will; this is in line with our Enochic author's concern with guarding his addressees against choosing retaliation as a response to suffering because persecution is in accordance with the will of God (cf. v. 9). The Enochic author's hidden paraenesis which is aimed at helping his addressees meet suffering head on and his focus on drawing out the benefits of their suffering also cohere with theories of post-traumatic growth which link the cognitive, relational, existential and spiritual changes brought on by trauma with growth.[66]

Furthermore, by employing identity-forming images that reinforce a common ingroup identity in opposition to the persecuting outgroups the author communicates another coping mechanism. One of the ways by means of which survivors of persecution overcome the temptation to conform so as to ease suffering is through embracing their new-found privileged identities. According to a study done on Christians persecuted in China, a key coping mechanism is their newly acquired Christian belief system and a religious identity that sees suffering as an integral consequence of Christian piety and as an occasion for divine triumph and future glory.[67]

From a theological perspective, Thomas Schirrmacher also argues for the need to stress in our theology of persecution the fact that the oppressed stand in a long tradition of God-fearing people whose persecution is recounted in both the Old and New Testaments.[68] As we have seen above, the

---

64. Esler 2005.
65. Wong-McDonald and Gorsuch 2000.
66. Tedeschi and Calhoun 2004.
67. Ting and Watson 2007.
68. Schirrmacher 2010:289.

author of 1 Enoch 108 does precisely this—he encourages his persecuted addressees by placing them in the *anawim* tradition that sees and interprets the persecution of the faithful as standing in continuity with the pious people of God.[69]

The Enochic author's elaborate treatment of impending judgment on oppressors and the condemnation of their acts as sin as well as the portrayal of the divine as judge is likely to speak to any modern occasion of religious persecution. The task of hearing the voice of 1 Enoch 108 in conflictual situations within the twenty-first century is also aided by the implicit resistance against hegemony and domination communicated through its apocalyptic genre with its assertions that "God governs time, that history unfolds according to God's plan, and that temporal powers are finite and transient."[70]

This is brought out by the text's narrative element of "point of view" which is communicated through an angelic being who relays "behind the scene" glimpses of the narrative world's dramatic unfolding of events. When the righteous *anawim* are being persecuted, it might seem that for the foreseeable future the winners are the powerful oppressors. But by employing the divine point of view, the author asserts that God, not the oppressors are in control - the persecution is transient and has taken place only because God has allowed it. Again that God is supreme over the persecutors is communicated through the narration of the heavenly inscription and the description of the judgment that awaits the sinners (vv. 3, 7). Verses 4–15 therefore emphatically denote that temporal powers are finite and that history unfolds in God's time.

In his teaching about the nature of religious life in a hostile world, the author of 1 Enoch 108 can thus be brought into dialogue with situations of persecution at times and places different from the social world of first-century Palestine. Indeed attempts to construct modern theologies of suffering can benefit from directly accessing the author of 1 Enoch 108 "so that, in spite of cultural and temporal distance, *cor ad cor loquitur*—'heart speaks to heart.'"[71]

---

69. See the persecution theology Scott Cunningham (1997) draws out from Luke-Acts.

70. See Portier-Young (2014:146), who identifies Daniel, the Apocalypse of Weeks (1 Enoch 93:1–10; 91:11–17) and the Book of Dreams (1 Enoch 83–90) as the earliest extant historical apocalypses. See also Portier-Young 2011:13–27.

71. Esler 2005:282 (taking up a favorite saying of St John Henry Newman).

11

Deus Victor

The Nature and Defeat of Evil in the Book of the Watchers (1 Enoch 1–36)

Philip F. Esler

The ancient Israelite work known as 1 Enoch is generally regarded as an Old Testament text by the Ethiopian and Eritrean Orthodox Churches. 1 Enoch has a continuous and honorable tradition of use among Ethiopian Christians since the fifth or sixth centuries CE when it was first translated into Ge'ez from Greek. This essay is aimed at demonstrating that the Book of the Watchers (1 Enoch 1–36) has an important theological contribution to make in our understanding of evil and the way in which God has dealt and will deal with it.[1]

Evil as the Central Problem in Theology

It has been said that all theology is a grappling with the problem of evil.[2] It would be more accurate to say that all theology is a grappling with the prob-

---

1. I gratefully acknowledge assistance received in the preparation of this essay from Dr Dee Carter, formerly of the University of Gloucestershire, and Professors Alan Torrance and Trevor Hart from the University of St Andrews. As far as Professor Torrance is concerned, this is one of many times over some fifteen years that I have greatly profited from theological conversations with him.

2. Mannion 2007:19, with reference to Lowe 1993.

lem of evil while insisting on the existence of God. For many philosophers, however, the reality of evil and the existence of God are incompatible. The problem has been set out by Nelson Pike like this: "If God exists, how can evils be explained? For an omnipotent being would have the power to prevent any and all evils if it wanted to; an omniscient being would know all about them; and a perfectly good being would want to prevent/eliminate all the evils it could. Thus, it seems, if God existed, and were omnipotent, omniscient, and perfectly good, there would be no evils."[3]

David Hume used the existence of evil in the world as positive proof of the non-existence of God.[4] In an influential essay published in 1990, the neo-Humean philosopher J. L. Mackie argued that not only did religious beliefs lack rational support but that they were positively irrational when confronted with the reality of evil.[5] While such philosophical attacks on God's existence have provoked strong reactions from other philosophers and theologians,[6] no one should doubt that this whole question of the co-existence of evil and God lies at the heart of theology and also of much human experience.

The very first point to be made about the significance of 1 Enoch 1–36 for contemporary theology is that its central interest lies precisely in this question of the terrible evils that affect humanity and what God has done and will do about them. The overall message of the book is an optimistic one: it begins with a blessing and message for those who will be present on the day of tribulation (vv. 1–3), which is followed soon after by a proleptic description of the theophanic arrival of God as warrior-king with his angelic war-band, apparently in the last days, to judge all and to destroy the wicked for their wicked deeds and for the proud and hard words they have spoken against him (vv. 4–9). Yet the text certainly does not present this as a quick or easy solution. For long eons evil will walk the earth among human beings—working death, havoc, misery and despair amongst them—and will only be partially dealt with by God before the final consummation.

The second respect in which 1 Enoch 1–36 speaks so directly to the experience of our age and to our theological reflection on it consists of its preoccupation with violence as the primary evil that humans face. In *Theology and Difference: The Wound of Reason*, Walter Lowe, writing in 1993, said this:

> Theology in our century was born amidst the darkness of war.
> It has been struggling ever since to emerge from the shadow

---

3. Pike 1964; cited by Adams 1999:7.

4. David Hume: "Is [God] willing to prevent evil, but not able? then is he impotent. Is he able, but not willing? then is he malevolent. Is he both able and willing? whence then is evil?" (Hume 1996 [1779]:261)

5. Mackie 1990.

6. See, for example, Adams 1999.

of mass violence cast by 'the Great War' and the events which followed in its wake. In the nineteenth century experience had become the touchstone for doing theology. With the twentieth century experience became unbearable. The sea of violence had, in Theodor Adorno's words, 'breached the barrier against stimuli beneath which experience, the lag between healing oblivion and healing recollection, forms.' For experience to crystallize as experience, there is required a certain psychic space. In the century of total war that space collapsed.[7]

The twenty-first century has not yet brought total war but it has brought numerous serious conflicts, including those of an inter-ethnic nature and those involving Islamic extremists bent on waging "jihad" with maximum killing and violence in forms that, in some cases, have not been seen for centuries. I first typed these words on 4th February 2015, the day after the world learned via the Web that some weeks previously members of Isis in Syria had doused a captured Jordanian pilot in petrol, locked him in a cage and set him alight. It should be noted that this act stiffened Jordanian resolution to oppose and defeat Isis.

The Phenomenology of Evil in the Book of the Watchers

"Dramatic Time" and "Narrative Time" in the Text

To appreciate the nature of evil in the Book of the Watchers in a manner that is sensitive to the structure of the work, it is useful to draw a distinction between "dramatic time" and "narrative time." Here "dramatic time" refers to the time during which the plot of the work, involving the secession of the Watchers from heaven and the description of Enoch's activities, takes place. "Narrative time," on the other hand, means the (much larger) sweep of time that embraces all of the events referred to in the drama of the Watchers and Enoch, which actually extend from the creation to the period of the final judgment (and beyond).[8] The following is a summary of the main events under both headings. It should be noted that the text does not always describe events in strictly chronological order, thus the Watchers descend to earth in 1 Enoch 6 (loosely based on Gen 6:1–4),[9] whereas it is not until 1 Enoch 12 that we hear that "before these things" Enoch was

---

7. Lowe 1993:1–2.

8. In Chapter 10 Sofanit Abebe encapsulates much the same distinction using the expressions "referential series," roughly equivalent to narrative time, and "plotted series," roughly equivalent to dramatic time,

9. On the relationship between the Watchers and Gen 6:1–4, see Wright 2013 and Seeman 2014.

taken (i. e. to heaven) which relates to an earlier period (of Gen 5:24). This is one of several signs in the text that the author well understands the broad chronological course of universal and Israelite history, even though he is capable of jumping from one time to another. A second indication of this comes later in the text, in 1 Enoch 26, where the angel accompanying him shows Enoch the site of Jerusalem long before a city had been dwelt there, as was appropriate, given Enoch's position in the remote past as the seventh patriarch. Accordingly, I must strongly demur from Paolo Sacchi's suggestion that "The author clearly uses scripture and history without attending to their chronological aspect. 'Before' and 'after' have no meaning for him."[10] The particular significance of my disagreement with Sacchi on this issue will appear below.

Dramatic Time	Narrative Time
	The creation ("the beginning") (1 Enoch 2:2)
	The refusal of the stars to rise (1 Enoch 18:13–16)[11]
	Expulsion of Adam and Eve from the Garden (1 Enoch 32:6)
	Cain murders Abel (1 Enoch 22:5–7)
Enoch is taken and is with God (= Gen. 5:24) and is with the watchers and the holy ones (12:1–2)[12]	
Descent of the Watchers (in the days of Jared)[13] (1 Enoch 6; cf. Gen 6:1–4)	

10. Sacchi 1990:55.

11. The date for this mysterious event is not mentioned; perhaps the Enochic scribes envisaged it happening after the expulsion of Adam and Eve from the Garden, or even after Cain's murder of Abel, but this seems less likely than that it preceded these events. Although Nickelsburg (2001:288–89) suggests this is a variant of the myth of the Watchers, the text conveys the impression of an entirely different event.

12. Note that, according to Gen 5:21–24, Enoch fathered Methuselah when he was 65, and thereafter "walked with God" for 300 years, at which time "he was not, for God took him," when he was thus 365 years old (having attained, as it were, a year of years).

13. For this dating, see 1 Enoch 6:6. Note that analysis of the geneaologies in Genesis 5 and the further dates given in Gen 9:28–29 shows that Noah was some 370 years old when Jared, his great, great grandfather, died. About 130 years later Noah began to have his sons (Shem, Ham and Japhet) and the flood occurred some 200 years after Jared's death. Bringing the material in 1 Enoch together with the dates in Genesis means that the events of Gen 6:1–4 must, in the mind of the Enochic author, have begun at least a hundred years before the birth of Noah's first son (to have occurred in the days of Jared).

Dramatic Time	Narrative Time
The Watchers take wives and teach them sorcery, charms and the cutting of roots and plants. The women produce giants, who beget Nephilim. The giants kill men and the earth brings accusation (1 Enoch 7)	
The secrets the Watchers reveal. As men perish, the cry goes up to heaven (1 Enoch 8)	
The four Archangels intervene with God on behalf of the earth (1 Enoch 9)	
God sends the four Archangels to sort things out on earth (1 Enoch 10–11)	
Good Watchers instruct Enoch to go and tell the Watchers on earth what is about to happen to them (1 Enoch 12–13:2)	
Enoch goes to them and they commission him to petition God on their behalf (1 Enoch 13:3–7)	
Enoch has a vision and reprimands the Watchers (1 Enoch 13:8)	
Enoch tells them that their petition will not be granted (1 Enoch 14:1–7)	
Enoch's ascent to heaven (1 Enoch 14:8–24)	
God sends Enoch back to the Watchers with the news of their judgment (1 Enoch 15:1–16:4)	
	Noah is warned, the Watchers are imprisoned and the giants killed as predicted will happen in 1 Enoch 10 but not described in the text.
Enoch's journeys (1 Enoch 17–36): we know these occur after the events predicted in 1 Enoch 10–11 have occurred since Enoch sees the imprisoned Watchers (1 Enoch 19:1; 21:7–10)	
	The distant generation (1:2)
	The day of tribulation (1:1)
	God will "come forth from his dwelling" (1 Enoch 1:4–9)

The Anatomy and Development of Evil in 1 Enoch 1–36

What type of evil does the author of 1 Enoch 1–36 have in mind? This is a text that categorizes human beings into polar opposites: the righteous (δίκαιοι) and chosen (ἐκλεκτοί) on the one hand, and the enemies (ἐχθροί), wicked (ἀσεβεῖς) and sinners (ἁμαρτωλοί) on the other. The former will inherit the earth, but for the latter there will be no salvation (5:6). Such a stark differentiation reflects a powerfully felt differentiation of ingroup vis-à-vis outgroup. Yet the ethnic dimension to this distinction that is so strongly expressed in the Animal Apocalypse (85–90) is not much felt here. Evil appears in the opening chapter in the form of "wicked deeds" (ἔργα τῆς ἀσεβείας) and "hard words" (σκληροὶ λόγοι) spoken by sinners against God (1:9). Another formulation of evil, in 1 Enoch 5:4, is that it involves acting against God's commandments (ἐντολαί), speaking proud and hard words with an unclean mouth against Him and being hard of heart.

When one turns to specifics, it is helpful to consider the way that sins are presented within narrative, not dramatic time. This will reveal that the first sin on earth was committed by a human being, not an angel, and it was a sin of violence. At one point on his journeying Raphael shows Enoch a mountain in which are four hollow places, three dark and one illuminated and with a fountain of water, intended to contain "spirits of the souls of the dead" until the day of judgment (1 Enoch 22:1–4). There Enoch sees "the spirit of a dead man making suit" and his lamentation went up to heaven (1 Enoch 22:5). Raphael replies to his question as to the identity of this person as follows:

> This is the spirit that went forth from Abel, whom Cain his brother murdered. And Abel makes a petition (ἐντυγκάνει; *yesakki*) about him until his seed perishes from the face of the earth, and his seed is obliterated from the seed of men. (1 Enoch 22:7)[14]

Then Raphael answers a question from Enoch about the reason for the four hollows, explaining (to summarize rather contradictory material)[15] that the illuminated hollow with the fountain is for the spirits of the righteous, and the other three are for sinners.

While it is often assumed that vv. 5–7 are presenting Abel as the first martyr, this view only developed after 1 Enoch 1–36 and the real point of the passage, as Nickelsburg notes, is to emphasize "not the righteousness of those who have been murdered, but the violence of their murderers and the

---

14. Nickelsburg 2001:300 (modified).
15. For the difficulties, see Nickelsburg 2001:302–3.

certain judgment that will befall them."[16] In fact, Cain is being presented as the prototypical murderer, especially since earlier in the text (but after the time of Cain), in 1 Enoch 9, mention is made of other "souls of men" who, using the same verb, "make a petition" (ἐντυγχάνουσιν; *yesakkeyu*; v. 3) and of the "spirits of the souls of men who have died" and "who make a petition" (ἐντυγχάνουσιν; *yesakkeyu*; v. 10) at a time when the blood of men is shed on the earth (v.9). Cain must be understood, therefore, as the prototypical evil-doer on the earth, the first person to engage in what for the Enochic scribe is the worst kind of evil—acts of violence, in the case of Cain, and by necessary implication, others after him, homicidal violence. Abel is the first, of many, to petition heaven on account of his murder.

An important consequence of this is that the frequently repeated view that the fall of the Watchers describes the origin of evil on earth and that this means that evil must be attributed to evil spirits and not to human beings is mistaken. Paolo Sacchi, for example, expresses this view,[17] while seeking to get around the reference to Cain's murder of Abel in 1 Enoch by arguing, as noted above, that there is no sense of chronological order in the text. But such order does exist and while the Watchers do bring ruinous evil upon the earth, it is a human being, Cain, and not a spirit, who invents evil, in the form of violent fratricide.

It is instructive to contrast the way Adam and Eve are presented in the Book of the Watchers. Toward the end of his cosmic journeys Enoch comes to the "paradise of righteousness" in which grows the tree of wisdom, "whose fruit the holy ones eat and learn great wisdom (1 Enoch 32:3)." Gabriel explains as follows:

> This is the tree of wisdom from which your father of old and *your mother of old* (אמך רבתא), who were before you, ate and learned wisdom. And their eyes were opened, and they knew *that they were naked* (די ערטליין), and they were driven from the garden. (1 Enoch 32:6)[18]

This translation depends upon the Ethiopic and Aramaic fragments (which survive for the words in italics).[19] Although the passage summarizes major

---

16. Nickelsburg 2001:306.

17. Sacchi 1990:22, 50, 54, 57 and 83.

18. ET Nickelsburg and VanderKam 2012:48; I have inserted the Aramaic from Milik 1976:357.

19. The Ethiopic here translates a different Greek translation from that found in Akhmin papyrus, since at this point it has simply, "This is the tree of knowledge, from which your father ate" (Τοῦτο τὸ δένδρον φρονήσεως ἐξ οὗ ἔφαγεν ὁ πατήρ σου; see Black 1970:36 and Charles 1906:75).

points in Gen 3:8–24, including the fact that "they were driven from the garden" (*tasaddu 'em-gannat*), this is a particularly restrained description of Adam and Eve eating from the tree. Moreover, there is no sense in which their actions, unlike those of Cain, in any way inaugurate or influence later forms of human evil. We are a very long way indeed from any idea of "original sin," from the view of Augustine that Adam and Eve were, in their sin, "human beings with the power fundamentally to harm all other human beings."[20]

That the Enochic scribes regarded Cain, and not Adam and Eve, as the originator of human evil, is confirmed in a later section of 1 Enoch, the Animal Apocalypse (Chapters 85–90). This text begins its narrative (in which biblical figures and ethnic groups are described under the guise of animals) with Enoch speaking as follows:

> Before I took your mother Edna (as my wife), I saw in a vision on my bed, and look, a bull came forth from the earth, and that bull was white. And after it a young heifer came forth. And with her two bull calves came forth; one of them was black, and one was red. And that black calf struck the red one and †pursued it over the earth.†[21] And from then on I could not see that red calf. (1 Enoch 85:3–4)[22]

Here the white bull is Adam, the heifer is Eve, the black calf Abel and the red one Cain. Again, the Enochic author says nothing adverse to Adam and Eve, and merely records their creation and Eve's giving birth to two sons. But of Cain he records that "he struck" (*gwad'a*) Abel so that he was no longer seen, meaning dead. In this later Enochic text, therefore, Cain is also seen as the prototypical human sinner and, once again, the prototypical sin is violence.

The next evil in chronological order is that of the Watchers desiring women and wanting to beget children from them (6:2).[23] Their leader recognizes this as a great sin (6:3). When the Watchers do this, they are said to "defile" (μιαίνεσθαι) themselves. The Watchers also impart knowledge to human beings. First we learn in general of their teaching of sorcery and charms, and the cutting of roots and plants (7:1) and later there is a list of which Watcher taught what: 8:1–3. After the account of Asael's teaching

---

20. Couenhoven 2005:381. That Augustine enhanced the significance of the sin of Adam and Eve is now widely recognized; which is not to say that there is not some support for his views in Paul.

21. The text seems confused here, since the pursuit should probably precede the striking: see Nickelsburg and VanderKam 2012:119.

22. ET Nickelsburg and VanderKam 2012:119–20.

23. On the tradition of the Watchers, see Wright 2013.

(curiously, concerning instruments of war, gold work, and silver work for women's bracelets and ornaments, and antimony, eye paint, precious stones and dyes), we are told that the sons of men made them for themselves and for their daughters, that they transgressed and led the holy ones astray. This last element seems to reflect a tradition that it was the women themselves who led the Watchers astray, a tradition in tension with the main thrust of the text, that the Watchers descended to earth with the purpose of taking human wives.[24] Consequently there was godlessness on earth and they made their ways desolate (8:1-2).

But the true horror of the Watchers' secession from heaven emerges only in the actions of their progeny, the giants to which their wives give birth:

> And the giants began to kill men and to devour them. And they began to sin against the birds and beasts and the creeping things and the fish, and to devour one another's flesh. And they drank the blood (7:4-5).[25]

The core of the evil they produce is violence, to the extent of killing and then eating human beings, the creatures of the earth and even themselves. Thus violence, initiated by Cain, re-appears in a most extreme form with the giants. So it is that when Michael, Sariel, Raphael and Gabriel look down from heaven upon earth they see much bloodshed, as (in some versions but not all) the earth is filled with godlessness and violence (9:1). They then complain to God that Asael has taught all "iniquities" ($\dot{\alpha}\delta\iota\varkappa\dot{\iota}\alpha\iota$) on earth and has revealed the eternal mysteries that are in heaven (9:6). The Watchers who took wives have defiled themselves with them and revealed to them all sins, as well as (in two versions) how to make hate-inducing charms (9:8). The whole earth is filled with iniquity (9:9).

It is to such at world that God will send his archangels, as predicted in 1 Enoch 10-11, although the process itself is not described, with Enoch's journeys around the cosmos occurring only after it has happened. But the critical thing to observe is that the actions the archangels take, to imprison the Watchers and kill their murderous progeny, the giants, are expressly not a permanent solution to the problem of evil on earth. In particular, we learn that the earth will continue to be plagued by evil spirits. Thus, in his address to Enoch in Chapter 15 God says at one point, in speaking about the giants:

> The spirits that have gone forth from the body of their flesh are evil spirits, for from humans they came into being, and from the

---

24. See Nickelsburg 2001:195-96.
25. ET Nickelsburg and VanderKam 2012:25.

holy watchers was the origin of their creation. Evil spirits they will be on the earth, and evil spirits they will be called (15:9).[26]

The true horror of what this means comes soon after:

> And the spirits of the giants <lead astray>, do violence, make desolate, and attack and wrestle and hurl upon the earth and <cause illness>. They eat nothing, but abstain from food and are thirsty and smite. These spirits (will) rise up against the sons of men and against the women, for they have come forth from them. (15:11)[27]

Then God explains the big picture to Enoch:

> From the day of slaughter and destruction and death of the giants (sc. contemporaneous with the flooding of the earth in the time of Noah), from the soul of whose flesh the spirits are proceeding, they are making desolate without (incurring) judgment. Thus they will make desolate until the day of consummation of the great judgment, when the great age will be consummated. (16:1)[28]

A further detail emerges during Enoch's travels. In 1 Enoch 19:1 Uriel shows Enoch certain spirits—which Nickelsburg reasonably observes should be interpreted as functionally equivalent if not identical with the evil spirits of 15:8–12[29]—and tells him that these bring destruction on men and "lead them astray to sacrifice to demons as to gods until the day of the great judgment."[30]

Putting all this together, it is clear that from the time of the destruction of most of humanity and of the giants in the days of Noah until the Endtime, the evil spirits of the giants will run amok upon the earth. It is a terrifying picture and raises real questions about the nature and justice of God.

---

26. ET Nickelsburg and VanderKam 2012:37. Note that although a different view is briefly announced at 1 Enoch 10:15, where God tells Michael to destroy the spirits of the half-breeds and the sons of the Watchers, this should be treated as discordant to the main thrust of the text as evident in the extended treatment in 1 Enoch 15:8—16:1.

27. ET Nickelsburg and VanderKam 2012:37.

28. ET Nickelsburg and VanderKam 2012:37.

29. Nickelsburg 2001:287.

30. ET Nickelsburg and VanderKam 2012:39.

The Problem of Evil and the Book of the Watchers

Understanding the contribution that the Book of the Watchers can make to the problem of evil and God's response to it must begin with contemporary theological approaches to the nature of evil.[31] At a general level, evil, which can be caused either by human or (on some views) nonhuman agency, involves harm that damages the capacity of its victims to act normally and is the most severe condemnation allowed by our moral vocabulary.[32]

The Nature of Evil

Evil as Illusion

Explanations of the nature of evil stretch along a spectrum. At one extreme are those views that evil does not exist but is an illusion. This was the Stoic position and taken up by Spinoza, while also being a feature of Christian Science belief. For Spinoza evil appeared to exist but this appearance was an illusion to which people succumbed because of misdirected desires. While there are good philosophical reasons for doubting this view,[33] its distance from ordinary human experience renders it hard to accept. In particular, Marilyn McCord Adams has identified a type of evil that she terms "horrendous," meaning that they are so serious that those who suffer them would have reason to doubt that their lives were a great good on the whole; in other words, an evil of such a nature that those suffering it would consider it was better that they had never been born.[34] For those such as these, the notion that the evil is illusory and a product of a misdirected desire will seem a trivial irrelevance.

Evil as a Privation of Good

A somewhat less extreme view is that evils are merely the privation of good. The view of Leibniz (in the *Theodicy* and other works) that the divinely created world was the best possible world did not mean that there was no imperfection in it, but this was simply because the world was not God: metaphysical evil was the essential non-divinity of the creature.[35] Leibniz claimed

31. See Adams and Adams 1990.
32. Kekes 1998:463.
33. Kekes 1998:465.
34. Adams 1999.
35. Barth 1960:316.

to have found this idea in the saying of Augustine *malum est privatio boni* ("evil is the privation of good"). Karl Barth argues, however, that Augustine well understood evil as privation to mean not just the absence of good but the direct attack on it: "Evil is related to good in such a way that it attacks and harms it." Leibniz, on the other hand, was only interested in *privatio* as negation, and hence unduly domesticated the notion of evil.[36]

Evil as a Distinct Power in the World

Passing now to the very opposite end of the spectrum, and thus deferring for a moment consideration of our preferred understanding of evil, we come to Manicheanism. According to this view, the universe is caught up in a dualist drama in the form of a continuous battle between two first principles, which are coequal and coeternal: God and the Prince of Darkness. These first principles produce good and evil substances that constantly battle for supremacy.[37] Two problems, among many with Manichean dualism, are that it provides little empirical support for its extravagant cosmology and that theists find it hard to accept that God is not an all-powerful sole creator.[38]

Evil as Nothingness (*Das Nichtige*)

Writing only a few years after the horrors of the Holocaust had occurred and then become known, Karl Barth formulated the problem of evil in terms of *Das Nichtige*, "nothingness." The Roman Catholic theologian Hans Urs Von Balthasar claimed that in framing this problem of evil in strictly theological terms, Barth had taken it "more seriously than [any] purely human experience or philosophical reflection [before]."[39] Barth regarded nothingness as a third, "alien factor," additional to God and his creation.[40]

What is *Das Nichtige*? It is a very paradoxical form of reality, since "Only God and His creature really and properly are."[41] And yet it exists, really exists.[42] "Nothingness is that from which God separates Himself and

---

36. Barth 1960:318.
37. Calder 2014.
38. Calder 2014.
39. Balthasar 1992:231.
40. Barth 1960:289–90.
41. Barth 1960:349.
42. Barth 1960:303.

in face of which He asserts Himself and exerts His positive will."[43] Moreover, "That which God renounces and abandons in virtue of his decision is not merely nothing. It is nothingness, and has as such its own being, albeit malignant and perverse." In addition, "Nothingness is that which God does not will. It lives only by the fact that it is that which God does not will. But it does live by this fact."[44] Sin is "the concrete form of nothingness because in sin it becomes man's own act, achievement and guilt. Yet nothingness is not exhausted in sin." For nothingness takes the form of evil and death as well as sin.[45] Nothingness is to be distinguished from nothing in that it has a destructive energy, it rebels against God, it takes negative positions, it is purposeful and mobile, it can affront God, it can conquer, and it can capture and enslave us.[46]

Finally, Barth considered that the origin and nature of the devil and demons lay in nothingness.[47] Like nothingness, "They are null and void, but they are not nothing . . . They are not divine but non-divine and anti-divine. On the other hand, God has not created them, and therefore they are not creaturely . . . They exist in virtue of the fact that His turning to involves a turning from, His election a rejection, His grace a judgment." In short, "They are nothingness in its dynamic, to the extent that it has form and power and movement and activity."[48]

While all of the above obtained prior to the coming of Christ, from a specifically Christian point of view nothingness is that "reality" (the inverted commas are important) on account of which (that is, against which) "God willed himself to become a creature in the creaturely world, yielding and subjecting Himself to it in Jesus Christ in order to overcome it. Nothingness is thus the 'reality' which opposes and resists God, which is subjected to and overcome by His opposition and resistance . . . the true nothingness is that which brought Jesus Christ to the cross, and that which He defeated there."[49] Yet Barth makes clear that his exposition of nothingness in no way absolves human beings from responsibility for sin:

> For the knowledge of sin it is formally decisive that it should be recognized as man's personal act and guilt, that man should be and be made responsible for it, and this in such a way that he

43. Barth 1960:351.
44. Barth 1960:352.
45. Barth 1960:310.
46. Barth 1960:319.
47. Barth 1960:522.
48. Barth 1960:523.
49. Barth 1960:305.

can neither renounce his liability nor impute it to others nor to an inexorable fate. It is essential that the direct climax should be seen which compels man to confess that alien and enemy, and to acknowledge his own treachery in giving entrance to the enemy. This is indeed the only serious knowledge of nothingness.[50]

Barthian Nothingness and Evil in the Book of the Watchers

The portrayal of evil in 1 Enoch can easily be brought into an enriching dialogue with Barth's understanding of evil and sin as nothingness. Indeed, I Enoch provides rich illumination, even clarification, of that approach. The negative power of nothingness makes its presence first clearly felt in relation to Cain's slaying of his brother. Its inexplicable perversity and opposition to divine order suddenly burst to the surface of human experience in an act of fratricide. Yet Cain cannot shed responsibility for his own act: Abel will continue to lay petition against Cain until his seed perishes from the face of the earth. The picture of the Watchers who secede from heaven, not just to marry human women, but to teach human beings forbidden knowledge, diverges somewhat from the Barthian picture of nothingness in that they are personalized, in some cases named, entities. Nevertheless, it is best to see them as exposed to and infected by the same anti-reality in the world as Cain was than to imagine them as the source of some *sui generis* evil force. For such a process would just push the problem of the origin of evil one level further up the hierarchy of beings.

Yet it is in the picture of the human condition from the period of the Flood to the End-Time, the period that we ourselves still inhabit—leaving aside for the moment the effect of the Incarnation—that the sophistication of the understanding of evil in the Book of the Watchers and its coherence with Barth's *Das Nichtige* are revealed. Nothing in the text suggests that humankind's potential to succumb to nothingness in the catastrophic way that first became evident in Cain's slaying of Abel has changed. There is, however, an added factor.

True it is that the Watchers who defected from heaven, many of them named, have been dealt with, given that what God instructed the archangels to do in 1 Enoch 10–11 has been accomplished. Asael has been buried in the wilderness until the End, when he will be led away to burning conflagration (1 Enoch 10:4–6). In addition, Shemihazah and all the Watchers with him

---

50. Barth 1960:306.

have also been bound for seventy generations in the valleys of the earth, until the day of judgment, when they too will be led away to the fiery abyss, to torture and eternal punishment (1 Enoch 10:11–13).

Yet the spirits of the giants, the latter the product of their miscegenation from Watchers and human women, will roam the earth until the End-Time. It is important to note that these are not named and they are not personalized. They assume many forms (1 Enoch 19:1). They are demonic forces rather than demons, appropriately seen as negative energies of nothingness with a particular animus towards human beings because they have partly sprung from them. Indeed, that this animus begins with violence (1 Enoch 15:11) indicates that its form reflects its original expression in Cain's murder of Abel. The corrosive power of nothingness expressed in violence has been shaped by this primordial origin in the human heart. The spirits of the giants are appropriately construed not as specific alien creatures but, in line with the Barthian picture, as the dynamism and activity of nothingness, which act on and through human agents. Sometimes they do this in ways that make it very clear that we are beholding a force for evil far greater than however people might be manifesting it in their own particular ways, even though individual responsibility cannot be ceded to its power. This is a vision of darkness similar to and at least as sophisticated as that of Dostoevsky, to judge from the following remark made by Rowan Williams in his work on that novelist: "We must bear in mind that, while Dostoevsky emphatically believed in the objective reality of the demonic, it is an objective reality that cannot be separated from actual human agents. It is not to be conceived (in Feramont's terms) as an infestation of identifiable alien creatures."[51]

Colin Gunton lends his weight to a very similar notion of the demonic. He cautions against a purely psychological account of evil that carries "the attendant danger of failing to do justice to the objective reality of evil." Furthermore, he suggests we must be wary of seeking to understand the biblical, here including (out of respect to the Ethiopian Orthodox tradition) the Enochic, picture of the demonic "in such tendentious terms that it appears ridiculously primitive." For in this area of discourse: "we meet an attempt to express the objectivity and irrationality of evil in the only way in which it can be adequately expressed: as a reality generating its own momentum and sweeping up human beings into its power."[52]

Interpreting Enochic evil in terms of *Das Nichtige* and *vice versa* allows for critical observations to be made of Walter Wink's important work

---

51. Williams 2008:99.
52. Gunton 1988:68.

Engaging the Powers (1992). Wink understands that human beings live under a "domination system" which is the expression of the activities of the dominions, rulers and powers mentioned in Col 1:15–17:

> He is the image of the invisible God, the first-born of all creation; for in him all things were created, in heaven and on earth, visible and invisible, whether thrones or dominions or principalities or powers (ἐξουσίαι)—all things were created through him and for him. He is before all things, and in him all things hold together. (RSV; slightly modified)

Wink regards these entities as collectively referred to as "the dominion (ἐξουσία) of darkness" in Col 1:13 from which believers have been delivered. Yet his acknowledgment that the four entities in v. 16 have been created by God forces him to the following position:

> They are not demonized as utterly evil; they are the good creations of a good God, and God, in the Genesis story of creation, needs no demons. But their rationale for existence is to serve human needs and values revealed as ultimate by the identification of Jesus with Wisdom and Christ. These Powers are the necessary social structures of human life, and it is not a matter of indifference to God that they exist. God *made* them.[53]

Wink astutely brings out in this book the extent to which human beings are subject to institutions and structures that inhibit the full expression and flourishing of a life under God because of the "powers." Nevertheless, the powers as he understands them are clearly not demons as understood by Barth, as nothingness in its dynamic form, with power and activity, which have a malignity far better expressed by the picture of the evil spirits of the giants in 1 Enoch 1–36. Moreover, Barth's nothingness was not created by God and this avoids the problems for theodicy posed by Wink's insistence on God's creation of the dominion or power of darkness in Col 1:13.

Taking Violence Seriously in the Book of the Watchers

I have already observed that we not only do we live in an age of violence but that violence is the pre-eminent evil as far as the Book of the Watchers is concerned. It is a theme that begins with Cain (22:6–7), finds extra energy when the giants begin to kill and eat living things of every type—human beings, animals, fish and even themselves (7:4–5)—and continues with Asael

---

53. Wink 1992:66 (italics original).

teaching human beings how to make weapons and instruments of war (8:1), which we must assume were used. Eventually the earth is filled with godlessness and violence (9:1). Even after the giants have been destroyed, their spirits will do violence (15:11).

A further dimension of the role of violence in the text is that it is foundational for and constitutive of a whole array of other evils. One formulation of evil in 1 Enoch 5:4, as already noted, is that it involves acting against God's commandments (ἐντολαί). For an Israelite author such as whoever composed 1 Enoch 1–36, these commandments should certainly be taken to include those spoken by God on Sinai in Exod 20:2–17, a detailed form of the Ten Commandments.[54] In this formulation the sixth commandment is "You shall not kill." It has recently been argued that we should not understand the ten commandments as self-contained entities, but rather view them as having a "perichoretic" nature in that each individual commandment nests in the others.[55] *Perichoresis* refers to co-indwelling, co-inhering, and mutual interpenetration and is usually applied in Christian theology to the relationship between the three members of the Trinity. In this context, however, it is being drawn into creative service to explain the inter-relationship amidst the commandments. While the Decalogue inevitably assumes a primary role for the first commandment, the perichoretic character of the sixth commandment can be demonstrated in relation to a number of other commandments.[56]

> At the most basic level, if the commandment not to kill is not kept, there seems to be little point in keeping the rest. 'You shall not kill' seems then to be the most basic of precepts, as it protects in general what the other commandments protect in a variety of more particular aspects: life itself.[57]

While the Matthean Jesus *expressly* extended this commandment also to embrace expressions of anger (Matt 5:22), this is not a huge step to take, given the way in which anger so often vents in violence and culminates in homicide. And when we learn in 1 Enoch 1:9 of "the proud and hard words" that wicked sinners uttered against God, we have behavior that both

---

54. This incident is mentioned in the Animal Apocalyse (89:28–30). I must regretfully part company from those scholars (such as Gabriele Boccaccini [1998]) who have argued that the law of Moses is marginalized in the Enochic corpus.

55. Wannenwetsch 2005.

56. Wannenwetsch 2005:148 (who follows certain Christian formulations in regarding the commandment not to kill as the fifth commandment).

57. Wannenwetsch 2005:149.

impliedly takes the Lord name in vain (Exod 20:7) but also infringes this extended understanding of "You shall not kill."

It is not hard to find some specific perichoretic linkages between this commandment and the others when we start to look for them. "Honor your father and mother" (Exod 20:12) extends to helping them preserve their life in old age and (in our modern times) not subjecting them, or even encouraging them, to euthanasia.[58] One way to illustrate the point is by considering what happens when David sees Bathsheba: "Watching bathing Bathsheba creates desire, desire becomes coveting, covering begets adultery, perhaps rape, which is followed by lying, deceit, murder, and making others complicit in another's sin."[59] One may amplify this by suggesting that David typifies some adulterers who would like to see the other party's spouse dead.

For good reason, then, the Book of the Watchers depicts violence as the central evil—which we interpret to mean that violence represents the most extensive field and opportunity for the operation of *Das Nichtige*. So much for the presence of evil in the world, epitomized in violence. We now proceed to the other half of the story: what God has done and will do about it.

God as Affected by Evil

Some construals of God, the hyper-Calvinist version for example, treat him as being unaffected by human evil. Yet this is certainly not the picture in the Book of the Watchers. In fact, the work announces with the blessing in its first verse that it is concerned precisely with the final termination of evil on earth and the deliverance of the righteous: "The words of the blessing with which Enoch blessed the righteous chosen who will be present on the day of tribulation, to remove all the enemies; and the righteous will be saved" (1 Enoch 1:1).[60] The manner of that deliverance, through the dramatic intervention of God with his angelic war-band, is described at length shortly afterwards, in 1 Enoch 1:4–9. The Book of the Watchers is a narrative that begins, therefore, with its ending, probably to reinforce the point that everything that is to be described in the book must be understood in terms of the ultimate victory that God will eventually deliver.

That is quite a reasonable way of proceeding, given that God is slow to react to the chaos unleashed on earth following the descent of the Watchers. In 1 Enoch 9 the four archangels (Michael, Sariel, Raphael and Gabriel) see

58. Wannenwetsch 2005:165–67.
59. Wannenwetsch 2005:162.
60. ET Nickelsburg and VanderKam 2012:19.

the bloodshed on earth and receive its petition to them (vv. 1-3). They then deliver a long address to God in which they first recite his glories, authority and knowledge (vv. 4-5), including his knowledge of what Asael and Shemihazah have done and of the horrors that have resulted (v. 6-9). They then urge him to look at what is happening on earth (v. 10) and, next, quite remarkably, actually tax him with not having given them the appropriate instructions:

> You know all things before they happen,
> and you see these things and you permit them,
> and you do not tell us what we ought to do to them
> with regard to these things. (v. 11)[61]

The Book of the Watchers, therefore, bears witness to the all too frequent complaint that human beings raise against God: that he acts too late or not at all. Thus the work recognizes both the sovereignty of God but also the grounds that humankind sometimes has for complaint against him.

Yet, eventually, react God does, in the form of his long instruction to the Archangels in 1 Enoch 10-11. We also see God's concern for what is happening on earth in his speech to Enoch in Chapters 15-16. The fact that all this has hit God rather personally is evident in his annoyance that the Watchers, who were eternal creatures, had departed the heavenly realm for earth. When God says: "The spirits of heaven, in heaven is their dwelling" (1 Enoch 15:7), one hears a monarch angered by the defection of his courtiers (much as Louis XIV used to be if his courtiers left the palace of Versailles without his permission).[62] In 1 Enoch 10-11 and 15-16 the text powerfully dramatizes a God determined, through seraphic agents, to deal with evil on earth. This produces for the audience of the text a picture with great clarity and a conviction of a God actively involved in his creation. It illustrates and yet also enriches Karl Barth's understanding of God's engagement with the world and opposition to the nothingness and evil besetting it.

In taking issue with what he regarded as Schleiermacher's belief that God is untouched by human sinfulness and actual sin,[63] Barth was moved to give magnificent expression to this theme:

> If it is his (sc. Schleiermacher's) serious contention that God Himself is not concerned with sin and evil, then man need not take them seriously nor acknowledge his own need of redemption from them.

---

61. ET Nickelsburg and VanderKam 2012:27.
62. Elias 1983.
63. Barth 1960:329-30.

But if he believes in man's need of redemption, in the culpability and punishment of sin, in the divine holiness which imputes it to him, and the justice which subjects him to evil as its consequence, then God himself is supremely involved in this mighty negation of nothingness, it is His own most intimate concern, He is holy and righteous not merely for us but in Himself, and he is the God of wrath and mercy.[64]

But let us now look more closely at just how God does respond to evil in 1 Enoch, and this brings us to the reality of *Deus Victor*: God the Victor.

Deus Victor in the Book of the Watchers

At one point in his *Second Oration Against the Arians* Athanasius notes (before disagreeing with) a possible view that God could have brought about human redemption otherwise than through Christ: "Yet some say, 'Although the Saviour was a creature, God was able merely to say the word and undo the curse.' We have also heard others saying in a similar way to one another, 'Even if he had not come amongst us at all, God was able merely to say the word and undo the curse.' But we must examine what is expedient for human beings and not consider what is simply is possible with God."[65]

Athanasius also mentions this notion in *De Incarnatione Dei Verbi*, when he cites people who claim: "If God wished to instruct and save human beings, He might have done so, not by His Word's assumption of a body, but merely by an act of will, just as He did long ago, when he created them out of nothingness."[66] To similar effect is Augustine's reference to those who ask: "What? Was God unable to free human beings from the misery of this mortality in any other way, that He should want the only-begotten Son, God co-eternal with Himself, to become a human being, by putting on a human soul and flesh, and having been made mortal to endure death?"[67]

---

64. Barth 1960:330.

65. Ἀλλ' ἠδύνατο, φασί, καὶ κτίσματος ὄντος τοῦ σωτῆρος μόνον εἰπεῖν ὁ θεὸς καὶ λῦσαι τὴν κατάραν. τὸ αὐτὸ δ' ἂν ἀκούσαμεν καὶ αὐτοὶ παρ' ἑτέρου λέγοντος ἠδύνατο καὶ μηδ' ὅλως ἐπιδημήσαντος αὐτοῦ μόνον εἰπεῖν ὁ θεὸς καὶ λῦσαι τὴν κατάραν. ἀλλὰ σκοπεῖν δεῖ τὸ τοῖς ἀνθρώποις λυσιτελοῦν καὶ μὴ ἐν πᾶσι τὸ δυνατὸν τοῦ θεοῦ λογίζεσθαι; *Against the Arians*, II.68 (text in Metzler 1998:245). All translations are my own unless otherwise indicated.

66. ὅτι ἔδει τὸν θεόν, παιδεῦσαι καὶ σῶσαι θέλοντα τοὺς ἀνθρώπους, νεύματι μόνον ποιῆσαι, καὶ μὴ σώματος ἅψασθαι τὸν τούτου Λόγον, ὥσπερ οὖν καὶ πάλαι πεποίηκεν, ὅτε ἐκ τοῦ μὴ ὄντος αὐτὰ συνίστη; Athanasius, *De Incarnatione Verbi Dei*, 44.1 (text in Kannengiesser 1973:424)

67. *Itane defuit deo modus alius quo liberaret homines a miseria mortalitatis huius*

References to such postulation of God's capacity to have saved human beings from evil, sin and death apart from Christ also appear in the works of other Fathers.[68]

None of these Patristic writers mentions the fact that precisely this scenario—of God acting to save humanity by the exercise of his own will or expression of his word, directly or through angelic agents but not via the Incarnation of his Son—had found detailed and mature expression centuries earlier in the Israelite text known as the Book of the Watchers. Perhaps they were not aware of this work or, if they were, chose to pass over it in silence, presumably because their interest lay elsewhere, in their insistence on the optimality of a redemptive process involving Christ.

To an extent there is a functional similarity in the broad structures of salvation history in 1 Enoch 1–36 and the Christian story of salvation in that both constitute a two-stage process. For the Enochic author there is period leading up to the decisive intervention, here in the time of Noah, when evil was partially dealt with, and then the period until the End during which evil will continue to exist. In the Christian story, although the events at the time of Noah are incorporated from the Old Testament, the decisive intervention comes in the Incarnation, death and resurrection of Jesus. After that there is also a period until the End-time during which, although the power of sin has been broken, God has not yet dealt with evil fully and finally.[69]

To come to terms with the Enochic picture in more detail, however, it is worth first considering the Christian understanding of how God addressed the problem of evil through the Incarnation, at which point we enter the theological topic of the atonement (the reconciliation of God and humanity). One of the most influential works on the atonement in the twentieth century was *Christus Victor*, by Gustav Aulén, published in 1931. Aulén was reacting to what he regarded as an excessive influence over Christian theology by the views of St Anselm (1033–1119) in *Cur Deus Homo*. According to Anselm's "satisfaction" theory of atonement, Christ suffered death on the cross as a substitute for all humankind to satisfy the demands of God's honor that had been affronted by human sin. By his death, Christ paid a debt of honor to

---

ut unigenitum filium deum sibi coaeternum hominem fieri uellet induendo humanam animam et carnem mortalemque factum mortem perpeti?; Augustine, *De Trinitate* 13.13.

68. See Aulén 1931:41–44.

69. Note what Barth says on this point: "For the fact that it (sc. nothingness) is broken, judged, refuted, and destroyed at the central point, in the mighty act of salvation accomplished in Jesus Christ is valid not merely at that point but by extension throughout the universe and its activity. This is not just visible or recognisable ... It took place once and for all, and is universally effective. Nothingness may still have standing and assume significance to the extent that the final revelation of its destruction has not yet taken place and all creation must still await and expect it" (1960:367).

God, His Father (not a debt, Anselm insisted, owed to Satan, as in earlier theories). To Aulén's mind, this view meant that Anselm regarded atonement as "that which Christ accomplishes as a man, of an offering made to God from man's side, from below."[70] In fact, according to Aulén, the "classic" way of conceiving the atonement was that Christ had been victorious over the demonic forces holding human beings in their thrall and he explained it as follows: "Its central theme is the idea of the Atonement as a Divine conflict and victory; Christ—Christus Victor—fights against and triumphs over the evil powers of the world, the 'tyrants' under which mankind is in bondage and suffering, and in Him God reconciles the world to Himself."

Needless to say, this theory has attracted much attention, some of it critical. Colin Gunton points out that a frequent criticism is that the book advocates too triumphalist a view of atonement and it does not sufficiently emphasize the human and tragic elements of the story.[71] Nevertheless, Gunton himself concedes that "there does appear to be biblical support for the general position that Aulén is advocating."[72] He regards the Bible as providing encouragement "for those who wish to see the metaphor of victory used in connection with God's saving activity," but against Aulén regards that material as not providing the basis for a theory of atonement.[73]

Yet whatever the merits of Aulén's view in relation to the *Christian* doctrine of atonement, if we substitute *Deus Victor* for *Christus Victor*, we have a very promising line of enquiry into the Enochic portrayal of atonement developed, as it is, without the incarnation of God's son. The passage *par excellence* for this substitution is 1 Enoch 1:4–9. God will come from his dwelling with his host, the Watchers will quake, and the earth will be shaken and torn apart, but he will protect the righteous. Then we encounter *Deus Victor* indeed:

> Look, he comes with the myriads of his holy ones,
>> to execute judgment on all,
>> and to destroy all the wicked,
>> and to convict all humanity
>>> for all the wicked deeds that they have done,
>>> and the proud and hard words that wicked sinners spoke against him (1 Enoch 4:9).[74]

---

70. Aulén 1931:88.
71. Gunton 1988:58.
72. Gunton 1988:57.
73. Gunton 1988:61.
74. ET Nickelsburg and VanderKam 2012:20.

He will execute judgment on all, destroying the wicked and convicting humanity for its wickededness. There is no specific mention of the spirits of the giants. As already noted from our Barthian perspective, however, they are not separate beings but expressions of nothingness embedded in human behavior, destructive energies that capture and enslave us. The consequences for the cursed and the blessed are set out in 1 Enoch 5:5-9.

The scale of the problem and the nature of the nothingness human beings are up against also elicited similar language from Karl Barth. Speaking of God's action in Jesus but in a manner equally applicable to 1 Enoch 1:4-9, Barth observed that "He has set Himself in opposition to nothingness, and in this opposition he is and was the Victor."[75] The setting for this drama is one in which we have "God's royal dominion on the one side, and creaturely existence, life and occurrence under his dominion on the other."[76] Closely consonant with the Enochic picture of a God as an enraged king is Barth's statement: "It is true, of course, that it (sc. nothingness) constitutes a threat to the salvation and right of the creature, but primarily and supremely it contests the honour and right of God the Creator."[77] And yet is this image of a warrior and victorious God to which the Book of the Watchers is committed theologically appropriate? To this, the last substantive issue in this essay, we now turn.

The Theological Appropriateness of *Deus Victor*

Miroslav Volf wrote *Exclusion and Embrace* from close personal experience of the violent disintegration of Yugoslavia in the 1990s.[78] The proponents of the Enlightenment, reacting against the religious wars in Europe in the sixteenth and seventeenth centuries, had believed that with the advance of reason violence would progressively decrease. The vicious warfare in the Balkans, however, was just the latest evidence that the idea that the civilizing process involved the reduction of violence had proved a naïve myth. Modernity, in fact, had made the Holocaust possible and contained no effective mechanisms for stopping it happening.[79] Yet the problem posed by this level of violence is twofold: what should human beings do and what should God do? The position Volf seeks to maintain is that absolute opposition by religious people to all nonviolence (including on God's part) is

75. Barth 1960:290.
76. Barth 1960:291.
77. Barth 1960:354.
78. Volf 1996.
79. Volf 1996:278-80.

not theologically viable. As such, his argument also stands in support of the Enochic picture of God's action in final judgment and condemnation.

Volf starts by discussing an essay by Giles Deleuze who argues that modernity's universal reason and the absolute God of Christianity are but two manifestations, one sacred and one secular, of the same system of terror.[80] According to Deleuze, the Apocalypse in the New Testament is really a revelation of cosmic terror even for those who end up in the Heavenly City.[81] After all, will we not witness the Word of God emerging as the white rider who "is clad in a robe dipped in blood" and who will "tread the wine press of the fury of the wrath of God the Almighty" (Rev 19:13, 15; RSV). True it is, agrees Volf, that the Cross breaks the cycle of violence.[82] But Jesus did not only fight violence by "absorbing" and "demasking" it. Proclaiming and enacting the kingdom of truth and justice is never just an act of mere positing but

> always already a transgression into spaces occupied by others. Active opposition to the kingdom of Satan, the kingdom of deception and oppression, is therefore inseparable from the proclamation of the kingdom of God . . . It takes the struggle against deception and oppression to transform nonviolence from barren negativity into a creative possibility, from a quicksand into a foundation of a new world.[83]

Diverging from John Milbank, he argues that you cannot just act as if sin was not there. You cannot suspend justice and truth. If you do, he says, in terms aligned with the various cries to heaven in 1 Enoch 1–36, "the world will remain forever awry, the blood of the innocent will eternally cry out to heaven. There can be no redemption unless the truth about the world is told and redemption is done."[84] Against proponents of universal salvation he argues that some human beings may be so evil that: "Ensnared by the chaos of violence . . . they have become untouchable for the lure of God's truth and goodness." It is here that there is a role for God's anger: "A nonindignant God would be an accomplice in injustice, deception, and violence."[85] In short, "the cross is not forgiveness pure and simple, but God's *setting aright the world of injustice and deception*."[86] To those who argue that it is unworthy

80. Volf 1996:286.
81. Volf 1996:287.
82. Volf 1996:290–91.
83. Volf 1996:293.
84. Volf 1996:294; citing Milbank 1990:411.
85. Volf 1996:297.
86. Volf 1996:298 (italics original).

of God to wield the sword, he ripostes that "one could further argue that in a world of violence it would not be worthy of God *not to wield the sword.*"[87]

Although Volf was writing in the context of Christian notions of atonement and the Last Judgment, virtually every point he makes has equal application to *Deus Victor* in 1 Enoch 1–36. This God will finally come in judgment, awarding salvation to some and eternal condemnation to others, those who, fatally invaded by and succumbing to *Das Nichtige* in the grossest and most violent ways, have put themselves beyond the reach of God's truth and goodness.

Conclusion

The central concern of the Book of the Watchers, God's defeat of evil, is arguably the central concern of theology. Common to 1 Enoch 1–36 and theology is the basic shape of the problem: (a) the objective reality of evil (even to the extent of its demonic dimensions); (b) the persistent tendency of humankind to cave in to evil, paradigmatically the evil of violence; (c) the fact that multitudes of human beings fall prey to others; and (d) the necessity of God's intervention to end our predicament.

In this essay I have sought to trace the beginnings of a dialogue between the two in such as way that the wider potential of the interaction is clear. The Enochic depiction of God as a victorious warrior king who will ultimately defeat evil coheres with our contemporary insight that evil as violent and merciless torture and killing of other human beings is so deeply implanted in the human domain that only a superior and divine countervailing force energetically deployed will ultimately defeat it.

---

87. Volf 1996:303 (italics original).

12

1 Enoch: An Artist's Response

Angus Pryor

Throughout the history of art, biblical, spiritual and ecclesiastical narratives have been a huge source of artistic inspiration. When visiting different cities around the world we judge the level of culture by what is exhibited in their galleries, museums and cathedrals. As tourists, we love to gaze upwards at spectacular ceilings and imagine the celestial behind the images.

I am fascinated and inspired by liturgy or ceremony and when it is reproduced into painting it can somehow translate to an entirely new audience, many of whom are not religious and have come to view the painting for many differing reasons. This gives the artist a huge licence to transcribe and expose hidden narratives and not only allows the public to see their art but also opens doors to further exploration. In this way, I aim to develop and reveal new themes and ideas through the visual imagery inspired by the Enoch text.

The Book of Enoch, or 1 Enoch, on which my series of paintings is based is one of the lost books of the Bible. It was widely known and read the first three centuries after Christ but was banned by the Council of Laodicea in the fourth century and therefore disappeared from the doctrine of the western Christian church. However, the Christian church in Ethiopia kept the Book of Enoch as part of its sacred scripture. An eighteenth-century traveller, James Bruce, procured a collection of Ethiopian manuscripts amongst which were three copies of the Book of Enoch. It was not until 1821 that Dr. Richard Laurence, an Oxford don, made the first English translation of the work.

1 Enoch has, probably because of this controversial past, been very under-represented in art history. Only William Blake and John Flaxman have attempted to make drawings from the text, both seeming to have been fascinated by the sensational coming together of humans and angels.

I came to Enoch's wonderful text purely from a perspective of biblical interpretation but wanted to take the imagery to another level of understanding by moving from the static nature of the word to the transcendental nature of painting. But I am now engaged on a project to paint 21 large paintings on themes and imagery from 1 Enoch, together with creating a large-scale model of an Ethiopian church illuminated with Enochic imagery, akin to a Church of St Enoch. I plan to exhibit them in 2020, in the Wilson Gallery in Cheltenham and in Gloucester and Canterbury Cathedrals.

Painting has its own language; it is unlike any other medium. Once you move beyond merely illustrating an idea you can create a new dynamic. With these works, I am exploring my own understanding of the Enoch text and trying to transcribe the words through images. I read and re-read the text (sometimes on a daily basis) to arrive at an understanding of the words themselves. I then begin the task of composition so that the extract I have chosen can be captured on canvas. This choice of text becomes the crux or the issue of the painting. Another artist may choose a different edit from the text and may display the theme in a different manner. I am very aware that I have the ability to take macro elements and transcribe them into the micro. Size, colour and composition are all the tools of the translator in this context. The power of the artist lies in putting these together in such a way that the end result is more than a mere reproduction of the text in imagery; an artist will actually add meaning to the text via the dialogue of using the paint as a medium. The artist is learned in this instance and by using (and at the same time challenging) art historical norms can create not only a meaningful interpretation, but also make an image that can exist on its own as art. Although the paintings inevitably refer to the Enochic text, the end product must be able to stand alone, independent of that text. It is the hope of the artist that the impact on the viewer encountering this exhibition will be a journey to discover the original written word. It is then that the audience's own interpretation of the text in relation to the images can really begin.

The Book of Enoch in its entirety is a narrative sequence that presents an exciting range of possibilities and challenges. The text is a self-contained unit which I treat as a "ready-made" (in the Duchamp sense). It can be read as a contemporary text, outlining as it does many of the challenges of contemporary society; faith, the thirst for knowledge, our relationship with God and the way our environment has an impact on our systems of belief. For the artist, the task is relatively simple; to take the concepts in the book of Enoch and translate them through the medium of painting so that a new and exciting element is introduced and further interpretation can take place.

The works themselves indicate that the process of painting is important to the end product. They also become a critique of the text as well as a commentary on it. The critical eye of the artist from an academic standpoint through the process of selection becomes crucial to how the Book of Enoch is perceived and received. Each element of the work is a contemplation on the text which operates at an individual level with its own particular meaning. However, a much greater impact occurs when the whole body of work is seen together. The sequence is important; it tells the whole story in its entirety so that the viewer has a complete series to view. The works are intended to overload the senses since I want the paintings to reveal themselves to the viewer. Clues exist throughout the paintings that make them multi-dimensional. It is an excess of knowledge that leads the viewer to a final understanding. This can only happen by absorbing the polyptych in its entirety and in its context within the exhibition.

Much like Blake and Flaxman, I find the text full of sensational imagery. A particular fascination lies in the dialogue between the mortal Enoch and the immortal angels and in his meeting with God ("The Head of Days"), which provide exciting source material.

My own paintings are a direct reflection of the text, which I have used as a contemporary typology. I interpret the text and, using a dialogue of reintroducing the objects to the paint, I build up a collage of painted images to replicate the narrative. By using everyday objects to interpret a religious text, a tension is created between the object chosen and the meaning of the image. I am experimenting with creating divine images from these everyday objects. I reflect the narrative with paint and objects so that the work becomes a three-dimensional representation of the Enochic text. I see these imprinted images as similar to the impression or essence left when someone has been sitting on a chair. I would like the impression of this exhibition to be a collective memory in which my paintings reflect the essence that the ancient Enoch text has left on a contemporary society.

The text deals with universal themes of life and death, shame, murder, sin, transcendence, faith and belief. Once an artefact is exposed to an audience and the work is released into the public sphere, it is open to interpretation. What is significant is not whether the audience likes or hates the work but that it acts as a translator of this lost text. I want the paintings to become a gateway to greater knowledge of the text of 1 Enoch.

For example, here is the extract where Enoch comes face to face with "The Head of Days."

LXXI Two earlier Visions of Enoch:

Verse:
10. And with them the Head of Days,
    His head white and pure as wool,
    And his raiment indescribable
11. And I fell on my face,
    And my whole body became relaxed,
    And my spirit was transfigured.

(ET R. H. Charles)

I was inspired to depict this moment when Enoch comes face to face with God, I chose to explore this theme by breaking it down into two separate images. The first image shows "The Head of Days" and the second depicts Enoch moving from a physical state to a spiritual state. I achieved the first by using a person to symbolize God (thereby taking literally the concept that man is made in God's image). I took a print of the (readymade) man and reprinted this onto the canvas. I then used objects to build up a collage of the Head of Days in order to represent the text. The interest for me lay in depicting the expression of Head of Days and this involved trying to imagine how the Head of Days would feel meeting Enoch. The entire composition is based around a really simple idea of the expression of the Head of Days, as an entity.

The second image of Enoch changing from man to spirit raises another question "Is there an after-life?" Whilst creating this image about Enoch's transition, I was thinking of other artists who have used the idea of transition, for example Mathias Grunewald's whose painting "Die Kreuzigung Christi," shows the crucified Christ figure changing before us as the body of a man (Christ) rots. This depiction leads the audience to believe that He is about to ascend to Heaven, leaving behind his suffering mortal body. I relate this directly to my own painting of Enoch transforming into a metaphysical being.

My research has involved an exploration of Ethiopic traditional painting and the imagery that reflects these traditions. The flatness of my previous paintings based on biblical scenes is in a modernist tradition. I am not exploring the allusion of space but trying to understand through the composition and medium the meaning of the image as a whole and a multi-layered narrative with reference to its self. This hermeneutical approach has a clear comparison to the tradition of Ethiopian paintings to which I am instinctively drawn because they are not describing anything other than themselves. This may appear naïve but I understand the relationship and how the works can be compared and contrasted in relation to a contemporary aesthetic.

The fact that the text of 1 Enoch was saved by the Ethiopian people has had a great impact on the work. The imagery reflects the language of painting, the book of 1 Enoch, my own interpretation and an understanding of Ethiopic artistic tradition. All the imagery pays homage to the Ethiopic tradition; the facial characteristics and clothes are painted in that style, the palette is one of muted and sombre earth colours which again reflects the Ethiopian paintings. On recent trips to Ethiopia, I have collected objects which not only formed part of my research but have also been used directly in the painting, both as a template for images and for printing directly onto the canvas. This process and methodology has enabled me to ensure an Ethiopian influence on the paintings whilst using recognizable contemporary objects, which signify a link between 1 Enoch, the contemporary world of Ethiopia, its traditions and its influence, and also as an act of gratitude for the Ethiopian conservation of the 1 Enoch text.

I believe that work exhibited in the public sphere has become increasingly polarised and wish to explore the relationship between the museum, the galley and other public spaces such as churches and cathedrals. I am attempting to enable these boundaries to be broken down and to give the work the space to become part of project designed to create more public awareness of the text.

Ultimately, my series of paintings deal with the systems for setting belief structures. I want the viewers of my works to learn the story of a transient individual who is undergoing a personal transformation as well as a universal one. The paintings will communicate this narrative via a travelling exhibition in which the work will be set in different contexts; the ecclesiastical setting (Canterbury Cathedral and Gloucester Cathedral) and within a contemporary gallery space (the Wilson in Cheltenham).

The ecclesiastical setting will provide the narratives with a site-specific undertone for an already biblically-informed audience, whereas within the gallery setting the impact of the imaginary will be seen in the context of contemporary painting. The juxtaposition of the two will result in the exhibition having a duality. These spaces have a sense of awe about them; both can be seen as meditative environments and both should provide the individual visitor with an opportunity to have their own contemplative relationship with the paintings in a reflective space.

Painting signifying belief is a powerful medium.

Bibliography

Abebe, Sofanit T. 2015. "The Significance of 1 Enoch 108 to 1 Peter: A Socio-Narrative Reading of Suffering, Liminality and *'Ānāwîm* Identity." MTh thesis, The Ethiopian Graduate School of Theology, Addis Ababa.
Abraha, Tedros. 2001. *La lettera ai Romani: Testo e commentari della versione Etiopica*. ÄthFor 57. Wiesbaden: Harrassowitz.
Adams, Marilyn McCord. 1999. *Horrendous Evils and the Goodness of God*. Ithaca, NY: Cornell University Press.
Adams, Marilyn McCord, and Robert Merrihew Adams, eds. 1990. *The Problem of Evil*. Oxford: Oxford University Press.
Adams, Samuel L. 2011. "Poverty and Otherness in Second Temple Instructions." In *The Other in Second Temple Judaism: Essays in Honor of John J. Collins*, edited by Daniel C. Harlow, Karina Martin Hogan, and Matthew J. Goff, 189–203. Grand Rapids: Eerdmans.
Aitken, James K. 2000. "Biblical Interpretation as Political Manifesto: Ben Sira in His Seleucid Setting." *JJS* 51:191–208.
Alehegne, Mersha. 2011. *The Ethiopian Commentary on the Book of Genesis: Critical Edition and Translation*. ÄthFor 73. Wiesbaden: Harrassowitz.
Amsalu, Tefera. 2015. *The Ethiopian Homily on the Ark of the Covenant: Critical Edition and Annotated Translation of Dərsanä Ṣəyon*. Texts and Studies in Eastern Christianity 5. Leiden: Brill.
Ande Berhan, Weldetense. 1994. *Commentari Etiopici sul Libro del Profeta Osea: Edizione critica da MSS inediti, Principi Ermeneutici, Temi Teologici*. ÄthFor 40. Wiesbaden: Harrassowitz.
Anonymous. 1988 EC. የቅዱስ ጳውሎስ መጽሐፍት. Addis Ababa: ትንሣኤ ማሳተሚያ ድርጅት.
Anonymous. 1998 EC. መዝሙረ ዳዊት ንባብ ከነትርጓሜው. Addis Ababa: ትንሣኤ ማሳተሚያ ድርጅት.
Anonymous. 1999 EC. መጽሐፍት ብሉያት፡ አሪት ዘፍጥረት (ዘልደት)፣ አሪት ዘፀአት. Addis Ababa: ትንሣኤ ማሳተሚያ ድርጅት.

Anonymous. 2000. መጽሐፍ፡ ቅዱስ የብሉይ የሐዲስ ኪዳን መጻሕፍት፡ *The Amharic Bible with the Old Testament based on Septuagint*. Addis Ababa: The Bible Society of Ethiopia.
Anonymous. 2003. መጽሐፈ ሄኖክ. Addis Ababa: ትንሣኤ ማሳተሚያ ድርጅት.
Antohin, Alexandra Sellassie. 2014. "Expressions of Sacred Promise: Ritual and Devotion in Ethiopian Orthodox Praxis." PhD diss., University College London.
Argall, Randal A. 1995. *1 Enoch and Sirach: A Comparative Literary and Conceptual Analysis of the Themes of Revelation, Creation and Judgment*. EJL 8. Atlanta: Scholars.
Asale, B. A. 2014. "The Ethiopian Orthodox Tewahedo Church (EOTC) Canon of Scripture: Neither Open nor Closed." Paper presented at the Society of Biblical Literature Annual Meeting, San Diego.
Assmann, Jan. 1999. *Fünf Stufen auf dem Wege zum Kanon: Tradition und Schriftkultur im frühen Judentum und seiner Umwelt*. Münstersche Theologische Vorträge 1. Münster: Lit.
Astley, Jeff. 2002. *Ordinary Theology: Looking, Listening and Learning in Theology*. Explorations in Practical, Pastoral and Empirical Theology. London: Routledge.
Astley, Jeff, and Leslie J. Francis. 2013. *Exploring Ordinary Theology: Everyday Christian Believing and the Church*. Explorations in Practical, Pastoral and Empirical Theology. London: Routledge.
Aulén, Gustaf. 1931. *Christus Victor: An Historical Study of the Three Main Types of the Idea of the Atonement*. Translated by A. G. Herbert. Reprinted, Eugene, OR: Wipf & Stock, 2003.
Aune, David E. 1997. *Revelation 1–5*. Word Biblical Commentary 52A. Dallas: Word.
Balthasar, Hans Urs von. 1992. *The Theology of Karl Barth: Exposition and Introduction*. Translated by Edward T. Oakes. San Francisco: Ignatius (German orig., 1951).
Barclay, John M. G. 2015. *Paul and the Gift*. Grand Rapids, Eerdmans.
Barker, Margaret. 2010. *Creation: A Biblical Vision for the Environment*. London: T. & T. Clark.
Barr, James. 1999. *The Concept of Biblical Theology: An Old Testament Perspective*. Minneapolis: Fortress.
Barth, Karl. 1960. *Church Dogmatics*, III/3: *The Doctrine of Creation*. Edited by G. W. Bromiley and T. F. Torrance. Edinburgh: T. & T. Clark.
Barton, John. 1999. "Canon and Old Testament Interpretation." In *In Search of True Wisdom: Essays in Old Testament Interpretation in Honour of Ronald E. Clements*, edited by Edward Ball, 37–52. JSOTSup 300. Sheffield: Sheffield Academic.
Bauckham, Richard. 2010. *Bible and Ecology: Rediscovering the Community of Creation*. Sarum Theological Lectures. London: Darton, Longman & Todd.
Bausi, Alessandro, and Siegbert Uhlig, eds. 2014. *Encyclopaedia Aethiopica*. Vol. 5: Y–Z, Addenda, Index. Wiesbaden: Harrassowitz.
Baynes, L. 2012. "Enoch and Jubilees in the Canon of the Ethiopian Orthodox Church." In *A Teacher for All Generations: Essays in Honor of James C. VanderKam*, edited by Eric F. Mason et al., 2:799–818. JSJSup 153. Leiden: Brill.
Bechtler, Stephen R. 1998. *Following in His Steps: Suffering, Community and Christology in 1 Peter*. SBL Dissertation Series 162. Atlanta: Scholars.
Beer, Georg. 1900. "Das Buch Henoch." In *Die Apokryphen und Pseudepigraphen des Alten Testaments*, edited by Emil Kautzsch and Georg Beer, 2:217–310. 2 vols. Tübingen: Mohr/Siebeck.

Bell, Catherine. 1988. "Ritualization of Texts and Textualization of Ritual in the Codification of Taoist Liturgy." *History of Religions* 27:366-92.
Berger, Klaus. 1984. "Hellenistische Gattungen im Neuen Testament." In *Aufstieg und Niedergang der römischen Welt* II.25.2: 1031-432, 1831-85.
Beyer, Klaus. 1984. *Die aramaïschen Texte vom Toten Meer*. Göttingen: Vandenhoeck & Ruprecht. [Corrected ed., 1994.]
Berry, Thomas and Brian Swimme. 1992. *The Universe Story: A Celebration of the Unfolding of the Cosmos*. New York: HarperCollins.
Bilen, Osman. 2008. "Environmental Ethics and Its Relation to Truth." In *Truth and Morality: The Role of Truth in Public Life*, edited by Wilhelm Dancă, 113-25. Washington, DC: Council for Research in Values and Philosophy.
Binns, John. 2013. "Out of Ethiopia—A Different Way of Doing Theology." *International Journal for the Study of the Christian Church* 13:33-47.
Black, Matthew, ed. 1970. *Apocalypsis Henochi graece*. Pseudepigrapha Veteris Testamenti Graece 3. Leiden: Brill.
Blenkinsopp, J. 1977. *Prophecy and Canon: A Contribution to the Study of Jewish Origins*. Studies of Judaism and Christianity in Antiquity 3. Notre Dame: Notre Dame University Press.
Boccaccini, Gabriele. 1998. *Beyond the Essene Hypothesis: The Parting of the Ways between Qumran and Enochic Judaism*. Grand Rapids: Eerdmans.
Boer, Jan H. 2003. *Nigeria's Decades of Blood*. Studies in Christian & Muslim Relations 1. Jos, Nigeria: Stream Christian Publishers.
Boring, M. Eugene. 1999. *1 Peter*. Abingdon New Testament Commentaries. Nashville: Abingdon.
———. 2007. "Narrative Dynamics in First Peter: The Function of Narrative World." In *Reading First Peter with New Eyes: Methodological Reassessments of the Letter of First Peter*, edited by Robert L. Webb and Betsy Bauman-Martin, 7-40. LNTS 364. New York: T. & T. Clark.
Boylston, Tom. 2013. "Review Essay: Orienting the East." The Anthropology of Christianity Bibliographic Blog. http://www.blogs.hss.ed.ac.uk/anthrocybib/2013/05/26/orienting-the-east/.
Brita, Antonella. 2010. *I racconti tradizionali sulla seconda cristianizzazione dell'Etiopia: il ciclo agiografico dei nove santi*. Studi africanistici, Serie Etiopica 7. Naples: Universita degli studi di Napoli L'Orientale.
———. 2012. "With the Saints Came the Manuscripts", http://www.manuscript-cultures.uni-hamburg.de/mom/2012_11_mom_e.html
Brown, Raymond E. et al., eds. 1990. *The New Jerome Biblical Commentary*. Englewood Cliffs: Prentice-Hall.
Bultmann, Rudolf. 1956. *Primitive Christianity in its Contemporary Setting*. Translated by R. H. Fuller. New York: Meridian.
Calder, Todd. 2014. "The Concept of Evil." In *The Stanford Encyclopedia of Philosophy*. Edward N. Zalta. http://plato.stanford.edu/archives/win2014/entries/concept-evil.
Campbell, Douglas A. 2010. *The Deliverance of God: An Apocalyptic Re-Reading of Justification in Paul*. Grand Rapids: Eerdmans.
Campenhausen, Hans von. 1968. *Die Entstehung der christlichen Bibel*. Beiträge zur historischen Theologie 39. Tübingen: Mohr/Siebeck.

———. 1972. *The Formation of the Christian Bible*. Translated by J. A. Baker. Philadelphia: Fortress.
Caquot, André. 1955. "L'homélie en L'honneur de l'archange Ouriel (Dersāna Urāēl)." *Annales d'Éthiopie* 1/1:61–88.
Carroll, Timothy. 2015. "Becoming Orthodox: Of People and Things in the Making of Religious Subjects." PhD. diss., University College London.
Cary, E. 1914. *Dio's Roman History*. Vol. 6. LCL. London: Heinemann.
Chaniotis, Angelos. 2003. "The Divinity of the Hellenistic Rulers." In *A Companion to the Hellenistic World*, edited by A. Erskine, 431–45. Blackwell Companions to the Ancient World. Oxford: Blackwell.
Charles, R. H. 1893. *The Book of Enoch*. Oxford: Clarendon. Reprint, Ancient Texts and Translations. Eugene, OR: Wipf & Stock, 2005.
———. 1906. *The Ethiopic Version of Book of Enoch: Edited from Twenty-Three MSS, Together with the Fragmentary Greek and Latin Versions*. Oxford: Clarendon.
———. 1912. *The Book of Enoch or 1 Enoch*. Oxford: Clarendon.
———, ed. 1913. *Apocrypha and Pseudepigrapha of the Old Testament*. 2 vols. Oxford: Clarendon.
Charlesworth, James H. 1983. *The Old Testament Pseudepigrapha*, Vol. 1: *Apocalyptic Literature and Testament*. Garden City, NY: Doubleday.
———. 2013. "The Date and Provenance of the Parables of Enoch." In *Parables of Enoch: A Paradigm Shift*, edited by Darrell L. Bock and James H. Charlesworth, 37–57. Jewish and Christian Texts in Contexts and Related Studies 11. London: Bloomsbury Academic.
Charlesworth, James H., and Ephraim Isaac. 2015. *O Livro de Enoque Etíope ou 1 Enoque*, 249–526. Translated by Orlando Iannuzzi Filho. Sao Paulo: Entre os Tempos.
Childs, Brevard S. 1970. *Biblical Theology in Crisis*. Philadelphia: Westminster.
———. 1974. *Exodus*. OTL. Philadelphia: Westminster.
———. 2001. *Isaiah*. OTL. Louisville: Westminster John Knox.
The Church of Ethiopia, a Panorama of History and Spiritual Life. 1970. Addis Ababa: Ethiopian Orthodox Church.
Cobb, John B., Jr., and David Ray Griffin. 1976. *Process Theology: An Introductory Exposition*. Louisville: Westminister.
Collins, John J. 1980. "The Heavenly Representative: The Son of Man in the *Similitudes of Enoch*." In *Ideal Figures in Ancient Judaism: Profiles and Paradigms*, edited by John J. Collins and George W. E. Nickelsburg, 111–33. Septuagint and Cognate Studies Series 12. Chico, CA: Scholars.
Coppens, Joseph. 1983. *Le Fils d'Homme vétéro- et intertestamentaire*. Bibliotheca Ephemeridum Theologicarum Lovaniensium 61. Leuven: Peeters.
Couenhoven, Jesse. 2005. "St. Augustine's Doctrine of Original Sin." *Augustinian Studies* 36:359–96.
Cowley, Roger W. 1971a. *Ṣedqa haymānot: ya-bēta krestiyān haymānot wesānēwoč*. Addis Ababa: Berhannena Selam.
———. 1971b. "Preliminary Notes of the *baläandəmta* Commentaries." *JES* 9/1:9–20.
———. 1972. "The Beginnings of the andem Commentary Tradition." *JES* 10/2:1–16.
———. 1974a. "Old Testament Introduction in the Andəmta Commentary Tradition." *JES* 12/1:133–75.

———. 1974b. "The Biblical Canon of the Ethiopian Orthodox Church Today." *OstSt* 23:318–23.

———. 1977. "New Testament Introduction in the Andəmta Commentary Tradition." *OstSt* 26.2/3:144–192.

———. 1978. "The Identification of the Ethiopian Octateuch of Clement, and Its Relationship to the Other Christian Literature." *OstSt* 27/1:37–45.

———. 1980. "Scholia of Ahob of Qatar on St John's Gospel and the Pauline Epistles." *Le Muséon* 98/3–4:329–43.

———. 1983a. *The Traditional Interpretation of the Apocalypse of John in the Ethiopian Orthodox Church*. University of Cambridge Oriental Publications. Cambridge: Cambridge University Press.

———. 1983b. "A Geez Prologue Concerning the Work of Mämhər Kəflä Giyorgis on the Text and Interpretation of the Book of Ezekiel." In *Ethiopian Studies: Dedicated to Wolf Leslau on the Occasion of His Seventy-fifth Birthday, November 14th, 1981*, edited by Stanislav Segert and András J. E. Bodrogligeti, 99–114. Sonderdruck aus Ethiopian Studies. Wiesbaden: Harrassowitz.

———. 1985a. "'The 'Blood of Zechariah' (Mt 23:35) In Ethiopian Exegetical Tradition." *Studia Patristica* 18/1:293–302.

———. 1985b. "The So-called 'Ethiopic *Book of the Cock*'—Part of an Apocryphal Passion Gospel, *The Homily and Teaching of Our Fathers the Holy Apostles*." *Journal of the Royal Asiatic Society* 1:16–22.

———. 1986. "Mämhər Esdros and His interpretations." In *Ethiopian Studies: Proceedings of the Sixth International Conference, Tel-Aviv, 14–17 April 1980*, edited by Gideon Goldenberg, 41–69. Boston: Balkema.

———. 1987. "A Ge'ez Document Reporting Controversy Concerning the Bible Commentaries of Ibn at-Taiyib." *Rassegna di Studi Etiopici* 30/1:5–13.

———. 1988. *Ethiopian Biblical Interpretation: A Study in Exegetical Tradition and Hermeneutics*. University of Cambridge Oriental Publications 38. Cambridge: Cambridge University Press.

———. 1989. "Zəkre and Pawli—Ethiopic Bible Translators or Interpreters." *Journal of Semitic Studies* 34:387–98.

Cunningham, Scott 1997. *Through Many Tribulations: The Theology of Persecution in Luke-Acts*. JSNTSup 142. Sheffield: Sheffield Academic.

Davidson, Ivor J. 2005. "'Not My Will but Yours Be Done': The Ontological Dynamics of Incarnational Intention." *International Journal of Systematic Theology* 7:178–204.

Davies, Donald M. 1987. "The Dating of Ethiopic Manuscripts." *Journal of Near Eastern Studies* 46:287–307.

Davies, John A. 2004. *The Royal Priesthood: Literary and Intertextual Perspectives on an Image of Israel in Exodus 19.6*. JSOTSup 395. London: T. & T. Clark.

Davies, Philip R. 1995. *In Search of 'Ancient Israel.'* JSOTSup 148. Sheffield: Sheffield Academic.

Delcor, M. 1976. "Le mythe de la chute des anges et de l'origine des géants comme explication du mal dans le monde dans l'apocalyptique juive: Histoire des traditions." *Revue de l'histoire des religions* 190:3–53.

Delio, Ilia 2013. *The Unbearable Wholeness of Being: God, Evolution, and the Power of Love*. Maryknoll, NY: Orbis.

DeSilva, David. 1992. "The Social Setting of the Revelation to John: Conflicts Within, Fears without." *Westminster Theological Journal* 54:273–302.

Dibelius, Martin. 1976. *James: A Commentary on the Epistle of James*. Edited by Heinrich Greeven. Translated by Michael A. Williams. Hermeneia. Philadelphia: Fortress.

Dillenberger, John, ed. 1961. *Martin Luther: Selections from His Writings*. Garden City, NY: Doubleday Anchor. Reprinted from *The Reformation Writings of Martin Luther*, vol. II, *The Spirit of the Protestant Reformation*. Translated by Betram Lee Woolf. London: Lutherworth, 1956.

Dillmann, August. 1851. *Liber Henoch Aithiopice*. Leipzig: Vogel. (See 2005)

———. 1853a. *Das Buch Henoch. Überstezt und erklärt*. Leipzig: Vogel.

———. 1853b. *Veteris Testamenti Aethiopici Tomus I: Octateuchus Aethiopicus*. Leipzig: Vogel.

———. 1907. *Ethiopic Grammar*. 2nd ed. by Carl Bezold. Translated by James A. Crichton. Reprinted, Ancient Language Resources. Eugene, OR: Wipf & Stock, 2005.

———. 2005. *The Ethiopic Text of 1 Enoch*. Reprint, with new bibliography by K. C. Hanson. Ancient Texts and Translations. Eugene, OR: Wipf & Stock. (See 1851)

Dimant, Devorah A. 1978. "1 Enoch 1–6: A Methodological Perspective." In *Society of Biblical Literature Seminar Papers*, edited by Paul J. Achtemeier, 1:323–39. Missoula, MT: Scholars.

Dryden, J. De Waal. 2006. *Theology and Ethics in 1 Peter*. WUNT 209. Tübingen: Mohr/Siebeck.

Dunn, James D. G. 1980. *Christology in the Making: A New Testament Inquiry into the Origins of the Doctrine of the Incarnation*. London: SCM.

Eco, Umberto. 1990. "Intentio Lectoris: The State of the Art." In *The Limits of Interpretation*, 44–63. Advances in Semiotics. Bloomington: Indiana University Press.

———. 1992. "Overinterpreting Texts." In *Interpretation and Overinterpretation*, edited by Stefan Collini, 45–66. Cambridge: Cambridge University Press.

Elias, Norbert. 1983. *The Court Society*. Translated by Edmund Jephcott. Oxford: Blackwell. (German original 1969).

Elliott, John H. 1986. "1 Peter, Its Situation and Strategy: A Discussion with David Balch." In *Perspectives on First Peter*, edited by Charles H. Talbert, 61–78. NABPR Special Studies Series 9. Macon, GA: Mercer University Press.

———. 1995. "The Jewish Messianic Movement: From Faction to Sect." In *Modelling Early Christianity: Social-Scientific Studies of the New Testament In Its Context*, edited by Philip F. Esler, 75–95. London: Routledge.

———. 1993. *What Is Social-Scientific Criticism?* Guides to Biblical Scholarship. Minneapolis: Fortress.

———. 2005. *A Home for the Homeless: A Social-Scientific Criticism: Its Situation and Strategy, with a New Introduction*. Reprint, Eugene, OR: Wipf & Stock.

Engelmann Helmut, and Reinhold Merkelbach. 1972. *Die Inschriften von Erythrai und Klazomenai*. 2 vols. Inschriften griechischer Städte aus Kleinasien 1–2. Bonn: Habelt.

Erho, Ted M., and Loren Stuckenbruck. 2013. "A Manuscript History of Ethiopic Enoch." *JSP* 23:87–133.

Esler, Philip F. 1987. *Community and Gospel in Luke-Acts: The Social and Political Motivations of Lucan Theology*. SNTSMS 57. Cambridge: Cambridge University Press.

———. 1994. "The Social Function of 4 Ezra." In *The First Christians in Their Social Worlds: Social-Scientific Approaches to New Testament Interpretation*, 110–30. New York: Routledge.

———. 2005. *New Testament Theology: Communion and Community*. Minneapolis: Fortress.

———. 2014. "Social-Scientific Approaches to Apocalyptic Literature." In *The Oxford Handbook of Apocalyptic Literature*, edited by John J. Collins, 123–44. Oxford Handbooks. Oxford: Oxford University Press.

Federal Democratic Republic of Ethiopia Population Census Commission. 2008. *Summary and Statistical Report of the 2007 Population and Housing Census: Population Size by Age and Sex*. Addis Ababa: UNFPA.

Feehan, John. 2010. *The Singing Heart of the World: Creation, Evolution and Faith*. Dublin: Columba.

Finsterbusch, Karin. 2005. *Weisung für Israel: Studien zu Religiösem Lehren und Lernen im Deuteronomium und in seinem Umfeld*. Forschungen zum Alten Testament 44. Tübingen: Mohr/Siebeck.

Flemming, Johann. 1902. *Das Buch Henoch Aethiopischer Text*. Texte und Untersuchungen zur Geschichte der altchristlichen Literatur. Leipzig: Hinrichs.

Fletcher-Louis, Crispin H. T. 2002. *All the Glory of Adam: Liturgical Anthropology in the Dead Sea Scrolls*. Studies on the Texts of the Desert of Judah 42. Leiden: Brill.

———. 2004a. "God's Image, His Cosmic Temple and the High Priest: Towards an Historical and Theological Account of the Incarnation." In *Heaven on Earth: The Temple in Biblical Theology*, edited by T. Desmond Alexander and Simon Gathercole, 81–99. Carlisle, UK: Paternoster.

———. 2004b. "The Worship of the Jewish High Priest by Alexander the Great." In *Early Christian and Jewish Monotheism*, edited by Loren T. Stuckenbruck and Wendy E. S. North, 71–102. JSNTSup 263. Edinburgh: T. & T. Clark.

———. 2004c. "The Temple Cosmology of P and Theological Anthropology in the Wisdom of Jesus ben Sira." In *Of Scribes and Sages: Early Jewish Interpretation and Transmission of Scripture*, edited by Craig A. Evans, 69–113. 2 vols. Library of Second Temple Studies 50–51. Sheffield: Sheffield Academic.

———. 2007. "Humanity and the Idols of the Gods in Pseudo-Philo's *Biblical Antiquities*." In *Idolatry: False Worship in the Bible, Early Judaism, and Christianity*, edited by Stephen C. Barton, 58–72. T. & T. Clark Theology. London: T. & T. Clark.

———. 2011. "Jewish Apocalyptic and Apocalypticism." In *Handbook for the Study of the Historical Jesus*, edited by Tom Holmén and Stanley E. Porter, 2:1569–607. 4 vols. Leiden: Brill.

———. 2014. "The *Similitudes of Enoch* (1 Enoch 37–71): The Son of Man, Apocalyptic Messianism & Political Theology." In *The Open Mind: Essays in Honour of Christopher Rowland*, edited by Jonathan Knight and Kevin Sullivan, 58–79. LNTS 522. London: T. & T. Clark.

———. 2015. *Jesus Monotheism*. Vol. 1, *Christological Origins: The Emerging Consensus and Beyond*. Eugene, OR: Wipf & Stock.

———. 2017 forthcoming. *Jesus Monotheism*. Vol. 2, *Philippians, the Synoptics and Questions in Need of an Answer*. Eugene OR: Wipf & Stock.

———. 2017/2018 forthcoming. *Jesus' Divine Identity, the High Priesthood and the Greco-Roman Ruler Cult in John 5*.

Fritsch, Emmanuel. 2012. "The Altar in the Ethiopian Church: History, Forms and Meanings." In *Inquiries into Eastern Christian Worship*, edited by Bert Groen, Steven Hawkes-Teeple, and Stefanos Alexopoulos, 443–510. Eastern Christian Studies 12. Leuven: Peeters.

Garcia, Miguel Angel. 1999. *Ethiopian Biblical Commentaries on the Prophet Micah*. ÄthFor 52. Wiesbaden: Harrassowitz.

———. 2010. "Tərgwame." In *Encyclopaedia Aethiopica*, edited by Siegbert Uhlig, Alessandro Bausi et al., 4:921–23. Wiesbaden: Harrassowitz.

Gathercole, Simon J. 2006. *The Preexistent Son: Recovering the Christologies of Matthew, Mark, and Luke*. Grand Rapids: Eerdmans.

Gieschen, C. A. 2007. "The Name of the Son of Man in the Parables of Enoch." In *Enoch and the Messiah Son of Man: Revisiting the Book of Parables*, edited by Gabriele Boccaccini, 238–49. Grand Rapids: Eerdmans.

Gignilliat, Mark. 2007. *Paul and Isaiah's Servants: Paul's Theological Reading of Isaiah 40-66 in 2 Corinthians 5:14—6:10*. LNTS 330. London: T. & T. Clark.

Ginzberg, Louis. 1925. *The Legends of the Jews*. Vol. 5. Philadelphia: Jewish Publication Society of America.

Goff, Matthew J. 2010. "Monstrous Appetites: Blood, Giants, Cannibalism and Insatiable Eating in Enochic Literature." *Journal of Ancient Judaism* 1:19–42.

Goldingay, John E. 1989. *Daniel*. Dallas: Word Books.

Gunton, Colin E. 1988. *The Actuality of Atonement: A Study of Metaphor, Rationality and the Christian Tradition*. Edinburgh: T. & T. Clark.

Haffner, Paul. 2008. *Towards a Theology of the Environment*. Leominster: Gracewing.

Hanks, William F. 1987. "Discourse Genres in a Theory of Practice." *American Ethnologist* 14:668–92.

Hanson, Paul D. 1977. "Rebellion in Heaven, Azazel, and Euhemeristic Heroes in 1 Enoch 6-11." *JBL* 96:195–233.

Harkins, Angela Kim, Kelley Coblentz Bautch, and John Endres C.S.J., eds. 2014. *The Watchers in Jewish and Christian Traditions*. Minneapolis: Fortress.

Hays, Richard B. 2002. *The Faith of Jesus Christ: The Narrative Substructure of Galatians 3:1—4:11*. Grand Rapids: Eerdmans.

Heldman, Marilyn et al. 1993. *African Zion: The Sacred Art of Ethiopia*. New Haven: Yale University Press.

Hellerman, Joseph H. 2005. *Reconstructing Honor in Roman Philippi: Carmen Christi as Cursus Pudorum*. SNTSMS 132. Cambridge: Cambridge University Press.

Hemer, Colin. 2000. *The Letters to the Seven Churches of Asia in their Local Setting*. Grand Rapids: Eerdmans.

Henten, William van. 2001. "The Honorary Decree for Simon the Maccabee (1 Macc 14:25–49) in Its Hellenistic Context." In *Hellenism in the Land of Israel*, edited by John J. Collins and Gregory E. Sterling, 116–45. Christianity and Judaism in Antiquity 13. Notre Dame: University of Notre Dame.

———. 2007. "Royal Ideology. 1 and 2 Maccabees and Egypt." In *Jewish Perspectives on Hellenistic Rulers*, edited by T. Rajak, S. Pearce, J. Aitken, and J. Dines, 265–82. Hellenistic Culture and Society 50. Berkeley: University of California Press.

Hobsbawm, Eric, and Terence Ranger, eds. 1983. *The Invention of Tradition*. Past and Present Publications. Cambridge: Cambridge University Press.

Horrell, David G. 2010. *The Bible and the Environment: Towards a Critical Ecological Biblical Theology*. Biblical Challenges in the Contemporary World. London: Equinox.

Hume, David. 1996 (1779). *Dialogues Concerning Natural Religion*. Part X in *Writings on Religion*, edited by Antony Flew. Chicago: Open Court.

Hunter, Richard. 2003. *Encomium of Ptolemy Philadelphus*. Hellenistic Culture and Society 39. Berkeley: University of California Press.

Hurtado, Larry W. 2003. *Lord Jesus Christ: Devotion to Jesus in Earliest Christianity*. Grand Rapids: Eerdmans.

Jahn, R. G., and B. J. Dunne. 2007; repr. 2004. "Sensors, Filters, and the Source of Reality." *Explore* 3:326–37.

Jenni, Ernst, and Claus Westermann, eds. 1997. *Theological Lexicon of the Old Testament*. 3 vols. Translated by Mark E. Biddle. Peabody, MA: Hendrickson.

Johnson, Elizabeth A. 2014. *Ask the Beasts: Darwin and the God of Love*. London: Bloomsbury.

Jorstad, Mari. 2016. "The Ground that Opened Its Mouth: The Ground's Response to Human Violence in Genesis 4." *JBL* 135:705–15.

Kane, Thomas Leiper. 1990. *Amharic-English Dictionary*. Vol. 2. Wiesbaden: Harrassowitz.

Kannengiesser, Charles, ed. 1973. *Athanase D'Alexandrie: Sur L'Incarnation du Verbe*. SC 199. Paris: Cerf.

Kekes, John. 1998. "Evil." In *Routledge Encyclopedia of Philosophy*, edited by Edward Craig, 3:463–66. London: Routledge.

Kelsey, David E. 2009. *Eccentric Existence: A Theological Anthropology*. Vol. 1. Louisville: Westminster John Knox.

Knibb, Michael A. 1978. *The Ethiopic Book of Enoch: A New Edition in the Light of the Aramaic Dead Sea Fragments*. 2 vols. Oxford: Clarendon.

———. 1988. "Hebrew and Syriac Elements in the Ethiopic Version of Enoch?" *Journal of Semitic Studies* 33:11–35.

Koester, Craig R. 2014. *Revelation: A New Translation with Introduction and Commentary*. Anchor Yale Bible Commentaries 38A. New Haven: Yale University Press.

LaCugna, Catherine Mowry. 1992. *God for Us: The Trinity and Christian Life*. San Francisco: HarperSanFrancisco.

Langlois, Michael. 2008. *Le premier manuscrit du Livre d'Hénoch: Étude épigraphique et philologique des fragments araméens de 4Q201 à Qumrân*. Lectio Divina. Paris: Cerf.

Laurence, Richard. 1821. *The Book of Enoch, The Prophet: An Apocryphal Production, Supposed to Have Been Lost for Ages; But Discovered at the Close of The Last Century in Abyssinia; Now First Translated from an Ethiopic Ms. in the Bodleian Library*. Oxford, Clarendon (Rev. eds. appeared in 1833, 1838, and 1842).

———. 1838. *Libri Enoch Prophetae Versio Aethiopica*. Oxford: Parke.

Lee, Ralph. 2011. "Symbolic Interpretations in Ethiopic and Ephremic Literature." PhD diss., School of Oriental and African Studies, University of London. (This work is pending publication by Peeters under the title *Symbolic Interpretations in Ethiopic and Early Syriac Literature*.)

———. 2014. "The Ethiopic 'Andəmta' Commentary on Enoch 2 (1 Enoch 6–9)." *JSP* 23:179–200.

———. 2017. *Symbolic Interpretations in Ethiopic and Early Syriac Literature*. Eastern Christian Studies 4. Leuven: Peeters.

Leslau, Wolf. 1987. *Comparative Dictionary of Ge'ez (Classical Ethiopic): Ge'ez–English/English–Ge'ez with an Index of the Semitic Roots*. Wiesbaden: Harrassowitz.

Levine, Donald N. 1965. *Wax & Gold: Tradition and Innovation in Ethiopian Culture*. Chicago: University of Chicago Press.

Levi-Strauss, Claude, and F. C. T. Moore. 1974. "How Myths Die." *New Literary History* 5:269–81.

Lied, Liv Ingeborg. 2008. *The Other Lands of Israel: Imaginations of the Land in 2 Baruch*. JSJSup 129. Leiden: Brill.

Lossky, Vladimir. 1974. "Tradition and Traditions." In *In the Image and Likeness of God*. Edited by John H. Erickson and Thomas E. Bird. Crestwood, NY: St. Vladimir's Seminary.

Lowe, Walter. 1993. *Theology and Difference: The Wound of Reason*. Indiana Series in the Philosophy of Religion. Bloomington: Indiana University Press.

Luz, Ulrich. 2014. *Theologische Hermeneutik des Neuen Testaments*. Neukirchner Theologie. Neukirchen-Vluyn: Neukirchener.

Macaskill, Grant. 2007. *Revealed Wisdom and Inaugurated Eschatology in Ancient Judaism and Early Christianity*. JSJSup 115. Leiden: Brill.

———. 2013a. *Union with Christ in the New Testament*. Oxford: Oxford University Press.

———. 2013b. "Matthew and the Parables." In *The Parables of Enoch: A Paradigm Shift*, edited by James H. Charlesworth and Darrell Bock, 218–29. T. & T. Clark Library of Biblical Studies. London: Bloomsbury T. & T. Clark.

Machinist, Peter. 2006. "Kingship and Divinity in Imperial Assyria." In *Text, Artifact, and Image: Revealing Ancient Israelite Religion*, edited by Gary Beckman and Theodore J. Lewis, 152–88. Brown Judaic Studies 346. Providence, RI: Brown Judaic Studies.

Mack, Burton L. 1985. *Wisdom and the Hebrew Epic: Ben Sira's Hymn in Praise of the Fathers*. Chicago Studies in the History of Judaism. Chicago: University of Chicago Press.

Mackie, J. L. 1990. "Evil and Omnipotence." In *The Problem of Evil*, edited by Marilyn McCord Adams and Robert Merrihew Adams, 25–37. Oxford: Oxford University Press.

Mair, A. W., and G. R. Mair. 1921. *Callimachus, Hymns and Epigrams*. LCL 129. Cambridge: Harvard University Press.

Malaty, Fr. Tadros. 1995. *The School of Alexandria (Book One): Before Origen*. Jersey City, NJ: St. Mark Coptic Orthodox Church.

Mannion, Gerard. 2007. *Ecclesiology and Postmodernity: Questions for the Church of Our Time*. Collegeville, MN: Liturgical.

Marlin, George J. 2015. *Christian Persecutions in the Middle East: A 21st Century Tragedy*. South Bend, IN: St Augustine's.

Marshall, Paul. 1998. "Persecution of Christians in the Contemporary World." *International Bulletin of Missionary Research* 22: 2–8.

———. "Present Day Persecution of Christians." *Evangelical Review of Theology* 24:19–30.

Martin, Francois. 1906. *Le Livre d'Hénoch*. Documents pour l'étude de la Bible: Les Apocryphes de l'Ancien Testament. Paris: Letouzey & Ané.

Martin, Michael Wade, and Brian A. Nash. 2015. "Philippians 2:6-11 as Subversive *Hymnos*: A Study in the Light of Ancient Rhetorical Theory." *Journal of Theological Studies* 66:90-138.

Maston, Jason. 2012. "Judaism and Hellenism: Rethinking Ben Sira's 'Opponents.'" In *Earliest Christian History: History, Literature, and Theology. Essays from the Tyndale Fellowship in Honor of Martin Hengel*, edited by Michael F. Bird and Jason Maston, 273-304. WUNT 2/320. Tübingen: Mohr/Siebeck.

Matthews, Mark. 2010. "Riches, Poverty and the Faithful: Perspectives of Wealth in the 2 Temple Period and the Apocalypse of John." PhD diss., Durham University.

———. 2013. *Riches, Poverty and the Faithful: Perspectives of Wealth in the 2 Temple Period and the Apocalypse of John*. SNTSMS 154. Cambridge: Cambridge University Press.

McConville, J. G. 2006a. *God and Earthly Power: An Old Testament Political Theology: Genesis-Kings*. T. & T. Clark Library of Biblical Studies 454. London: T. & T. Clark.

———. 2006b. "Old Testament Laws and Canonical Intentionality." In *Canon and Biblical Interpretation*, edited by Craig G. Bartholomew et al., 259-81. SHS 7. Milton Keynes, UK: Paternoster.

McFague, Sallie. 1993. *The Body of God: An Ecological Theology*. Minneapolis: Fortress.

Meeks, Wayne E. 1972. "The Man from Heaven in Johannine Sectarianism." *JBL* 91: 44-72.

Metzler, Karin, and Kyriakos Savvidis, eds. 1998. *Athanasius Werke: Erster Band: Erster Teil: Die Dogmatischen Schriften 2. Lieferung*. Orationes I et II ContrArianos. Berlin: de Gruyter.

Meyers, Carol L. 2005. *Exodus*. New Cambridge Bible Commentary. Cambridge: Cambridge University Press.

Milbank, John. 1990. *Theology and Social Theory: Beyond Secular Reason*. Oxford: Blackwell.

Milik, J. T. 1976. *The Books of Enoch: Aramaic Fragments of Qumran Cave 4*. With the collaboration of Matthew Black. Oxford: Clarendon.

Minchakpu, Obed. 2004. "Eye for an Eye: Christians Avenge February Murders, Spark Muslim Retaliation." *Christianity Today* 48:17.

Mohammed, Girma. 2012. *Understanding Religion and Social Change in Ethiopia: Toward a Hermeneutic of Covenant*. New York: Palgrave Macmillan.

Morris, Michael Ashley. 2012. *Concise Dictionary of Social and Cultural Anthropology*. West Sussex, UK: Wiley-Blackwell.

Mosala, Itumeleng J. 1993. "Biblical Theology and Black Hermeneutics in South Africa: The Use of the Bible." *The Bible and Liberation: Political and Social Hermeneutics*, edited by Norman K. Gottwald and Richard A. Horsley, 51-73. 2nd ed. Maryknoll, NY: Orbis.

Naess, Arne, 1973. "The Shallow and the Deep, Long Range Ecology Movements." *Inquiry* 16:95-100.

Newsom, Carol A. 1980. "The Development of 1 Enoch 6-19: Cosmology and Judgment." *Catholic Biblical Quarterly* 42:310-29.

Nickelsburg, George W. E. 2001. *1 Enoch 1: A Commentary on the Book of 1 Enoch, Chapters 1-36, 81-108*. Hermeneia. Minneapolis: Fortress.

———. 2003. "Revisiting the Rich and Poor in 1 Enoch 92-105 and the Gospel of Luke." In *George W. E. Nickelsburg in Perspective: An Ongoing Dialogue of Learning*, edited by Jacob Neusner and Alan J. Avery-Peck, 2:541-71. JSJSup 80. Leiden: Brill.

Nickelsburg, George W. E., and James C. VanderKam, 2012a. *1 Enoch 2*. Hermeneia. Minneapolis: Fortress.

———. 2012b. *1 Enoch: A New Translation Based on the Hermeneia Commentary*. Minneapolis: Fortress.

Northcott, Michael S. 2013. *A Political Theology of Climate Change*. Grand Rapids: Eerdmans.

Nyberg, Richard. 2004. "Pastors Killed, Churches Burned: New Wave of Violence Begins." *Christianity Today* 48.6:17.

Oberman, Heiko A. 2003. "Luther and the Via Moderna: The Philosophical Backdrop of the Reformation Breakthrough." *Journal of Ecclesiastical History* 54:641-70.

Parker, K. I. 1992. "Solomon as Philosopher King? The Nexus of Law and Wisdom in I Kings 1-11." *Journal for the Study of the Old Testament* 53:75-91.

Parry, Donald W., and Emanuel Tov, eds. 2004-2005. *The Dead Sea Scrolls Reader*. 6 vols. Leiden: Brill.

Pedersen, Kirsten Stoffregen. 1995. *Traditional Ethiopian Exegesis of the Book of Psalms*. ÄthFor 36. Wiesbaden: Harrassowitz.

Pike, Nelson, ed. 1964. *Good and Evil: Readings on the Theological Problem of Evil*. Contemporary Perspectives in Philosophy Series. Englewood Cliffs, NJ: Prentice-Hall.

Piovanelli, Pierluigi. 2007. "'A Testimony for the Kings and the Mighty Who Possess the Earth': The Thirst for Justice and Peace in the Parables of Enoch." In *Enoch and the Messiah Son of Man: Revisiting the Book of Parables*, edited by Gabriele Boccaccini, 363-79. Grand Rapids: Eerdmans.

Pop, Simion. 2011. "Eastern Orthodox Christianity as Anthropological Object: Conceptual and Methodological Considerations." *Studia Ubb Sociologia* 56/2:93-108.

Portier-Young, Anathea. 2011. *Apocalypse against Empire: Theologies of Resistance in Early Judaism*. Grand Rapids: Eerdmans.

———. 2014. "Jewish Apocalyptic Literature as Resistance Literature." In *The Oxford Handbook of Apocalyptic Literature*, edited by John J. Collins, 145-62. Oxford Handbooks. Oxford: Oxford University Press.

Propp, W. H. 2006. *Exodus 19-40: A New Translation with Introduction and Commentary*. Anchor Bible 2A. New York: Doubleday.

Rad, Gerhard von. 1972. *Genesis: A Commentary*. 2nd ed. Translated by John H. Marks. OTL. Philadelphia: Westminster.

Reese, Günter. 1999. *Die Geschichte Israels in der Auffassung des frühen Judentums: Eine Untersuchung der Tiervision und der Zehnwochenapokalypse des äthiopischen Henochbuches, der Geschichtsdarstellung der Assumptio Mosis und der des 4 Esrabuches*. Bonner Biblische Beiträge 123. Berlin: Philo.

Rogerson, John. 1991. *Genesis 1-11*. Old Testament Guides. Sheffield: Sheffield Academic.

Roszak, Theodore. 1995. *The Voice of the Earth*. New York: Simon & Schuster.

Roth, S. John. 1997. *The Blind, the Lame and the Poor: Character Types in Luke-Acts*. JSNTSup 144. Sheffield: Sheffield Academic.

Rowland, Christopher. 2000. "Jude." In *The Oxford Bible Commentary*, edited by John Barton and John Muddiman, 1284-87. Oxford: Oxford University Press.

———. 1995. "In This Place: The Center and the Margins in Theology." In *Reading from This Place: Social Location and Biblical Interpretation in Global Perspective*, edited by Fernando F. Segovia and Mary Ann Tolbert, 169-82. Minneapolis: Fortress.

Rubin, Alissa J. 2014. "ISIS Forces Last Iraqi Christians to Flee Mosul." *The New York Times*, July 19.

Ruether, Rosemary Radford. 1992. *Gaia and God: An Ecofeminist Theology of Earth Healing*. New York: Harper Collins.

Russell, Norman. 2004. *The Doctrine of Deification in the Greek Patristic Tradition*. Oxford: Oxford University Press.

Sacchi, Paolo. 1990. *Jewish Apocalyptic and Its History*. Translated by William J. Short OFM. Journal for the Study of the Pseudepigrapha Supplements 20. Sheffield: Sheffield Academic.

Sanders, James A. 1987. *From Sacred Story to Sacred Text: Canon as Paradigm*. Reprint, Eugene, OR: Wipf & Stock, 2000.

———. 1993. "Introduction: Why the Pseudepigrapha?" In *The Pseudepigrapha and Early Biblical Interpretation*, edited by James H. Charlesworth and Craig A. Evans, 13–19. Journal for the Study of the Pseudepigrapha Supplements 14. Sheffield: JSOT Press.

Santmire, H. Paul. 1985. *The Travail of Nature: The Ambiguous Ecological Promise of Christian Theology*. Philadelphia: Fortress.

Schechter, Solomon. 1902. *Midrash ha-gadol. Genesis*. Cambridge: Cambridge University Press.

Schirrmacher, Thomas. 2010. "Theses on a Theology of Martyrdom." In *Suffering, Persecution and Martyrdom: Theological Reflections*, edited by Christof Sauer and Richard Howell, 287–314. Religious Freedom Series 2. Johannesburg: AcadSA.

Seebass, Horst. 2003. "Erstes oder Altes Testament." In *Die Einheit der Schrift und die Vielfalt des Kanons*, edited by John Barton and Michael Wolter, 27–43. BZNW 118. Berlin: de Gruyter.

Seeman, Chris. 2014. "The Watchers' Traditions and Gen 6:1–4 (MT and LXX)." In *The Watchers in Jewish and Christian Traditions*, edited by Angela Kim Harkins et al., 25–38. Minneapolis: Fortress.

Sjöberg, Erik. 1945. *Der Menschensohn im äthiopischen Henochbuch*. Skrifter utg. av Kungl. Humanistiska vetenskapssamfundet i Lund 41. Lund: Gleerup.

Smith, Anthony D. 2003. *Chosen Peoples*. Oxford: Oxford University Press.

Smith, Morton. 1971. *Palestinian Parties and Politics that Shaped the Old Testament*. New York: Columbia University Press. 2nd corrected ed., London: SCM, 1987.

Sparks, H. F. D., ed. 1984. *The Apocryphal Old Testament*. Oxford: Clarendon.

Stuckenbruck, Loren T. 1990. "Revision of Aramaic-Greek and Greek-Aramaic Glossaries in The Books of Enoch: Aramaic Fragments of Qumran Cave 4 by J. T. Milik." *JJS* 41:13–48.

———. 2000. "201 2–8. 4QEnochA ar." In *Qumran Cave 4. XXVI. Cryptic Texts and Miscellanea Part 1*, edited by Stephen J. Pfann et al., 3–7. Discoveries in the Judean Desert 36. Oxford: Clarendon.

———. 2002. "Genesis 6, 1–4 as the Basis for Divergent Readings during the Second Temple Period." *Henoch* 24: 99–106.

———. 2007. *1 Enoch 91–108*. Commentaries on Early Jewish Literature. Berlin: de Gruyter.

———. 2013. "The Book of Enoch: Its Reception in Second Temple Jewish and in Christian Tradition." *Early Christianity* 4:7–40.

———. 2014. *The Myth of the Rebellious Angels: Studies in Second Temple Judaism and New Testament Texts*. WUNT 335. Tübingen: Mohr/Siebeck.

Sweeney, Marvin A. 2010. "Synchronic and Diachronic Considerations in the DtrH Portrayal of the Demise of Solomon's Kingdom." In *Birkat Shalom: Studies in the Bible, Ancient Near Eastern Literature, and Postbiblical Judaism Presented* to Shalom M. Paul on the Occasion of His Seventieth Birthday, edited by Chaim Cohen et al., 175–89. Winona Lake, IN: Eisenbrauns.

Tamrat, Tadesse. 1984. "Feudalism in Heaven and Earth: Ideology and Political Structure in Medieval Ethiopia." In *Proceedings of the Seventh International Conference of Ethiopian Studies, University of Lund, 26–29 April, 1982*, edited by Sven Rubenson, 195–200. Addis Ababa: Addis Ababa University Press.

Taylor, Charles. 1992. *The Sources of the Self: The Making of the Modern Identity*. Cambridge: Cambridge University Press.

Tcherikover, Victor. 1979. *Hellenistic Civilization and the Jews*. Philadelphia: Jewish Publication Society.

Tedeschi, Richard G., and Lawrence G. Calhoun. 2004. "Posttraumatic Growth: Conceptual Foundations and Empirical Evidence." *Psychological Inquiry* 15:1–18.

Theisohn, Johannes. 1975. *Der auserwählte Richter: Untersuchungen zum traditionsgeschichtlichem Ort der Menschensohngestalt der Bilderreden des Äthiopischen Henoch*. Studien zur Umwelt des Neuen Testaments 12. Göttingen: Vandenhoeck & Ruprecht.

Thesleff, H. 1965. *The Pythagorean Texts of the Hellenistic Period*. Acta Academiae Aboensis, Ser. A, Humaniora 30.1. Åbo: Åbo Akademi.

Thiselton, Anthony C. 2006. "Introduction." In *Canon and Biblical Interpretation*, edited by Craig G. Bartholomew et al., 1–30. SHS 7. Milton Keynes, UK: Paternoster.

Tibebu, Teshale. 1995. *The Making of Modern Ethiopia: 1896–1974*. Trenton, NJ: Red Sea.

Tiller, Patrick A. 1993. *A Commentary on the Animal Apocalypse of I Enoch*. EJL 4. Atlanta: Scholars.

Tilling, Christopher. 2012. *Paul's Divine Christology*. WUNT 2/323. Tübingen: Mohr/Siebeck.

Ting, R. S. K., and T. Watson. 2007. "Is Suffering Good? An Explorative Study on Religious Persecution among Chinese Pastors." *Journal of Psychology and Theology* 35:202–10.

Trible, Phyllis. 1984. *Texts of Terror: Literary-Feminist Readings of Biblical Narratives*. Overtures to Biblical Theology. Philadelphia: Fortress.

Turcan, Marie, ed. 1971. *Tertullien, la toilette des femmes*. SC 173. Paris: Cerf.

Turner, Victor W. 1974. *Dramas, Fields, and Metaphors: Symbolic Action in Human Society*. Ithaca, NY: Cornell University Press.

———. 1967. *The Forest of Symbols: Aspects of Ndembu Ritual*. Ithaca, NY: Cornell University Press.

———. 1969. *The Ritual Process: Structure and Anti-Structure*. Lewis Henry Morgan Lectures, 1966. Ithaca, NY: Cornell University Press.

Uhlig, Siegbert. 1984. *Der äthiopische Henochbuch*. Jüdische Schriften aus hellenistisch-römische Zeit 5/6. Gütersloh: Gütersloher.

Uhlig, Siegbert et al., eds. 2003, 2005, 2007. *Encyclopaedia Aethiopica*, Vols. 1–3. Wiesbaden: Harrassowitz.

Uhlig, Siegbert, Alessandro Bausi et al., eds. 2010. *Encyclopaedia Aethiopica*, Vol. 4. Wiesbaden: Harrassowitz.

Underwood, Paul A. 1950. "The Fountain of Life in Manuscripts of the Gospels." *Dumbarton Oak Papers* 5:41–138, figs. 34–38, 26, 30, 53–55.

VanderKam, James C. 1984. *Enoch and the Growth of Apocalyptic Tradition*. Catholic Biblical Quarterly Monograph Series 16. Washington, DC: Catholic Biblical Association of America.

———. 2000. *Revelation and Canon: Studies in the Hebrew Bible and Second Temple Literature*. JSJSup 62. Leiden: Brill.
———. 2004. "Open and Closed Eyes in the Animal Apocalypse (1 Enoch 85–90)." In *The Idea of Biblical Interpretation: Essays in Honor of James L. Kugel*, edited by Hindy Najman and Judith H. Newman, 279–92. JSJSup 83. Leiden: Brill.
Volf, Mirolslav. 1996. *Exclusion and Embrace: A Theological Exploration of Identity, Otherness, and Reconciliation*. Nashville: Abingdon.
Vonnahme, Nathan. 2012. "Christian Environmental Ethics." http://enteuxis.org/nathan/portfolio/writing/1999/xian_environmental_ethics.html.
Wagner, J. Ross. 2007. *Heralds of the Good News: Isaiah and Paul "in Concert" in the Letter to the Romans*. Novum Testamentum Supplements 101. Leiden: Brill.
Walck, Leslie W. 2012. "The Social Setting of the Parables of Enoch." In *A Teacher for All Generations. Essays in Honor of James C. VanderKam*, edited by Eric F. Mason et al., 669–86. JSJSup 153. Leiden: Brill.
Wannenwetsch, Bernd. 2005. "You Shall not Kill—What Does It Take? Why We Need the Other Commandments If We Are to Abstain from Killing." In *I Am the Lord Your God: Christian Reflections on the Ten Commandments*, edited by Carl E. Braaten and Christopher R. Seitz, 148–74. Grand Rapids: Eerdmans.
Webster, John. 2001. *Word and Church: Essays in Christian Dogmatics*. Edinburgh: T. & T. Clark.
———. 2003. *Holy Scripture: A Dogmatic Sketch*. Current Issues in Theology 1. Cambridge: Cambridge University Press.
White, Lynn, Jr. 1967. "The Historical Roots of Our Ecologic Crisis." *Science* 155:1203–7.
Williams, Ron G., and James W. Boyd. 1993. *Ritual Art and Knowledge: Aesthetic Theory and Zoroastrian Ritual*. Studies in Comparative Religion. Columbia: University of South Carolina Press.
Williams, Rowan. 2008. *Dostoevsky: Language, Faith and Fiction. The Making of the Christian Imagination*. London: Continuum.
Wilson, Bryan R. 1975. *Magic and the Millennium: Religious Movements of Protest among Tribal and Third-World Peoples*. London: Heinemann.
Wink, Walter. 1992. *Engaging the Powers: Discernment and Resistance in a World of Domination*. The Powers 3. Minneapolis: Fortress.
Winter, Irene J. 1997. "Art in Empire: The Royal Image and the Visual Dimensions of Assyrian Ideology." In *Assyria 1995: Proceedings of the 10th Anniversary Symposium of the Neo-Assyrian Text Corpus Project, Helsinki, September 7–11, 1995*, edited by. S. Parpola and R. M. Whiting, 359–81. Helsinki: Neo-Assyrian Text Corpus Project. Reprinted in Winter, *On Art in the Ancient Near East*. Vol. 1, *Of the First Millennium BCE*, 71–108. Culture and History of the Ancient Near East 34.1. Leiden: Brill, 2009.
Wolter, Michael. 2003. "Die Vielfalt der Schrift und die Einheit des Kanons." In *Die Einheit der Schrift und die Vielfalt des Kanons*, edited by John Barton and Michael Wolter, 45–68. BZNW 118. Berlin: de Gruyter.
Wong-McDonald A., and R. L. Gorsuch. 2000. "Surrender to God: An Additional Coping Style?" *Journal of Psychology and Theology* 28:149–61.
Wright, Archie T. 2013. *The Origin of the Evil Spirits*. 2nd ed. WUNT 198. Tübingen: Mohr/Siebeck.
Young, Frances M. 1997. *Biblical Exegesis and the Formation of Christian Culture*. Cambridge: Cambridge University Press.

Author Index

Abebe, Sofanit T., 11, 168, 197
Adams, Marilyn McCord, 167, 176, 197
Adams, Robert Merrihew, 176, 197
Adams, Samuel L., 77, 78, 197
Aitken, J. K., 99, 197
Alehegne, Mersha, 45, 197
Amsalu, Tefera, 31, 197
Ande Berhan, Weldetense, 45, 197
Anonymous, 47, 48, 56, 58, 161, 197
Antohin, Alexandra Sellassie, 4, 5, 41, 198
Argall, Randal A., 23, 24, 198
Asale, B. A., 48, 198
Assefa, Daniel, 6, 7, 9, 10, 198
Assmann, Jan, 20, 198
Astley, Jeff, 5, 198
Aulén, Gustaf, 186, 187, 198
Aune, David E., 75, 198

Balthasar, Hans Urs von, 177, 198
Barclay, John M. G., 145, 198
Barr, James, 21, 198
Barth, Karl, 12, 176, 177, 178, 184, 185, 186, 188, 198
Barton, John, 16, 198
Bauckham, Richard, 9, 124, 198
Baynes, L., 163, 198
Bechtler, Stephen R., 162, 198
Beer, Georg, 136, 198
Bell, Catherine, 37, 199
Berry, Thomas, 111, 199

Bilen, Osman, 111, 199
Binns, John, 30, 199
Blenkinsopp, Joseph, 17, 199
Boccaccini, Gabriele, 74, 182, 199
Boer, J. H., 163, 199
Boring, M. Eugene, 149, 199
Boyd, James W., 37, 199
Brown, Raymond E., 154, 199
Bultmann, Rudolf, 114, 199

Calder, Todd, 177, 199
Calhoun, L. G., 164
Campbell, Douglas A., 145, 199
Campenhausen, Hans von, 135, 199
Caquot, André, 29, 35, 36, 200
Carroll, Timothy, 35, 200
Cary, E., 90, 200
Chaniotis, Angelos, 99, 200
Charles, R. H., 1, 66, 116, 136, 200
Charlesworth, James H., 1, 90, 200
Childs, Brevard S., 16, 135, 144, 200
Cobb, John, Jr., 111, 200
Collins, John J., 137, 200
Coppens, Joseph, 136, 200
Couenhoven, Jesse, 173, 200
Cowley, Roger W., 5, 6, 45, 46, 55, 56, 57, 58, 59, 200
Cunningham, Scott, 165, 201

Davidson, Ivor J., 140, 201
Davies, J. A., 96, 201

Davies, P. R., 17, 201
Delcor, M., 129, 201
Delio, Ilia, 124, 201
deSilva, David A., 75, 201
Dibelius, Martin, 152, 202
Dillenberger, John, 15, 202
Dillmann, August, 1, 62, 68, 125, 202
Dimant, Devorah, 129, 202
Dryden, J. De Waal, 158, 160, 202
Dunn, James D. G., 106, 202
Dunne, B. J., 111, 202

Eco, Umberto, 19, 20, 21, 202
Elias, Norbert, 184, 202
Elliott, John H., 156, 157, 159, 202
Engelmann, H., 99, 202
Erho, Ted M., 2, 202
Esler, Philip F., 147, 148, 149, 156, 158, 163, 164, 165, 202

Feehan, John, 124
Finsterbusch, Karin, 24, 203, 203
Flemming, Johann, 1, 125, 203
Fletcher-Louis, Crispin H. T., 8, 90, 93, 98, 104, 106, 107, 108, 203
Francis, Leslie J., 5, 198
Fritsch, Emmanuel, 31, 204

Garcia, Miguel Angel, 45, 204
Gathercole, S. J., 108, 204
Gieschen, C. A., 93, 204
Gignilliat, Mark, 136, 204
Ginzberg, Louis, 48, 204
Goldingay, John E. 23, 204
Gorsuch, R. L., 164, 204
Gunton, Colin E., 180, 187, 204

Haffner, Paul, 124, 204
Hanks, William F., 33, 204
Hanson, Paul D., 129, 204
Hays, Richard B., 149, 204
Hellerman, Joseph H., 108, 204
Hemer, Colin, 75, 204
Henten, William van, 102, 204
Hobsbawm, Eric, 28, 204
Horrell, David G., 113, 115, 122, 204
Hume, David, 167, 205
Hunter, R. L., 99, 205

Hurtado, Larry W., 106, 205

Isaac, Ephraim, 1, 205

Jahn, R. G., 111, 205
Jenni, Ernst, 126, 205
Johnson, Elizabeth A., 124, 205
Jorstad, Mari, 10, 205

Kane, T. L., 68, 205
Kannengiesser, Charles, 185, 205
Kekes, John, 176, 205
Kelsey, David E., 143, 205
Knibb, Michael A., 49, 51, 52, 53, 55, 66, 116, 125, 205
Koester, Craig R., 76, 205

LaCugna, C. M., 163, 205
Langlois, M., 125, 205
Laurence, Richard, 1, 205
Lee, Ralph, 5, 6, 30, 31, 36, 45, 56, 161, 205
Leslau, W., 68, 205
Levine, Donald Nathan, 47, 206
Levi-Strauss, Claude, 40, 206
Lied, Liv Ingeborg, 126, 206
Lossky, Vladimir, 29, 30, 206
Lowe, Walter, 166, 167, 168, 206
Luz, Ulrich, 3, 206

Macaskill, Grant, 8, 10, 11, 23, 136, 139, 140, 206, 206
Machinist, P., 98, 206
Mack, Burton L., 100
Mackie, J. L., 167, 206
Mair, A. W., 100, 206
Mair, G. R., 100, 206
Malaty, Fr. Tadros, 27, 206
Mannion, Gerard, 166, 206
Marlin, G. J., 163, 206
Marshall, Paul, 163, 206
Martin, F., 66, 206
Martin, M. W., 109, 206
Maston, J., 98, 206
Matthews, Mark, 75, 207
McConville, J. Gordon, 3, 4, 19, 96, 207
McFague, Sally, 111, 207
Meeks, Wayne E., 156, 207

Merkelbach, H., 99, 207
Metzler, Karin, 185, 207
Meyers, Carol L., 98, 207
Milbank, John, 189, 207
Milik, J. T., 1, 125, 207
Minchakpu, O., 163
Mohammed, Girma, 31, 207
Moore, F. C. T., 40, 207
Morris, Michael Ashley, 159, 207
Mosala, Itumeleng J., 19, 207

Naess, Arne, 111, 207
Nash, B. A., 109, 207
Newsom, Carol A., 129, 207
Nickelsburg, George W. E., 14, 21, 24, 63, 65, 66, 67, 69, 74, 75, 77, 78, 81, 82, 90, 117, 128, 138, 148, 151, 169, 173, 174, 175, 183, 184, 187, 207
Northcott, Michael S., 124, 208
Nyberg, Richard, 163, 208

Oberman, Heiko A., 140, 208

Parker, K. I., 96, 208
Parry, Donald W., 118, 125, 208
Pedersen, Kirsten Stoffregen 45, 208
Pike, Nelson, 167, 208
Piovanelli, P., 90, 208
Pop, Simion, 28, 208
Portier-Young, Anathea, 165, 208
Propp, W. H., 96, 97, 98, 208
Pryor, Angus, 13

Rad, Gerhard von, 114, 208
Ranger, Terence, 28, 208
Reese, G., 64, 208
Rogerson, John, 114, 208
Roszak, Theodore, 111, 208
Roth, S. John, 153, 208
Rowland, Christopher, 18, 20, 21, 22, 25, 208
Rubin, A. J., 163, 208
Russell, Norman, 139, 208
Ruether, Rosemary Radford, 111, 115, 208

Sacchi, Paolo, 169, 209

Sanders, James A., 17, 21, 209
Santmire, Paul, 115, 209
Schechter, Solomon, 48, 209
Schirrmacher, Thomas, 164, 209
Schmid, H. H., 126, 209
Seebass, Horst, 17, 209
Seeman, Chris, 168, 209
Sjöberg, Erik, 136, 209
Smith, Anthony D., 36, 209
Smith, Morton, 17, 209
Sparks, H. F. D.
Stuckenbruck, Loren T., 2, 7, 9, 11, 20, 21, 49, 50, 51, 73, 79, 81, 84, 86, 125, 127, 130, 147, 149, 150, 151, 152, 153, 154, 161, 163, 209
Sweeney, Marvin A., 96, 209
Swimme, Brian, 111, 199

Tamrat, Tadesse, 31, 32, 210
Taylor, Charles, 143, 210
Tcherikover, Victor, 77, 210
Tedeschi R. G., 164, 210
The Church of Ethiopia 30, 210
Theisohn, Johannes, 136, 210
Thesleff, H., 92, 210
Thiselton, Anthony C., 18, 210
Tibebu, Teshale, 31, 210
Tiller, Patrick A., 63, 64, 65, 66, 67, 210
Tilling, Christopher, 93, 210
Ting, R. S., 164, 210
Tov, Emanuel, 118, 125, 210
Trible, Phyllis,, 18, 210
Turner, Victor W., 12, 41, 159, 160, 161, 162, 210

VanderKam, James C., 7, 65, 73, 75, 90, 136, 138, 173, 174, 175, 183, 184, 187, 210–211
Volf, Miroslav, 188, 189, 190, 211
Vonnahme, Nathan, 111, 211

Wagner, J. Ross, 136, 211
Walck, L. W., 90, 211
Wannenwetsch, Bernd, 182, 183, 211
Watson, T., 164, 211
Webster, John, 135, 140, 211
White, Lynn, Jr., 8, 111, 115, 211
Williams, Ron G., 37, 211

Williams, Rowan, 180, 211
Wilson, Bryan, 12, 156, 157, 158, 211
Winter, I., 98, 211
Wink, Walter, 180, 211
Wolter, Michael, 17, 20, 211

Wong-McDonald A., 164, 211
Wright, Archie T., 7, 168, 173, 211

Young, Frances, 19, 211

Scripture Index[1]

Old Testament

Genesis

1:4	114	6–11	116
1:9	101	6	9, 116
1:10	114	6:1–4	168, 169
1:11–13	117	6:1–2	116, 117
1:11–12	117	6:4	116
1:12	114	6:5—8:22	116
1:18	114	6:5	116
1:20–22	117	6:11–12	116
1:21	114, 117	7–9	129
1:24–30	117	9:1	121
1:24–25	117	9:15	129
1:25	114	9:28–29	169
1:26–28	9, 96, 114, 115	13:10	126
1:28	121	15:18	126
1:31	114, 117	22:5	47
2	7, 69	35:12	127
2:7–10	69		
2:7	68, 114		
3:8–24	173		
4:22	48		
5:21–24	150, 169		
5:24	169		
5:28–32	116		

Exodus

14	64
14:31	64
15:25–26	64
15:25b–26	64, 65
15:29	65
16–17	64

1. This Index lists canonical and apocryphal/deutero-canonical books in their order in the Catholic Bible, except for inserting 1 Enoch and Jubilees, which are Old Testament scripture for the Ethiopian and Eritrean Tewahedo Churches, after the Prophets.

Exodus (continued)

20:2–17	182
20:7	183
20:12	183
23:20–23 (LXX)	98
24:4–8	35
25	95
28	98
28:2	98, 101
28:9–12	101
28:21	101
28:29	101
28:40	98, 101
29	96, 97
32	97
33:3	127
39	96

Leviticus

2	97
10	97
10:18	85
14:34	127
18:25	127

Numbers

29:7	150

Deuteronomy

7–15	7, 71
7:12–14	72
8:13–19	83
8:13–14	72
8:17–18	83
14:22	72, 78
15:4–5	72
15:4	72
15:5	72, 73
15:7	72
15:10	73
15:11	73
15:18	72, 78
16:29	150

16:31	150
17	95
17:14–20	97
17:16–17	96
17:20	96
23:27	150
23:32	150
28:48	78, 85
33	95
33:27	14

Judges

2:18	85

Ruth

3:4	69

1 Samuel

8–12	95
8:5	95
10–20	95
13:7–14	97
17:56	68, 69
26:3	68

1 Kings

3–8	96
3:1–2	96
4	96
9:10—14:20	96
10–11	96
10	96
10:14—11:8	96
10:26–29	96
11:1–8	96

1 Chronicles

29:20	99

2 Chronicles

26:16–21	97

Judith

9:11	151, 153

(Greek) Esther

11:6–12	153
11:11	151

1 Maccabees

1:14	73
2:29	77
3:3–9	102
3:9	102
13:47	74
14:4–15	102
14:10	102

2 Maccabees

6–7	151
7:34	92
9:5–12	92
12:40	74

Job

3:4–5	78
3:4	84
5:11	151
15:23	78, 84
21:19	69
38:1–40:2	9, 114

Psalms

2	92
8:5–8	96
8:6–8	101
10:2	85
37:10–11	152
37:11	151
40	17
42:7	78
45	99
49:5–11	78
49:6–7	83
49:6	83
50	17
52:7	83
52:9	83
69:29	155
80:17	23
82	6, 47, 50
82[81]:3	151, 152
86:1	152
89:11	152
104	9, 114
104:1–2	100
109:31	152
119:84	85
119:86	85
119:150	85
119:161	85
131:2	152
132:15	152
138[137]:6	151, 152

Proverbs

1:19	81
8	24
3:33	77
5:18	77
10:2	81
10:6	77
10:22	77
11:22	77
11:28	78, 81, 83
13:28	81
15:27	81
16:19	151
18:11	81
18:16	81
20:17	81
20:21	81
23:4–5	81
23:23–27	81

Proverbs (continued)

24:25	77
28:1	81
28:16	81
28:22	81
29:3	81
29:23	151

Wisdom

4:20–5:15	92
5:8	78

Sirach

3:17–29	23
3:30	83
4:11–19	23
5:1	83
5:8	78
6:18–37	23
7:32	77
10:30–31	83
10:14	151
11:12	151
11:14	83
11:22	77
13:3–5	77
13:18	77
14:20–15:10	23
17:22	83
18:25	83
24	102
24:1–23	98, 100
24:10	98
24:33	24
29:23	83
31:4	77
31:8	77
32:21–26	153
34:1–8	23
36:1–22	101
39:1–11	23
40:13	83
40:18	83
40:17	83
40:24	83
44–50	102
44:1	98
44:8	102
44:14	102
44:19	98
45:6–22	100
46:12	102
46:19	101
47:10	102
47:13	102
47:16	102
47:18	102
47:19	101
47:23–25	101
48:15–16	101
48:17–21	99
49:4	101
49:14	98
49:16	101
50	8, 98, 99, 100, 101, 102
50:1–21	98, 99, 100, 102
50:1–4	99, 100, 101
50:1	101
50:2–3	99
50:2	101
50:3	101
50:4	101
50:5–21	100
50:5–7	100, 101
50:7	98
50:11–13	101
50:11	100
50:15	99
50:20	102
50:21	98

Isaiah

10:1–2	152
11:2–5	92
14:4–20	92
42:6	23
48:4	23
48:22	78
49:6	23

57:15	152	3:12	151
57:21	78		
65:21–22	121	## Malachi	
66:2	152		
		2:7	57, 98

Jeremiah

1 Enoch

9:23	78	1–36 (the Book of the Watchers)	
17:11	83		1, 12, 13, 62, 166,
22:6	82		167, 171, 181, 182
22:13	77	1:1–3	167
22:16	83	1:1	14, 170, 183, 186,
			189, 190
## Ezekiel		1:2	62, 66, 170
		1:4–9	167, 170, 183,
1:26–28	98		187, 188
		1:4	129
## Daniel		1:9	2, 21, 182
		2:2	169
7	23, 92, 105	2:3	125
7:13	92, 109	5:4–6	152
8:10	92	5:4	78, 81, 182
12:1	155	5:5–9	188
12:2	79, 80	5:5	78
		5:6	171
## Hosea		5:8	67
		6–11	9, 121, 123
6:6	17	6–8	12
		6–5	25
## Joel		6	168, 169
		6:1–2	117
1:2—2:17	9, 114	6:1	120, 130
2:2	84	6:2	129, 173
2:28—3:21	115	6:3–6	117
		6:3	51, 173
## Amos		6:5	52
		6:6	129
4:1	72	6:8	52
5:18	78, 84	7	170
5:20	84	7:1	173
		7:3–5	117, 121
## Zephaniah		7:3a	117
		7:3b	117
1:15	78, 84	7:4	117
2:3	152		
3:11–12	152		

1 Enoch (continued)

7:4–5	174, 181
7:5–6	128
7:5	52
7:5a	117
7:5b	117
7:6	9, 128
8	170
8:1–3	117, 173
8:1–2	174
8:1	52, 182
8:4	118, 128
9	24, 170, 172, 183
9:1	56, 118, 128, 174, 182
9:1–3	184
9:1–2	128
9:2	9, 10, 52, 118, 128
9:3	172
9:4–5	184
9:6–9	184
9:6	174
9:9	128, 172
9:10	128, 172
9:11	184
10–11	170, 174, 179, 184
10	56
10:1–3	118
10:2	51
10:4–6	179
10:7	130
10:9	118, 155
10:12	125, 155
10:11–13	180
10:15	175
10:16	120
10:17	120
10:18	9, 120, 121
10:19	120
10:21–22	9, 121
10:21	130
11:1	121, 130
11:2	121
12–17	22
12—13:2	170
12	168
12:1	130
12:1–2	169
12:3	22
12:4	129, 130
12:5–6	22
12:5	78, 81
12:6	155
13:1	78
13:2	130
13:3–7	170
13:8	170
14:1–7	170
14:6	53
14:8–24	170
14:8	53
14:19	53
14:20	22
15–16	184
15:1—16:4	170
15	174
15:3	22, 129, 130
15:4	22
15:7	22, 184
15:8—16:1	175
15:8–12	175
15:9	175
15:11	22, 175, 180, 182
15:12	130
16:1	22, 175
16:4	78, 81
17–36	4, 29, 35, 170
17:2	22
18:1–9	5
18:13ff.	22
18:13–16	169
19:1	170, 175, 180
20:7	55
20:4	56
21:2	125
21:7–10	170
22	58
2:1–4	171
22:3	130
22:5–7	12, 169, 171
22:5	130, 171
22:6–7	181
22:7	155, 171
25:3	128
26	169

26:2	129	53:5	90
27:1	126	54:2	90
32:2	125	55:4	90, 98, 125
32:3	172	56:5	127
32:6	12, 62, 169, 172	56:6	125, 126
37–71 (the Similitudes/Parables)		56:7	126
	8, 10, 63, 92, 98, 104, 106, 107, 109, 133	60:9	125
		61:5	79
		61:8	98
38:1	136	62:1	63, 90
38:2	136	62:2–3	92, 98
38:4–5	90	62:3	90, 98
38:4	126	62:5	98, 137
39:1	130	62:6	90
39:4–8	137	62:9	90, 93
39:5	130	63:1	90
39:12	125	63:8	93
40:5	137	63:9	92
40:9	130, 137	64:1	130
42	23, 102	63:12	90
42:2	130	65:1	125
45:1	137	65:5	128
45:2	125	65:6	125
45:3–5	138	67:2	129
45:3	92, 98	67:8	90
46:1	98	67:12	90
46:3	93	69:6	130
46:4–6	90	69:8	130
46:4–5	93	69:12	130
46:5	98	69:14	130
46:7	91, 92	70:1	140
46:8	85	70:5	11, 141
48	11, 23, 93	71	98
48:2–3	141	71:4	11, 134, 143
48:3	141	71:10–12	194
48:4–6	93	71:14–17	94
48:5	98, 141	71:14	137, 140
48:6	141	72–82 (the Astronomical Book)	
48:8	90, 92	72–79	119
48:10	92	80	9, 118
49:3	92	80:2–6	119
49:4	93	80:2	126
50:1	138	80:4–6	152
50:11–19	104	83:5	128
51:1	79	84:4–17	119
51:3	98, 137	84:5	129
52:5–9	92	84:6	129
53:2	92, 125		

1 Enoch *(continued)*

85–90 (the Animal Apocalypse)
                        6, 61, 127, 171, 173

85:3–4	173
85:3	129
85:8	128
86:1ff.	22
86:6	130
86:8	130
87:2–3	56
88:2	130
89	25
89:15–16	128
89:21	63
89:25	63
89:28–30	182
89:28	64, 65
89:28a	64
89:28b	64
89:32–33	7, 65
89:38	128
89:40	127
89:41	65
89:44	66
89:53	66
89:54ff.	66
89:57ff.	128
89:59ff.	22
89:74	66
90:6	66, 67
90:7	66
90:20	54, 127
90:28	127
90:32	67
90:35	67
91:10	79, 80
91:11–17	127, 165
91:12	82

92–105/107 (the Epistle of Enoch)
                        7, 63

92:2–5	80
92:2–3a	79
92:2	152
92:3	7, 80
92:4	80
92:5	84
93:1–10	127, 165
93:10	67
94:1	77
94:3	77
94:4	77
94:5	23
94:5b	77
94:6	81
94:6—95:2	81
94:6d	77
94:7	77, 78
94:7a	82
94:7b	82
94:7b–8b	78
94:8	83
94:8a	83
94:9	7, 83, 84, 85
95:2	81
95:2b	84
95:3	24, 82
95:3–7	85
95:4–7	81
95:5	8, 85
95:6	78
95:7	85
95:9b	85
96:4–8	81
96:5	155
97:8	83
97:10	81
98:6	81
98:9—99:2	81
98:11	78
98:15	74, 86
98:16	78, 81
99:2	86
99:2a	78, 85
99:5	155
99:6	84
99:8	63
99:13	81
99:16	82
99:16a	82
100:3	84
100:5	79, 80
100:6	130
100:7–9	81
101:3	78, 81
101:8	125

102:1–3	130	108:4–6	156
102:3	78, 81, 130	108:4–5	148, 151
102:4	79	108:5–6	150
103:2	155	108:6–10	148
103:3	84, 86	108:6–7	149
103:3a	86	108:6	153, 154, 162
103:4a	80	108:7–9	160
103:5–8	81	108:7	56, 85, 149, 151, 153, 155, 175
103:7–8	85		
103:8	78, 81	108:7a	150
103:9	77	108:7b	150
103:9–15	24	108:7c	150
103:11	78, 85	108:8–10	149
104:1	56	108:8	149, 150, 152, 153, 162
104:2	79, 80, 88		
104:6	79	108:8b	149
104:10–11	152	108:9	151, 154, 155, 158, 162, 164
104:12–13	67		
105:2	81	108:9a	149
106:2	63	108:9b	149
106:8ff.	63	108:9c	150
106:15	125	108:10–14	150
106:16	125	108:10	162
107	63	108:10a	150
107:1	125	108:10c	149, 150
107:3	129	108:11–15	152, 153
108 (The Eschatological Admonition)		108:11–12	149
	12, 147, 148, 149, 150, 151, 152, 153, 156, 157, 158, 159, 160, 161, 162, 163, 164, 165	108:11	151, 152, 155
		108:12	155, 162
		108:13–15	149
108:1	148, 149, 151, 154	108:13	151
108:1b–2	160	108:15	150
108:2–3	148, 150		
108:2	154, 155, 157	Jubilees	
108:3	155, 162, 165		
108:4–15	165	5	50
		23:23–24	85

New Tetament

Matthew

5:3	153	6:25–34	115
5:10–44	85	10:23	85
5:22	182	11:5	153
6:1–4	153	13	115

Matthew (continued)

19:21	153
19:23	87
19:24	87
23:1–36	153
25:31	109, 137
25:31–46	21
26:9	153
27:57	87

Mark

4	115
8:38	109
10:4	84
10:21	153
10:25	87
10:35–45	108
10:35–44	108
10:45	108
12:42–43	153
13	115
13:9–13	85
14:5	153
14:7	153

Luke

1:49	85
1:52	151
6:17–49	79
6:20–26	81
6:20	79
6:24	87
9:58	109
12:13–21	79
14:13	153
14:21	153
16:19–31	87
16:20	153
16:22	153
18:25	87
19:8	153
21:12	85

John

5:16	85
10	26
11:51–52	97
14:1	79
15:20	85

Acts of the Apostles

7:56	107

Romans

6–8	138
8:19–23	115
12:2	142

1 Corinthians

2:9	84
10:4	144

2 Corinthians

1	138
3:6	27

Galatians

2:20	143

Ephesians

1–2	138

Philippians

1:21	143
2:6–11	83, 94, 108, 109
3:8–9	143

Colossians

1:13	181
1:15–17	181

1:15–20	115, 122
1:16	181
2:16–19	22

1 Timothy

6:9	87
6:10	87
6:17–18	78

Hebrews

11:16	84
12:2	142
12:18	78, 84

James

1:9–11	153
1:9	151
2:5–12	153
2:6	87
5:1–6	153
5:1	87

1 Peter

2:4–10	138
3:19	21

2 Peter

2:17	78, 84
3:10–13	9, 113, 115

Jude

1	22
6	22
8	22
12	22
13	78, 84
18	22
25	22
14–15	2, 21

Revelation

1:9	85
1:13	107
1:20	58
2:2	86
2:20	86
3:5	155
3:10	82
3:17	83
3:18a	83
5:1	86
5:6–10	54
5:6	54
6:4	47, 59, 81
6:11	58
6:12—7:17	55
6:17	85
7:1	55
7:2–4	82
8	81
8:4	59
8:8	21
8:13	81
9:4	82
9:12	81
9:20	82
17:4	83
11	138
11:1–2	82
11:3	57, 59
11:4	59
11:6	59
11:14	81
11:18	80
12:12	81
12:14	79
13:8	86
14:7	85
14:14–20	56
14:14	56, 107
14:15	56
14:20	8, 84
15:1–8	55
15:1	55
16:10	85
16:11	8, 85
17:8	57, 86

Revelation *(continued)*

18:10	85
18:11–12	83
19:8	86
19:13	189
19:15	189
20:4–6	80
20:5	7, 80
20:6	80
20:15	86
20:12	56
21:1—22:5	115
21:9	55
21:27	86

Jewish Sources Index

Dead Sea Scrolls

CD (A)

vi 14–21	153
vi 14–17	81
vi 21	151
viii 4–6	81
ix 2–5	85
xi 15	81

CD (B)

xix 19	81

CD (B)

xix 9–10	153
xix 19	81, 151

1QHab

vi 3–4	151
vi 20	81
x 34	151
xiii 13–14	151
xiii 20–22	151
xix 25	151
xxiii 14	151

1QM

xiv 7	151

1QpHab

viii 8–12	87
ix 5	81
xii 10	81

4QpIs(a)

1–2 ii 8–10	151
1–2 ii 16–20	151

1QS

ii 8	78, 84
v 14–15	81
v 19	81
v 20	81
ix 8–9	81
x 18	85

1QS (B)

4–5	103, 104

1Q203 1

| 3.1 | 78 |

4Q417

| f2i:17–19 | 78 |

11QTemple Scroll

| 56.12–59.21 | 103 |

Q24

| 8.2 | 78 |

Josephus

Jewish/Judean Antiquities

13.301—14.491	103
14.168–176	91
14.398	91
14.490–491	103
16.24	91
16.140	91
16.146	91
16.150	91
16.156–158	91
16.157–158	91
16.158	91
17.304–310	91

Jewish/Judean War

1.70–357	103
1.293	91
7.260–261	77

Old Testament Pseudepigrapha

2 Baruch

| 54.21 | 85 |

2 Enoch

| 1–21 | 94 |
| 22–67 | 94 |

4 Esdras

| 2.32–36 | 58 |

4 Ezra

9.45	153
14.13	151
14.13–15	153

Psalms of Solomon

| 17–18 | 94, 103 |

Sibylline Oracles

2.25	81
2.70–72	81
2.100–102	81

Testament of Levi

| 8 | 97 |

Testament of Moses

| 6.1–4 | 91 |
| 10.2 | 98 |

Classical Sources Index

Athenaeus
Deipnosophistae
6.253e — 99

Callimachus
Hymns
4.165–166 — 100

Cassius Dio
Roman History
52.35.1–2 — 90

Cicero
De Inventione Rhetorica
1.24 [34] — 103

Hecataeus of Abdera
40.3.5 — 98

Quintilian
Institutes
3.7.9 — 91

Stobaeus
4.7.61 — 92

Theocritus
Hymn to Ptolemy II Philadelphus
8 — 99

www.ingramcontent.com/pod-product-compliance
Lightning Source LLC
Chambersburg PA
CBHW020407230426
43664CB00009B/1222